21st-Century Dylan

21st-Century Dylan

Late and Timely

Edited by Laurence Estanove, Adrian Grafe,
Andrew McKeown and Claire Hélie

BLOOMSBURY ACADEMIC
NEW YORK • LONDON • OXFORD • NEW DELHI • SYDNEY

BLOOMSBURY ACADEMIC
Bloomsbury Publishing Inc
1385 Broadway, New York, NY 10018, USA
50 Bedford Square, London, WC1B 3DP, UK
29 Earlsfort Terrace, Dublin 2, Ireland

BLOOMSBURY, BLOOMSBURY ACADEMIC and the Diana logo are trademarks of
Bloomsbury Publishing Plc

First published in the United States of America 2021
This paperback edition published in 2022

Copyright © by Laurence Estanove, Adrian Grafe, Andrew McKeown and Claire Hélie, 2021
Each chapter © of Contributor

Cover design: Louise Dugdale
Cover photo by Jo Hale/Redfern/Getty images

All rights reserved. No part of this publication may be reproduced or transmitted in any form or by any means, electronic or mechanical, including photocopying, recording, or any information storage or retrieval system, without prior permission in writing from the publishers.

Bloomsbury Publishing Inc does not have any control over, or responsibility for, any third-party websites referred to or in this book. All internet addresses given in this book were correct at the time of going to press. The author and publisher regret any inconvenience caused if addresses have changed or sites have ceased to exist, but can accept no responsibility for any such changes.

Whilst every effort has been made to locate copyright holders the publishers would be grateful to hear from any person(s) not here acknowledged.

A catalog record for this book is available from the Library of Congress.

ISBN: HB: 9781501363696
PB: 9781501371240
ePDF: 9781501363719
eBook: 9781501363702

Typeset by RefineCatch Limited, Bungay, Suffolk

To find out more about our authors and books visit www.bloomsbury.com and sign up for our newsletters.

Contents

List of Figures	vii
List of Tables	viii
Editors	ix
Contributors	x
Acknowledgements	xii
Introduction: Some Variations on Late Dylan *Adrian Grafe*	1

Part One   Honest with Me: Late Dylan's Performing Personae

1. 'I Made It So Easy for You to Follow Me': Making a Case for Dylan's *Revisionist Art* (2012)   *Nina Goss* — 15

2. Masked, Anonymized and Chronicled: Dylan's Fatal Auto-Mythos for the New Millennium   *Jim Salvucci* — 27

3. Performativity, Subversion and Mask-ulinity: Dylan *on* Screen, Dylan *as* Screen   *Sara Martínez* — 43

4. *No Direction Home*: When Dylan Does Look Back   *Charles Bonnot* — 57

5. Dylan Does Adverts. Surely Not? Surely?   *Andrew McKeown* — 71

6. Bringing the Margin to the Centre: Dylan's Visible Republic   *Erin C. Callahan* — 83

7. Creation and Re-Creation in Dylan's Performances of 'Blowin' in the Wind' (1963–2016)   *Julie Mansion-Vaquié* — 99

8. 'Behind Every Beautiful Thing There's Been Some Kind of Pain': Melancholia in Dylan's Songs and Paintings   *Anne-Marie Mai* — 121

Part Two   Roll on Bob: Late Dylan in Text and Tribute

9. 'A-Journeying over the Shadow and the Rain': Dylan's Late Style(s)   *Jean Du Verger* — 135

10	'The Last Outback at the World's End': Dylan's Sense of an Album's Ending *M. Cooper Harriss*	149
11	'No Success Like Failure'? Dylan's Awards, from Princeton to the Nobel *Denis Feignier*	165
12	'How Could It Be Any Other Way?' Dylan's Editorial Decisions in *The Lyrics: 1961–2012* *Simon McAslan*	179
13	Dylan's Resources *Christopher Ricks*	197
14	Dylan Nobelized? Dylan Ricksified? *Adrian Grafe*	203

Coda: Late and Timely, Rough and Ready: A Review of *Rough and Rowdy Ways*   *Adrian Grafe and Andrew McKeown*   217

Index   227

Figures

7.1 Stage plan of 1963 Newport version of 'Blowin' in the Wind' (VS1b) 114
7.2 Stage plan of 1971 Madison Square Garden version of 'Blowin' in the Wind' (VS2) 115
7.3 Video still from 2016 Berkeley version of 'Blowin' in the Wind' (VS3) 116
7.4 Stage plan of 2016 Berkeley version of 'Blowin' in the Wind' (VS3) 117

Tables

7.1 Duration and tempo of various versions of 'Blowin' in the Wind'   105
7.2 Structure of the song 'Blowin' in the Wind' – the *Freewheelin'* album version   106
7.3 Structures of the five versions of 'Blowin' in the Wind' studied   107
7.4 Instrumentation of the five versions of 'Blowin' in the Wind' studied   108
7.5 Keys used in the five versions of 'Blowin' in the Wind' studied   109
7.6 Harmonica playing in three versions of 'Blowin' in the Wind'   109
7.7 Distribution of lyrics between Dylan and backing singers in the 1963 Newport version of 'Blowin' in the Wind'   110
7.8 Separate shots from 1963 TV version of 'Blowin' in the Wind' (VS1; video stills)   113

Editors

Laurence Estanove is an independent scholar and co-editor of the online journal *FATHOM*. She has published articles in Britain, the USA and France and co-edited *Thomas Hardy, Poet: New Perspectives* (2015) with Adrian Grafe. Her more recent research focuses on popular music and digital sociability, and she is currently working on a book-length study of the Glasgow music scene.

Adrian Grafe, Professor, Université d'Artois, France, BA Hons. (Oxon), PhD, Fellow (Corresp.) of the English Association, is the author of monographs on Hopkins (2003) and Emily Dickinson (2009). He is author-editor or co-editor of several books on British poetry. He has published broadly on poetry, literature and popular music in Britain, Europe and America. His novel *Back to Vienna* is due from Addison & Highsmith in 2022.

Andrew McKeown teaches English at the University of Poitiers, France, and co-hosts *Half Men Half Biscuits*, a weekly radio show on Radio Pulsar, 95.9 FM. He has written a number of articles on poetry and fiction and most recently co-edited with Adrian Grafe *Roads from Arras* (2018), a centenary tribute to the writing of Edward Thomas. *You What?*, a jumble of sardonic verses, was published by Glib Books in 2017 and is to be followed by *Spurts*, a novelette due out autumn 2020.

Claire Hélie holds a PhD on North of England Poetry and is a Senior Lecturer at the Arts Department at Université de Lille, France. She has published several articles on contemporary poetry, drama and translation, and co-edited *No Dialect, Please, You're a Poet: English Dialect in Poetry in the 20th and 21st Centuries* (Routledge, 2019).

Contributors

Charles Bonnot, Associate Professor, Université Sorbonne Nouvelle Paris 3, France, holds a PhD on the discourse of music documentaries from Robert Johnson to LCD Soundsystem.

Erin C. Callahan, Professor, San Jacinto College, Houston, focuses her research on identity construction with a special emphasis on film and music. Her next major project will focus on Don Robey and the history of blues music in Houston, Texas.

Jean Du Verger, Associate Professor, ENSMM Institute of Engineering, Besançon, France, is a specialist of contemporary British drama who has authored many articles on various subjects such as TV series, counterculture in the USA in the 1960s, and David Bowie.

Denis Feignier, Civil Servant, France, has published 'Lord Byron Goes Electric: Lord Byron & Bob Dylan, Reluctant Voices of their Generations' (2008), and met Bob Dylan when he worked at the French Ministry of Culture.

Nina Goss, Adjunct Professor, Fordham University, New York, USA, co-edited *Tearing the World Apart: Bob Dylan and the 21st Century* released in 2017 and *Dylan at Play* in 2011. She also taught classes on Bob Dylan and has delivered papers at conferences including MLA, Arkansas State University's Delta Symposium and University of Southern Denmark's 'New Approaches to Bob Dylan's Songs' (2018).

M. Cooper Harriss, Associate Professor, Indiana University, USA, is the author of *Ralph Ellison's Invisible Theology* (NYU Press, 2017), and he has published widely in periodicals including *The Journal of Religion*, *African American Review*, *Biblical Interpretation* and *Soundings*, among others. He is presently at work on a book titled *Muhammad Ali and the Irony of American Religion*.

Anne-Marie Mai, Professor, Syddansk Universitet, Denmark, has edited the anthology *Hvor dejlige Havfruer svømmer – om Dylans digtning* (Where Lovely

Mermaids Flow – On Bob Dylan's Poetry), 2012, published the monograph *Bob Dylan – the Poet* (2018) and introduced the Danish translation of *Tarantula* (2018). She organized the international conference 'New Approaches to Bob Dylan's Songs' in 2018 and has edited the proceedings (University of Southern Denmark, 2020).

Julie Mansion-Vaquié, Senior Lecturer, Université Nice Sophia Antipolis, France, holds a PhD in musicology from the University Sorbonne-Paris IV. Her research focuses in particular on stage performance in popular music. She is also a composer of electro-acoustic music and her work has been performed in Europe and in Mexico.

Sara Martínez, Associate Lecturer, Lancaster University, UK, holds a PhD in English Literature. Her thesis was entitled '"I celebrate myself, and sing myself": Insight into Bob Dylan's Chameleonic Masculinity. Writings and Songs 1956–1970' and she is currently working on adapting it into a book.

Simon McAslan, English Professor, Vanier College, Montreal, Canada, first started teaching a course on Bob Dylan in 2007. His research interest is in literature informed by the ethos of rock music.

Christopher Ricks is a Professor of the Humanities at Boston University, USA, having formerly been Professor of English at Bristol and at Cambridge, and the Professor of Poetry at Oxford, UK, 2004–2009. *Dylan's Visions of Sin* appeared in 2003; with Lisa Nemrow and Julie Nemrow, he edited *The Lyrics: Since 1962* (2014).

Jim Salvucci, Dean of Faculty, Union College, Kentucky, USA, taught several advanced courses on Bob Dylan that focused on the lyrics, the music, the cultural significance and the satiric stances of Dylan's work. He has presented on Dylan in the USA, Asia and Europe, and has also blogged on Dylan.

Acknowledgements

The essays in this book arose out of a conference on Twenty-First-Century Dylan which took place at Université d'Artois in Arras, France, 3–5 December 2018. It is to this conference that Christopher Ricks refers in his chapter. The editors would like to thank the head of the research centre *Textes et Cultures* at Artois, Professor Anne-Gaëlle Weber, for supporting the conference, as well as the research centres *FoReLL* (Université de Poitiers), directed by Isabelle Gadoin, and *CECILLE* (Université de Lille), directed by Constantin Bobas. We would like to thank all those who took part in that conference; *Textes et Cultures* chief administrator Nathalie Cabiran, as well as Sophie De Clerck and Olivier Rota, for their logistical help and skill; and all the friends, students, colleagues – especially Michael Hearn, Kevin Dwyer, Julie Assouly, Jaime Cespedes, Marie-Thérèse Bernat and Yannick Boutier – and members of the public who attended the event.

The conference was accompanied by *Twenty-First-Century Dylan*, an exhibition at the Artois University Library, opened by Christopher Ricks, to whom Artois Vice-President for Culture, Professor Brigitte Buffard-Moret, and Head Librarian Corinne Leblond paid tribute. The exhibition was mounted by librarians Virginie Lecouteux, Ambre Lesage, Yannick Machon and Rafael Szwarcensztein, whom we thank for their expertise and enthusiasm. Mylène Douriez, who gave much-appreciated logistical help during the conference, and the late Jonathan Dickinson kindly lent materials for the exhibition. A long-time friend and fan of Bob Dylan's, Jonathan died while this book was in preparation. He is much missed.

We are grateful to our editor, Leah Babb-Rosenfeld, Bloomsbury staff members Amy Martin and Rachel Moore and the Bloomsbury editorial board for welcoming our project. Leah and the anonymous reviewers of our project made many helpful suggestions.

Introduction: Some Variations on Late Dylan

Adrian Grafe

Bob Dylan's late work is not so much work as works: disparate creations in different fields and genres that form an intricate, multilayered, multi-textured world, the reflection of a restless, constantly active artist who has not only created new works but devoted a good part of each year, since 1988, to his life and trade as a concert artist travelling the miles across America and globally. But, first, what do we mean by 'late'? 'Late' here points – mainly – to the chronology of the artist's life. In Dylan's case, we can if we wish date the beginning of his late period from the release of the *Time Out of Mind* album (1997), an artistic rebirth seven years after *Under the Red Sky* (which critics considered as generally weak), and two albums of non-original songs, *Good As I Been to You* (1992) and *World Gone Wrong* (1993). This book, then, is intended mainly, though not exclusively, to cover the period from 1997 up to the present. In 1997 Dylan was fifty-six; he will be eighty in 2021. As the wise man has it: 'To everything there is a season and a time'. How far does Dylan's late work reflect this particular 'season' of life?

To paraphrase the title of the first chapter of Edward Said's *On Late Style*, 'Timeliness and Lateness', Dylan's work over the past twenty years or so has been both timely and late (Said 2006: 3). Timely because he has retained the ability to speak to his time, able to retain listeners of his own age, while gathering new, young listeners – and performers – to his music: young artists as diverse as Ed Sheeran, Kate Tempest and Passenger either express their admiration for Dylan directly or sing his songs. Late because of his age; the size of his back-catalogue, built up over a whole adult lifetime devoted to songwriting, means that he is not obliged to carry on writing songs (for performance in the studio or on stage, or for financial reasons). But age does not, in Dylan's case, necessarily mean decrepitude in mind or body. An attempt to apply Shakespeare's 'seven ages of man' monologue (*As You Like It*, II. vii.) to Dylan is, in fact, bound to fail: 'the lover, … with a woeful ballad made to his mistress' brow' – Shakespeare's third age after the infant and the schoolboy – chimes perfectly with the speaker/singer of 'Love Sick', who is 'sick of love' but no less 'in the thick of it' (Dylan 2016a: 559). Or the last lines of 'Long and Wasted Years' in which the singer and his lover first weep, and then he says, in a twist that manages both to be cool and yet even more desolate: 'So much for tears / So much for those long and wasted years' (Dylan 2016a: 652). Jaques's 'sixth age', with its 'lean and slippered pantaloon', 'spectacles on nose' and, above all, 'big manly voice, / Turning again towards childish treble', could hardly resemble Dylan less. And if he sings high notes occasionally, he never 'pipes' (*As You Like It*, II vii 139ff).

And yet Dylan's work over the past twenty-five years has also been both timely and late because some songs and some performances have a valedictory quality to them, and show an increasing awareness of mortality. Does Dylan break into what Said calls 'a new idiom' in his late phase (Said 2006: 6)? It depends on which aspect of Dylan's production one considers, as well as on one's understanding of the adjective 'new'. Said is especially interested not in a 'ripeness is all', serene expression of old age such as he finds in Rembrandt and Bach, among others, but in the unresolved tensions that the late work of some artists manifests. Hence, Ibsen's last plays 'suggest an angry and disturbed artist for whom the medium of drama provides an occasion to stir up more anxiety, tamper irrevocably with the possibility of closure, and leave the audience more perplexed and unsettled than before' (Said 2006: 7). Dylan's massive recent output in various media does suggest a certain refusal of 'closure', although he fully accepts the reality of death. He has retained his lyrical aggressiveness, when the occasion calls for it: 'I'll dress up your wounds with a blood-clotted rag / I ain't afraid to make love to a bitch or a hag' ('Early Roman Kings', Dylan 2016a: 657); also 'Pay in Blood' (2016a: 654): 'You bit your lover in the bed / Come here I'll break your lousy head'.

Dylan's twenty-first-century original songs often, in fact, express discontent and disgust. The protean persona alternates apocalyptic imagery with delicate, sometimes Christian spirituality which counters that discontent and disgust: 'I can hear a sweet voice gently calling / Must be the Mother of our Lord', with a capital *M* for Mother ('Duquesne Whistle', Dylan 2016a: 645). He has survived personally (though interviews filmed for the 2019 Martin Scorsese film *Rolling Thunder Revue: A Bob Dylan Story* show him with a nervous tic) and creatively, and more than survived, far longer than many. A well-known remark from T. S. Eliot's essay 'Ezra Pound, His Metric and Poetry' offers a possibly relevant reflection: 'Any poet, if he is to survive beyond his twenty-fifth year, must alter;

he must seek new ... influences; he will have different emotions to express' (Eliot 2014: 639). Assuming Dylan is a poet, as this volume at times does, Dylan's restlessness has always led him to explore new influences, however old those influences may have been.

Has Dylan mellowed over the years? On stage his adrenalin-charged delivery of 'Things Have Changed' suggests not. Even though he still performs 'Like a Rolling Stone' he sometimes seems to have given up his spirit of revenge. His old weapons have been left on the shelf. What, if anything, has remained unchanged is Dylan's enthusiasm for performance, and his ability to make you believe in what he's singing, even when the song in question is by someone other than him. He does not consider his versions of standards from the American Songbook as covers. He takes them over almost as if he had written them himself – and perhaps he did, for each new interpretation is a creation.

Like the simple time signatures of most of these old songs, Dylan's own time signatures are and have always been the stock in trade of folk, blues and rock: almost always four-four, sometimes two-four, very occasionally three-four (as in 'Huck's Tune', Dylan 2007); his chosen instrumentation is more often than not rudimentary, like that of the blues and hillbilly artists he admires. This is his bedrock. These elements mean that the slightest variation takes on gigantic proportions: for example the offbeat lead-in to the chorus of 'Love Sick' (Dylan 1997); or the violin, banjo and bow across the bass of 'Scarlet Town' (Dylan 2012a), all of which reinforce the song's plangent quality. His singing voice in the current century is worn down, as well it might be after a lifetime's exercise on the road or in the studio, combined with a chain-smoking habit. Yet despite this, Dylan's work challenges us to find new ways to express our response to his music, and to his art.

Here are four features out of many which characterize Dylan's work in the new millennium, opening up four possible pathways, beaten or otherwise, to look at his work: praise, predecession, profundity, and a special concern of this book – persona. Some things have been strengthened. There are signs of patterns of reconciliation. Perhaps a less blatant truculence. At times, a stronger imagination.

1. Praise

One clue as to how one might respond to late Dylan in words may be found in Dylan's own response to artists and their work. Dylan is an appreciator of the first order. He brings his own gift for words to his expression of gratitude to, and his enjoyment of, artists he loves and admires, even if in some cases they are obscure or we cannot necessarily find in them what he finds. He has naturally dropped the spirit of early emulations, of Joan Baez and Woody Guthrie for instance, where his gratitude mingled with the message: Look out, I'm coming up behind you. About Baez when Dylan was starting out, he considered that while they were both heading the same way, he was a long way behind her 'at the moment' (Dylan 2004: 256). At the moment, perhaps, but not for long!

Most of the time, Dylan gets asked about himself in interviews, but he often seems at his best when discussing other artists. In public pronouncements over the past twenty years or so, he has turned his attention more and more to other people's work, sometimes in connection with his own work but often as a matter of appreciation. Dylan's (quasi-?)autobiography chronicles his early days in New York City and the musicians whose live performances he appreciated and learnt from: he divides them into those who waited for you to respond, and others, like Ramblin' Jack Elliott, who reached out to the audience. 'Most folk musicians waited for you to come to them. Jack went out and grabbed you' (Dylan 2004: 251). In Jack Elliott's records Dylan would hear 'the compelling poise of self' (2004: 252). When he listened to Jack Elliott, Dylan would not hear the compelling voice of the singer, nor the compelling voice of the self. Dylan pinpoints a certain sort of calm, of (apparent) self-assurance, that radiated from Elliott when he was performing, an unblinking expression on his face, and appropriated it, took it over for himself. Not only took it over from Jack Elliott. He, as it were, overtook Jack Elliott, partly because Elliott did not, generally speaking, write his own material: he seemed to sing whatever he could find and work from that.

Part of Dylan's blurb for his *Beaten Path* exhibition reads: 'If there is a soundtrack to this compilation of paintings, I would say it could be recordings by Peetie Wheatstraw in some places, Charlie Parker in others, Clifford Brown or Blind Lemon, maybe Guitar Slim – artists that make us a lot bigger when listening to them. It would have to be that way. Absolutely' (Dylan 2016b). Artists that make us a lot bigger? More generous, more forgiving? More serious? We don't *feel* a lot bigger thanks to such artists. We *are* a lot bigger.

Great music, then, expresses something bigger than itself, bigger than the composer. We remember Mahler's remark: 'The essence of music does not lie in its notes' (Le Guay 7).¹ Where then does it lie? In the emotions it makes the listener feel, thanks to its blend of thought and feeling. The essence of poetry and song lyrics does not lie in their words alone, but in their combination or alchemy. And that combination has to sound good.

2. Predecession

One might include in this category older songs of which unfamiliar versions or variants have only much later come to light, such as a totally different version of 'You're Gonna Make Me Lonesome When You Go', the lyrics of which appeared in autumn 2018 and contain the words: 'I see things inside my mind, the things Milton saw after he went blind' (Dylan 2018). This is surely the only lyric of Dylan's in which he names Milton. From Milton one might turn to his older contemporary Donne, in the Nobel Lecture: 'John Donne …, the poet-priest who lived in the time of Shakespeare, wrote these words, "The Sestos and Abydos of her breasts. Not of two lovers, but two loves, the nests." I don't know what it means, either. But it sounds good. And you want your songs to sound good' (Dylan 2017). Sound over meaning is Dylan's principle. This might explain why there are so many variants in the numerous printed (and online) versions of Dylan's lyrics. These variants – or variables – with regard to those that have appeared with the artist's own imprimatur, represent a 'meditation of self versus self' (*Simon McAslan*),² 'versus' putting one in mind of the Yeatsian adage according to which 'We make out of the quarrel with others, rhetoric, but of the quarrel with ourselves, poetry' (Yeats 1997: 411). Dylan has always made art out of his quarrel with others *and* with himself, and indeed, as Richard Elliott (2017: 169) has put it, Dylan 'battles his way out of lyrical dilemmas' in a broader sense than Elliott perhaps intended his remark. On the page, but even more so in performance, 'every text [is] eternally written here and now'; for Dylan, the creation of both art and personae is 'a fluid, changeable process ruled by a permanent state of reinvention that resembles theatre-making' (*Sara Martínez*).

In his Nobel Lecture, Dylan quotes Donne who alludes to a classical myth. So that there's Dylan's voice, Donne's, and that of the classical world, for one's

---

1   My translation from French. Le Guay quotes (or possibly misquotes) Mahler in French: 'L'essentiel de la musique n'est pas dans les notes.'
2   References to chapters in this volume appear as the author's name in italics and in parentheses. Please note that this Introduction was written some time before the release in June 2020 of *Rough and Rowdy Ways*. On the latter album, see Chapter 15.

reading of these lines might be enriched by one's knowing that Sestos and Abydos are central to the Greek myth of Hero and Leander, in which Leander swims across the Hellespont strait from Abydos to Sestos to join Hero. Hero lights a lamp to guide him but on a stormy night her lamp is blown out and he himself is nearly drowned; in some versions of the story they are both drowned. From Ovid, to Shakespeare, to Donne, to Byron, to Keats, all these poets have rewritten the myth. They're all in Dylan:

> I had read a lot of poetry by the time I wrote those early songs. I was into the hard-core poets. I read them the way some people read Stephen King. I had also seen a lot of it growing up. Poe's stuff knocked me out in more ways than I could name. Byron and Keats and all those guys. John Donne.
>
> Cott 2017: 463

Dylan may love the loving way in which Donne describes his lover's bosom. From Donne to Keats in the 'Bright Star' sonnet: 'pillow'd upon my fair love's ripening breast'. From Donne and Keats to Dylan's song, 'Narrow Way': 'I'm still hurting from an arrow that pierced my chest / I'm gonna have to take my head and bury it between your breasts' (Dylan 2016a: 649). With the verb 'bury', Dylan strikes a note of Keatsian balance between, if not love and theft, love and death.

Dylan also proves here his own line from 'Thunder on the Mountain', in which the speaker (though this is not the only possible interpretation) says he has been reading the *Ars amatoria* (Dylan 2016a: 605), with his attention to Donne's – and Ovid's – love lines. What is new in this century is how Dylan brings together in the same song his own words, quotations from blues or folk songs, and lines from the ancient poets. This is both new and unique in contemporary songwriting and perhaps in any songwriting ever, this bringing together of two strains or kinds of culture usually thought of as separate: classical poetry as a tough or now-elitist medium, and blues and popular culture as supposedly more accessible.

Something Dylan said in 2015 enlightens a line of his from the song 'Working Man's Blues # 2': 'I sleep in the kitchen with my feet in the hall' (Dylan 2016a: 612). The singer hears the sounds of the night birds calling and the lover's breathing: the erotic life of nature and of people; heartwarming. Whether or not 'I sleep in the kitchen with my feet in the hall' is heartwarming, it sounds chastening to the singer. This song attracted particular attention when Cliff Fell, a New Zealand poet and teacher, discovered that some of the lines in it were taken word for word from a translation of Ovid (Fell 2006). The line in question is neither by Ovid nor Dylan. It's a variant on a line by Billy Lee Riley, whom Dylan discussed in his MusiCares speech. 'Billy's hit song was called "Red Hot", and it was red hot. It could blast you out of your skull and make you feel happy about it. Change your life' (Dylan 2015). Part of the lyric of 'Red Hot' (as sung on the original 1957 version) goes: 'Well I got a gal six feet four / Sleeps in the kitchen with her feet out the door' (Riley 1957). Love and theft go together, or they do since Dylan came along. And if one were Dylan, there'd be only one thing to do with a great line: steal it. You steal what you love. Steal it, and change it slightly. In fact the line is so great that Riley may have stolen it himself. There is a song of Robert Johnson's entitled 'They're Red Hot': 'I got a girl she's long and tall / She sleeps in the kitchen with her feets in the hall' (Johnson 1937). However this line also appears in Cisco Houston's 'Talking Blues': 'I got a gal she's six feet tall / And sleeps in the kitchen with her feet in the hall' (Houston n.d.). In chronological order, one might say in order of predecession, this line travels from Robert Johnson (1911-1938), to Cisco Houston (1918-1961), to Billy Lee Riley (1933-2009), to Dylan. The important thing is not the borrowing in itself but, as with the example from Donne, what the borrowing brings to the new work, how it fits into that context, how, if it sounds good, it may even add to, or highlight, the profundity of the whole.

3. Profundity

Profundity is not as common a critical criterion as it might be. According to T. S. Eliot, Lawrence's novels are all surface and no depth, while Eliot writes of 'that profundity which James, if he did not always get it, was at least always after' (Eliot 2015: 89). One might ask whether Dylan himself does not in his lyrics achieve a level of profundity worthy of his praise of e. e. cummings, 'for my money the most profound poet of the twentieth century' (Dylan 2012b), proffered just after his reading of cummings' poem 'dying is fine)but Death'. (Whether the poem itself is profound or not is another matter and, perhaps, a matter of opinion.) Profound and profundity are not terms that Dylan used in *Chronicles*, nor does he seem to have used them in writing elsewhere. We assume he chooses the word carefully.

However, profundity in Dylan lies not necessarily in deep statements about life and death but about what he calls 'turning things on their heads'. He quotes a line from a Johnny Cash song: 'A freighter said, "she's been here but she's gone boy she's gone." That's high art. If you do that once in a song, you usually turn it on its head right then and there' (Cott 2017: 460). Dylan goes on:

> Someone gave me a book of François Villon poems and he was writing about hard-core street stuff and making it rhyme. It was pretty staggering, and it made you wonder why you couldn't do the same thing in a song. I'd see Villon talking about visiting a prostitute and I would turn it around. I won't visit a prostitute. I'll talk about rescuing a prostitute. Again, it's turning stuff on its head . . . I didn't invent this you know. Robert Johnson would sing some song and out of nowhere there would be some kind of Confucius saying that would make you go, 'Wow, where did that come from?' It's important to always turn things around.
>
> Cott 2017: 463–4

The lyrics of recent songs offer some possible examples: 'When you think you've lost everything / You find out you can always lose a little more' ('Tryin' to Get to Heaven', Dylan 2016a: 564); 'Try to make things better for someone, sometimes you just end up making it a thousand times worse' ('Sugar Baby', 2016a: 597).

And let's not forget that Dylan takes himself seriously as an interpretative singer. He is indeed a profound interpreter. Why spurn – all too easily – his 2009 album *Christmas in the Heart*? If we set aside whimsical tunes like 'It Must Be Santa' (judging from the video, it must be whisky), that still leaves, among other valid renderings, the stark arrangement of 'O Little Town of Bethlehem' (Dylan 2009). Journalist's question: 'On "O Little Town of Bethlehem" you sound like a true believer.' Dylan's answer: 'Well, I *am* a true believer!' (Flanagan 2009). It is true that Dylan does not specify the object of his belief (nor, alas, does the journalist ask him to); yet this album is one of Dylan's many faces, and perhaps his seemingly mysterious answer typifies Dylan.

4. Persona

Then there is Dylan's 'lifelong persona-building project' (*Jim Salvucci*): Dylan populates his works with 'a chaos of characters' – one of whom is 'Bob Dylan'. Indeed, perhaps Dylan's 'persona-building' comes as naturally to him as the web to the spider, except that to try and interpret the personae is to 'play an enervating game of bogus hermeneutics' (*Nina Goss*), since it is the persona as a manifestation of creativity which is most thought-provoking, not what it does, even less what it is or represents (isn't all the world a stage?). Dylan's agreement to be filmed for the

Pennebaker documentary *Dont Look Back*, and for the latter to be revisited by Scorsese with Dylan's cooperation and participation in *No Direction Home*, reveals a willingness to be filmed both onstage and off, thus in a sense blurring the two. Through the use of flashbacks to the earlier film, Scorsese enables the audience 'to read the passing of time on the faces of Dylan and other witnesses' (*Charles Bonnot*) – the face that in recent years, on stage, Dylan sometimes turns more towards his band than to the audience (*Julie Mansion-Vaquié*). It was indeed on the stages of Greenwich folk clubs that Dylan discovered and forged his (first) stage persona. Song, in performance, may be 'gleefully or poignantly or thrillingly open to a multiplicity of re-creations' (*Christopher Ricks*). Perhaps one could say the same of Bob Dylan's personae? Dylan's persona(e) in his four (now five) most recent original albums make(s) the 'journey into old age' (*Jean Duverger*), in 'eschatological' accents (*M. Cooper Harriss*): Dylan as prophet of the end-time, a role he has often played when it suited him over the years, but now combined with the approach of the end of the artist's own mortal time. However, Dylan himself dislikes being identified too closely with the viewpoints expressed in his songs: hence he has said that the intimations of mortality listeners saw (or, rather, heard) in the *Time Out of Mind* album were not to be taken as intimations of his own mortality. This provides a true example of the poetic 'persona', or even the notion of the dramatic monologue, in which the speaker is a creation of the author and not the author speaking as himself: 'People say the record deals with mortality – *my* mortality for some reason!' (Cott 2017: 441).

But still, that author's self remains open to question. 'There was a missing person inside myself, and I needed to find him' (Dylan 2004: 147). Dylan's quest as an artist might be bound up with this sense of needing to find a lost part of himself, which could be an alter ego, or several selves. Perhaps he did 'find him' in his radio show *Theme Time Radio Hour*, within his persona as DJ, for the time the show ran. In this persona, 'Bob meets Bob' (*Andrew McKeown*). Hence 'authenticity' bobs up not in one single 'Bob' but in the encounter of (at least) two 'Bobs'. Along with 'authenticity', the term 'Dylan-ness' was waiting to be invented (by *Denis Feignier*); this 'painfully shy' artist clearly has reservations about appearing in public as himself (whoever that may be).

Authenticity turns out to be one of the volume's major concerns: the tension between the apparent care taken by the artist to project an authentic image of himself – authentic here meaning uncommodified, 'untainted by consumerism *en masse*' (*Erin C. Callahan*) – and his willingness to take part in commercials in the twenty-first century when he can hardly pretend to be the icon of youth (and fashion?) he may once have been (not that he cares one way or the other). Rather than in terms of authenticity or otherwise alone, one may be better off seeing Dylan and his work as not only enigmatic but also 'oxymoronic' (*Anne-Marie Mai*): the works' very ability to combine contradictory feelings and traits, in songs, as in the *Brazil Series* paintings, accounts for their singularity and effectiveness. And it is finally Dylan's very 'Dylan-ness' that makes it impossible for anyone or anything to transform or appropriate him and his work from the outside, whether it be the Nobel Committee or literary appreciation of the highest and most insightful kind (*Adrian Grafe*).

Although the various events and phases in Dylan's life and career have a tendency to turn into myth, usually rather quickly, there is at least always an element of surprise to them. Hence it was that on 27 March 2020, in the midst of a sanitary lockdown in America and much of the rest of the world, Dylan released for the first time a song which 'we recorded a while back',[3] focusing on the assassination of President Kennedy on 22 November 1963. To a jazz-influenced, semi-improvised-sounding musical backdrop made up mainly of piano, violin, bow across the bass and drums, playing a simple chord sequence, Dylan's semi-spoken vocal mixes an approach to the assassination, the latter seeming to unfold with the lyric, with a vast roll-call of American popular culture from mainly the 1960s onwards, but not entirely: for example, he mentions the nineteenth-century African-American spiritual 'Freedom Oh Freedom'. Over the years, Dylan has occasionally responded in different media, in work both officially published and unpublished, to the Kennedy assassination.[4] But 'Murder Most Foul', the song in question, provides his richest response to it. The song represents Dylan's mythopoesis of Kennedy's assassination, and the lyrics reveal a close historical interest in the details of the event. Through the lyrics, Dylan lends his voice to Lee Harvey Oswald who claimed, after being accused of the assassination, that he was a 'patsy' ('I'm just a patsy like Patsy Cline'), and to (presumably) Kennedy when he asks the DJ Wolfman Jack to play various songs, including a song 'for me and for Marilyn Monroe' (Dylan 2020a). Given that behind this lyric pattern resounds a possible echo of 'Mr Tambourine Man' ('play a song for me'), one might argue that Dylan's own voice, that of the sixties icon, lies behind Kennedy's, placing them both (Kennedy and Dylan)

---

[3] Bob Dylan's official Facebook page, 27 March 2020. Available online: https://m.facebook.com/story.php?story_fbid=10163074736115696&id=11955325695 (accessed 14 April 2020).
[4] The most extensive account of Dylan's interest in this event is by James O'Brien (2013).

alongside that other contemporary icon, Monroe. The song name-checks, or name-drops, dozens of artists, and song or tune titles, including the very same song when the singer tells the DJ in the last words of the song, 'play "Murder Most Foul"' (Dylan 2020a). Given the apparent free association and series of names in the lyrics, the latter resemble the liner notes to Dylan's 1964 album *The Times They Are A-Changin'*, entitled '11 Outlined Epitaphs', with their 'love songs of Allen Ginsberg / an' jail songs of Ray Bremser' (Dylan 1964). 'Murder Most Foul' is an elegy not only for Kennedy but a lament for a certain idea of America and for a particularly American, constitutional ideal – 'the soul of a nation' as Dylan calls it (Dylan 2020a). Dylan followed this song up by releasing online (on 17 April 2020) a much shorter song, 'I Contain Multitudes', again highly allusive (as is apparent right from the Whitman quotation that forms the title; Dylan 2020b), though it is far more light-hearted, and the speaker, through welcoming the tension between unity and multiplicity, seems to have come to a sense of reconciliation with himself and the world. These songs heralded the album *Rough and Rowdy Ways*, released in June 2020 and gratefully responded to in the Coda to this volume (*Grafe and McKeown*).

This volume considers that if Dylan is to be found at all, it is through his work and his creativity. Or perhaps one must ultimately, in timely compliance, ask Jack Fate. Or for Fate read Frost: late Dylan still has miles to go before he sleeps.

References

Cott, J., ed. (2017), *Bob Dylan: The Essential Interviews*, New York: Simon and Schuster.
Dylan, B. (1964), '11 Outlined Epitaphs' [Album liner notes], *The Times They Are A-Changin'*. Available online: www.bobdylan.com/albums/the-times-they-are-a-changin/ (accessed 14 April 2020).
Dylan, B. (1997), *Time Out of Mind* [Album], USA: Columbia Records.
Dylan, B. (2004), *Chronicles, Volume One*, New York: Simon and Schuster.
Dylan, B. (2007), 'Huck's Tune' [Song], *Lucky You: Music from the Motion Picture*, USA: Columbia Records.
Dylan, B. (2009), *Christmas in the Heart* [Album], USA: Columbia Records.
Dylan, B. (2012a), 'Scarlet Town' [Song], *Tempest*, USA: Columbia Records.
Dylan, B. (2012b), 'Episode 49: Death and Taxes', *Theme Time Radio Hour*. Available online: www.themetimeradio.com/episode-49-death-taxes/ (accessed 14 April 2020).
Dylan, B. (2015), 'Read Bob Dylan's Complete, Riveting MusiCares Speech', *Rolling Stone*, 9 February. Available online: www.rollingstone.com/music/music-news/read-bob-dylans-complete-riveting-musicares-speech-240728/ (accessed 3 April 2020).

Dylan, B. (2016a), *The Lyrics: 1961–2012*, New York: Simon and Schuster.
Dylan, B. (2016b), 'In His Own Words: Why Bob Dylan Paints', *Vanity Fair*, 2 November. Available online: www.vanityfair.com/culture/2016/11/why-bob-dylan-paints (accessed 14 April 2020).
Dylan, B. (2017), 'Nobel Lecture', *The Nobel Prize* website. Available online: www.nobelprize.org/prizes/literature/2016/dylan/lecture/ (accessed 3 April 2020).
Dylan, B. (2018), *Mondo Scripto*, London: Halcyon Gallery.
Dylan, B. (2020a), 'Murder Most Foul' [Single], USA: Columbia Records.
Dylan, B. (2020b), 'I Contain Multitudes' [Single], USA: Columbia Records.
Eliot, T. S. (2014), 'Ezra Pound: His Metric and Poetry', *The Complete Prose of T. S. Eliot: The Critical Edition: Apprentice Years, 1905–1918*, 626–47, eds J. S. Brooker and R. Schuchard, Baltimore: Johns Hopkins University Press.
Eliot, T. S. (2015), 'The Contemporary English Novel', *The Complete Prose of T. S. Eliot: The Critical Edition: Literature, Politics, Belief, 1927–1929*, 83–94, eds F. Dickey, J. Formichelli and R. Schuchard, Baltimore: Johns Hopkins University Press.
Elliott, R. ([2015] 2017), *The Late Voice: Time, Age and Experience in Popular Music*, New York: Bloomsbury.
Fell, C. (2006), 'An Avid Follower of Ovid', *The Nelson Mail*, 7 October. Available online: http://nzetc.victoria.ac.nz/iiml/bestnzpoems/BNZP06/nelson_mail.pdf (accessed 14 April 2020).
Flanagan, B. (2009b), 'Dylan for the Holidays', *Street Roots*, 10 December. Available online: https://news.streetroots.org/2009/12/10/dylan-holidays (accessed 14 April 2020).
Houston, C. (n.d.), 'Talking Blues' [Song]. Lyrics available online: www.ciscohouston.com/lyrics/talking_blues.shtml (accessed 14 April 2020).
Johnson, R. (1937), 'They're Red Hot' [Single], USA: Vocalion/ARC Records. Lyrics available online: www.robertjohnsonbluesfoundation.org/track/hot-tamales-theyre-red-hot/ (accessed 14 April 2020).
Le Guay, C.-M. (2018), *La vie est plus belle en musique*, Paris: Flammarion.
O'Brien, J. (2013), 'Researching Dylan's Fugitive Writings: The Kennedy Assassination – Margolis and Moss and (the Non-Fugitive) Revisionist Art', *ISIS* [Fanzine], 163 (March–April): 26–33. Available online: https://static1.squarespace.com/static/5b16b7e4e749408e659d0fbd/t/5cf019e9d135c900019f0490/1559239151415/2013__DylanKennedyArticle_ISISno167.pdf (accessed 14 April 2020).
Riley, B. L. (1957), 'Red Hot' [Single], USA: Sun Records. Available online: www.youtube.com/watch?v=Nxt_7sD9znM (accessed 14 April 2020).
Said, E. W. (2006), *On Late Style: Music and Literature Against the Grain*, New York: Pantheon Books.
Yeats, W. B. (1997), *The Major Works: Including Poems, Plays and Critical Prose*, ed. E. Larrissy, Oxford: Oxford University Press.

Part One

Honest with Me: Late Dylan's Performing Personae

1

'I Made It So Easy for You to Follow Me': Making a Case for Dylan's *Revisionist Art* (2012)

Nina Goss

In his review of *More Blood, More Tracks: Bootleg Series 14* (2018), *New Yorker* music critic Alex Ross judges the set as 'both more and less than what Dylan obsessives have been tiresomely clamoring for' (Ross 2018). If Ross archly includes himself among the clamouring herd of obsessives, the archness is too subtle for me. What comes through is the familiar critical register conveying both sensibility and expertise that are uncorrupted by obsession. This kind of hygienic distance is peculiarly common in Dylan studies, in which the condescending and objectionable term 'Dylanologists' is generally used to maintain the normative epistemic hierarchy of popular culture. Obsessives accumulate unvetted quantities of knowledge and experience in an irrational field of desire. The professional critics discriminate, evaluate, provide rational structures of meaning and value and justify/modulate their own ardour, should they bear any.

I choose instead Roland Barthes on obsessive excess: in *A Lover's Discourse*, he writes: 'I pass beyond the limits of satiety, and instead of finding disgust, nausea, or even drunkenness, I discover ... *Coincidence* ... I adhere to the Image, our proportions are the same: exactitude, accuracy, music: I am through with not enough' (Barthes 1978: 55; orig. emphasis).

I use Barthes as a companion in this chapter, rather than a methodology, because elements of his work can be a good friend to the swarming, fervent and combative field that Bob Dylan's audience has made of Bob Dylan. In the passage above from *A Lover's Discourse*, Barthes offers a relation to an image – an apprehended face – that certainly differs from the ethical severity of Levinasian alterity, in which facing down the presented Other entails submitting to that

Other's singular inviolability. Barthes, I hope, restores *eros* to the confrontation with Image. Beyond the limit of even the most comprehensive and engaged apprehension is 'coincidence' of the lover and the beloved: a climactic be-coming of the self and the Image that consummates via 'exactitude', and not through a sublime flooding or mingling of the self and the beloved Other. Barthes manages to have his alterity and eat it too. I insist this is the consummation of the art encounter, in which we are revised by the precise lineaments of an exquisite too-much of an artefact or a performance. As Ross demonstrates, critics task themselves with defining where exactitude and *eros* are permitted to ignite in the listener/viewer/reader, and when the condition of obsession demeans an audience to a clamouring indistinct mass. Bob Dylan's audience is a special case of exactitude and clamour. Although Dylan's audience is voracious, expert and minutely attentive, a combination that brings an insatiable and very sensitive appetite to his work, we can be tiresome to those who do not pass with us beyond the limits of satiety. In this chapter, I test satiety and take on what is arguably the most discouraging post-2000 project bearing the name Bob Dylan: *Revisionist Art*. Appearing in 2012, *Revisionist Art* comprises silk-screened mock magazine covers, in some cases legitimate publications whose logos are accurately reproduced, as well as fabricated samples. The project entailed gallery exhibitions and an exhibition catalogue produced by Gagosian Gallery, which mounted the exhibition in New York, and which does not reproduce every item from the combined exhibitions. Absent one textual allusion, Bob Dylan's presence is his name displayed as the author of the project, and to whom 'All artworks' are copyrighted. Inscribing Bob Dylan into this project ultimately tests only the peculiar gains of the ordeal of inscribing.[1]

Barthes writes also in *A Lover's Discourse*: 'The ego discourses only when it is *hurt*; when I am fulfilled or remember having been so, language seems pusillanimous: I am transported, beyond language' (Barthes 1978: 55; my emphasis).

---

[1] This project was mounted with different items in different locations: I'm working with the published catalogue to the exhibition and my own two trips to the Gagosian in New York in 2012. Dylan's personal involvement in the project was not detailed in the published material accompanying the exhibitions, nor has he explicated this project in interviews. There are internet rabbit holes speculating on Richard Prince's role in the project, or Dylan's collaboration with Prince. I eschew any speculation regarding what Bob Dylan did to conceive, sponsor, manufacture, or curate the exhibitions and the physical objects themselves, as well as his involvement with the transparently facetious catalogue text by B. Clavery. I accept responsibility for refusing to sleuth out what is not in plain and public sight (i.e. Bob Dylan identified as the project's artist and to whom each and all the works are copyrighted).

I want to link to Edward Said's *On Late Style: Music and Literature against the Grain* (2007) Barthes's claim that, in love, we speak when we are *not* fulfilled, when the beloved forbids 'adher[ing]' to his/her 'Image' (Barthes 1978: 55). Said's thoughts on 'late style' were influenced by Adorno's writing on Beethoven's late works. Said takes on the tiny set of supreme artists who in hard old age still suffered intensities of productivity and consciousness that manifest in 'an inherent tension in late style that abjures mere bourgeois aging' (Said 2007: 17). These works '[insist] on the increasing sense of apartness and exile and anachronism, which late style expresses' (17). Said cannot merely submit to relishing the 'essentially unrepeatable, uniquely articulated aesthetic works written not at the beginning but at the end of a career'. Instead, he writes of the 'paradox' (Said 2007: 17–18) by which these 'unrepeatable, uniquely articulated' late works can yet be accessible influences for new artists. He further insists on terms of alienation, such as *apartness, exile, anachronism, unacceptable*, and *intransigence* and emphasizes the impermeability in the work of, in this case, the elder Beethoven. Said speaks like a lover vexed by implacable potency and appetite in a beloved who has aged out of natural potency and appetite: he pits vitality against currency. Said is not seeking a technical musicological vocabulary for the choices made by Beethoven in, say, 1822. He is theorizing a strangeness in the greatness of no-longer-young artists, which he cannot assimilate.

Bob Dylan post-2000 is prosaically unacceptable, as at this point we must never accept what he gives us as is. Henry Timrod, Abraham Lincoln, F. Scott Fitzgerald, Robert Fagles' Homer, John Greenleaf Whittier – all of these voices and more are camouflaged in the late style of Bob Dylan's compositions and we presume they await our discovery and analysis. Christopher Ricks's elegant benediction that Dylan 'repay[s] attention' (Ricks 2004: 311) has perhaps unfortunately come to describe a festering ritual of picking through a new Dylan work for whatever plundered loot he's hiding in plain sight, and then domesticating this new misbred creation into the canon. In our exhausting toil of inscribing and reinscribing late Bob Dylan, we can identify ourselves by linking Said's vexations with Barthes's now classic assertion in 'Death of the Author' that 'the reader is simply that someone who holds gathered into a single field all the paths of which the text is constituted' (Barthes 1967: 6). Bob Dylan sings his songs, paints his paintings, attaches his name to a set of mock magazine covers, and we stand at the ready as the agents of his late-style relevance; we inscribe the 'single field' that is not Bob Dylan, but inscriptions that we name 'Bob Dylan'.

The first image reproduced in the *Revisionist Art* catalogue is the actual 6 November 1964 *Life* magazine cover showing actress Shirley Eaton as Jill Masterson from the Bond film *Goldfinger*. The photo and date are authentic (although the scarlet lipstick appears enhanced) and are accompanied by fake headlines including 'Revolutionary new procedure turns flesh to gold.' In *S/Z*, Barthes writes: 'Meaning is golden …' (Barthes 1974: 9) – and indeed it is. To confer meaning on anything is the only way to give it life and value in the marketplace of signs; gold has been the marketplace's standard of value. Read this *Revisionist* image against Rembrandt's *Danaë* (1636), who raises her hand in a gesture, ambiguously greeting and alarmed, at the cascade of gold in her chamber. Danaë is the elected permeable one for the god who, as transcendent signified, can will himself into becoming the currency of supreme value. The first fake cover, then, is the woman consummated with the showered gold, which makes her the living sign. A golden woman is the best of all possible worlds: sex, illumination, money. She's lit up with the affected rapture of being the gate to *Revisionist Art*'s ersatz world and the title, *Life*, becomes an irony both trite and radical. It may be easy to write her as the composite portrait of Dylan's lineage of frozen idealized female characters. These are the women in his songs who are pinned, inviolable and manipulated all at once, from the self-sufficient artist who belongs to the songwriter, to the ageless girl from the Red River shore whose life becomes a shadow for the restive exhausted singer. Can we begin our inscribing by suggesting that, when framed with the name Bob Dylan, Shirley Eaton's phony Danaë speaks to Johanna, or the woman who might be in Tangier, or the lover drifting like a satellite, or the girl from the Red River shore? Or, by opening the published text (i.e. the version that is fixed in time and place, as a gallery visit is not) to this image, am I tempted to set up Dylan as satirizing his audience of ultra-obsessives, via insinuating he is a Midas who turns to gold everything he sets his hand to?

In hard truth, these questions play with reading through the name Bob Dylan and can't be answered. As Barthes puts it: 'Once the Author is gone, the claim to "decipher" a text becomes quite useless. To give an Author to a text is to impose upon that text a stop clause, to furnish it with a final signification, to close the writing' (Barthes 1967: 5). This kind of reverse reading accepts the slimmest invitation to impute an Author named Bob Dylan to a text, and leads right away to playing out allusions that are momentarily suggestive and exciting. This is also what Barthes calls *passionifying*: '[T]ake a bunch of roses: I use it to signify my passion. Do we have here, then, only a signifier and a signified, the roses and my passion? Not even that; to put it accurately, there are here only "passionified" roses' (Barthes 1972: 111). To passionify *Revisionist Art* with fugitive and satisfying meaning turns out to be appropriately taxing.

The prestigious Gagosian Gallery, located on the empyrean Upper East Side of Manhattan at Madison Avenue and 77th Street, is neither guarded nor welcoming. If you already know that (i) anyone may walk right in from the street; (ii) the desk guard will ignore visitors who stride past him to summon the elevator; and (iii) anyone may wander the upper floor to find the gallery which is neither clearly marked nor restricted, then you are perfectly welcome to spend as much time as you like in the gallery. Revisionist Art itself? The cheap silk-screened Photoshopping and the ludicrous text flung themselves idiotically off those white walls. There was not a square inch of authenticity. Adjusting to this facetious realm, where all signifying was obviously a game, took me no work at all – who would be tricked by this?

Getting things right and jeering at what is wrong is the work of taking in *Revisionist Art*. The project is legible primarily to those of us entitled to do this work, which Barthes helped introduce with his early demonstrations of semiotic literacy, collected in *Mythologies*. Although this anthology has largely fallen from syllabi, its lessons have become reflexive and, as ever, a class dividing line. Culture is code, the code reveals social meaning and systems of control, and the ironic and analytical consciousness that is both tool and reward of cracking these codes accrues to each succeeding entitled generation. I never questioned that signs of accessibility indicated *my* access; I read instantly the artful low quality of the objects; and epistemological privilege felt natural, as it tends to feel.

The chief form of text in *Revisionist Art* is the headline, which indicates remote and grounding phenomena, and I require numerous further fluencies to identify what Barthes would call the *indices* of the headline as text. I have to know which term in the headline is the variable substituting for the remote text; I also have to identify the *levels of description* in the value of the absent text – chronological, demographical, cultural significance.

Revisionist Art is a bedlam of discourse: lies, fictions, confabulations, anachronisms, *non sequiturs* and vacuities. Due to my competence in the codes, I can efficiently recognize in *Revisionist Art* Harry Frankfurt's definition of bullshit: 'For the essence of bullshit is not that it is *false* but that it is *phony*' (Frankfurt 2007: 14; orig. emphasis).

But phoniness is no obstacle to interpretation, and I begin my obsessive's work of excavating and inscribing. Reading *Revisionist Art* means carefully locating one emptiness after another. I distinguish a variety of fake discourses, from fallacies to nonsense, some of them rabbit holes, all of which require some prior knowledge, however trivial, to evaluate. What follows is a very brief cross-section of the work reproduced in the catalogue, which, as mentioned, is itself not comprehensive.

- Anachronisms:
  - 'Fall of Saigon' dated 1967 (Dylan 2012: 29).
  - 'Nixon's Body Exhumed' dated 2005 (2012: 41).
  - 'Muhammad Ali Using "Rope A Dope"' Knocks Out George Foreman in 8th' dated 2005 (89).
  - 'OPEC Oil Embargo Ends!' dated 1961 (117).
  - 'The Beatnik Craze' dated 1997 (81).
  - 'Portugal Establishes a Democracy' dated 1961 (129).

- Pseudo-events implicating public personalities:
  - 'Burt Reynolds' "car crash"' (25).
  - 'Gwen Stefani to Appear at Guantanamo' (33).
  - 'Mel Gibson Insists 3D Version of *The Ten Commandments* will be ready for Sundance' (25).
  - 'David Crosby Busted in Italy!' dated 1999 – Crosby was arrested in 1982 and 2004 and served prison time (65).

- Vacuous references elevated to teasing due to celebrity subjects – a thin and obvious satire of celebrity culture, if even that:
  - 'Bon Jovi Rides All Night' (33).
  - 'Billy Joel Goes for a Walk in the Park' (101).
  - 'Warren Beatty Makes a Comeback' (137).

- Misidentified images
  - 'Frank Sinatra and Joey Bishop Have a Laugh …' The photo shows Frank Sinatra, Jr., not Bishop (133).

- Allusive generic noun and adjective phrases that are conventional teaser headlines:
  - 'Houses of the East Coast' (49).
  - 'The Rocky Road to Fame' (41).
  - 'American Muscle' (137).

- Inanities that are funny – it is telling how rare *funny* is in this material:
    - 'Big Fat Pineapples Are Quite Alright' (81).
    - 'Stoicism and Divorce' (77).
    - 'Cindy Oppenheimer: Animal Psychic' (125).

There are also rabbit holes: for example, the *Sports Illustrated* cover on page 93 lists nine female names including fictional and real women, one of whom is the model on the cover of the Cars' first album. There are lies: 'Oliver Stone's New Movie "Apocalypse Now" Breaks New Ground' – no apologies to Francis Ford Coppola and the cover is dated 1997, eighteen years after the film's release (Dylan 2012: 105). Cameron Chambers (2012: 53) and Barry Sandler (2012: 97) are among the names of Googleable living people innocent, apparently, of any connection to this project. Indeed, the extensive endnote annotations are themselves vertiginous fictions involving contemporary figures, and that are something more than rabbit holes hidden in plain sight. Falsehoods range from an erroneous publication history for Stephen King's novel *Christine* (Dylan 2012: 152) to the not quite appropriate claim that US Supreme Court Justice Elena Kagan once appeared in *Playboy* magazine (2012: 160).

That the work of tracing, exposing and verifying these references is a parody of the manic sleuthing of appropriations Dylan's audience has been carrying out this millennium is self-evident. One could construct a conspiracy narrative from *Revisionist Art*: decide that Bob Dylan has embedded an entire fabulous disordered history within the numerous covers dated 1961, when the Bob Dylan Period of western culture began. One could also bring critical savvy to this project: use it to construct a tedious critique of our current info-culture, from moribund print journalism to the wormhole of the Internet to fake news as a category of journalism. I add this 'quixotic code' to the list Barthes offers in *S/Z*. The hours spent assembling this taxonomy of baloney yield a heap of verifiable facts that offers no coherent reality, given that the project is explicitly and completely counterfeit. All I've done is bullshit myself as a discursive subject.

Yet the themes of futility, flippancy, vacuum, and hard work are the ingenious triumph of 'Buckets of Rain', which concludes *Blood on the Tracks* (Dylan 1975). Dylan has not offered many faces of this song to the world. The twelve takes/remakes and one rehearsal on *More Blood, More Tracks* are fairly uniform, and the one live performance in 1990 was faithful to the studio versions (Dylan 2018). In the canon, 'Buckets of Rain' is comparatively stable, humble and very deceptively simple. The song is the coda to the masterwork of *Blood on the Tracks*: it is the curtain raised to reveal a stagehand taking down the set. All the pain and beauty of the previous nine songs is finally and cartoonishly just emptying into buckets of tears. The voice that has captivated and astonished us for nine songs is now only a little poet hard at work toting buckets of cliché moonbeams. I also hear an allusion to William Carlos Williams' iconic red wheelbarrow reduced to a toy red wagon, and perhaps the hard-driven car in 'Tangled Up in Blue' (Dylan 1975) has ended up another child's plaything, a little red bike. The verse completes the disillusionment with the philistine's motto 'I know what I like' – all poetry is just a toy chest. In 'Buckets', the beloved is finally metonymized to her simple charms always to hand for the singer, her smile, her fingertips, her sashaying hips, and the lover's 'misery' is witty and seriocomic. Bitterness, rage, inspiration, loss, fugitive love, murder – everything that is *Blood on the Tracks* – winds down into a common man's labour handed over playfully to his beloved at the end of a tiring day. The show is over, 'Buckets of Rain' tells me, the spell is broken. How felicitously Dylan disabuses himself of a masterpiece in which the range and depth of performance is equal to the range and depth of the material. In 1975, Dylan himself depassionifies greatness, while late-style Dylan has made me a one-person folly of bogus hermeneutics, playing enervating games with *Revisionist Art* in order to make Dylan mean something, anything. Said helps me appreciate that the 'unacceptable' nature of great artists' late style is not immanent in the work, but emergent in the scrutiny of an audience who may charitably be called demanding.

In *Roland Barthes*: '*I like. I don't like … My body is not the same as yours*' (Barthes 1977: 117; orig. emphasis). I also want to argue for a Barthes-worthy *eros* that may be excavated here, as a reward for some dirty work. *Revisionist Art* curiously contains one persistent image pattern, which is repeated images of bloody men and display-case women. Both sexes are presented more or less unclothed. Both present as narrative elements in which the men signify the moment after an encounter, and the women the moment preceding one.

The men appear in lurid grainy newsprint close-ups with bloody eyes, bloody mouths, blood on their bare necks and chests. Their eyes are often glazed. All the photos show the aftermath of some staged episode of masculine action (i.e. theatrical or sporting violence). Each man could be the winner or the loser in his bout. Each has survived and not yet recovered. How does this blood matter? Whose side should I be on?

The women of *Revisionist Art* create a Trump-ist paradise of universally available sex. Even the cover of *Modern Philosophy* features a topless woman. Furthermore, they are cast from the outmoded fantasies of the Trump-ish man: they are all white, young, pin-up voluptuous and clad in girlish bits of clothing. Each makes her cover beckon to pleasures within the pages that the headlines do not indicate. Each woman invites an ecstasy in this discordant world that has no regard for truth or falsehood.

The ironies here of commodified sex and violence and the possibility of a critique of toxic masculinity don't interest me. Instead I refer to *A Lover's Discourse*: 'I love the other not according to his accountable qualities but according to his existence' (Barthes 1978: 222). I choose to distribute the Never Ending Bob Dylan himself across these battered men and available women. This is the Bob Dylan who revealed himself to us in 'What Was It You Wanted?' in 1989, when the Never Ending Tour was getting underway. 'I definitely needed a new audience', he confides in *Chronicles*, 'because my audience at that time had more or less grown up on my records and was past the point of accepting me as a new artist and this was understandable' (Dylan 2004: 155). He gave himself a three-year plan for revitalization: numerous concerts would lead to a process of attrition and renewal as the older fans lost interest in the repetition and younger fans increasingly joined the parade. He was terribly wrong about his older fans; he was right about attracting younger audiences; he underestimated his own stamina or compulsiveness; and he could not have predicted that after fifteen or thirty shows, young fans develop the attitude of old fans thus requiring him to find another new audience, and then another. The result is the juggernaut we continue to refer to as the Never Ending Tour.

And this is when Dylan became the story told by the men and women of *Revisionist Art*. For thirty years now, he has come round and round the globe with about five other rotating and changing musicians, playing small and large venues in major and minuscule markets, over and over again. Consecutive set lists have contained surprises, one-offs, or been identical throughout a tour. He has given us the chance to gorge ourselves or to pass as he comes through, believing we will have another chance soon enough. Dylan's performing schedule for these thirty years has created a new kind of communal and combative subculture, whose participants compete with charts and maps and spreadsheets and life lists. One may at this point now configure Earth as a topography of Bob Dylan's performances of 'All Along the Watchtower'.

And so there is the battered and bloody Dylan – enduring the relentless vivisection of his every utterance and action, not to mention empty seats, the nights the breath may not be up to it, the trolls who pay to scorn, the nowhere venues and ugly cheap arenas, the one or two hundred shows a year as he does what he must do, ageing onstage, in real time. Here's a body blow: Michael Gray himself confessed at the October 2018 Southern Denmark University conference, 'New Approaches to Bob Dylan', that he has not listened to *Triplicate* all the way through even once.[2]

'What Was It You Wanted?' is the anthem of Never Ending Bob Dylan (Dylan 1989). The song is a mystery of patience. Embattled by the desire of his anonymous companion, the singer remains present and available to the floating and obscure 'it' that binds and separates them. 'Tell me again . . . You can tell me . . .' He promises they can start the cryptic 'it' over. 'What's going on in your show?' he asks with a stunning about-face (Dylan 1989). Bob Dylan tirelessly reaches out from his own mask, his own shadow world of *show* to find the authentic self in another person, because he knows there is such a thing. Even when the singer retreats from the words of availability, his very breath continues to signal his presence via the fierce and candid harmonica phrases. The fourteen unanswered uses of the indefinite pronoun *what* are all legitimate questions. The singer even leaves and returns, and is unafraid of a third presence in shadow, who may be a rival. This song is the late-style 'Eternal Circle' from 1963: both songs use light, shadow and desire to compose portraits of the artist trapped by his art. In 'Eternal Circle', the young artist is trapped by excess of breath and words and creativity – his song is so long, his art is so full, that desire has to wait (Dylan 1991). In 'What Was It You Wanted?' the old artist has sung so very many songs, for so very, very long. 'What Was It You Wanted?' is the peculiar beauty of anachronistic and intransigent desire, to borrow Said's terms.

In all the heavy-handed pretense of images and texts, there is only one unmistakable albeit indirect reference to Bob Dylan. The 14 February 1964 *Life* mockup shows Jack Ruby at his Carousel Club with two of his dancers and bears the headline 'Song & Dance Man from Dallas Shoots Alleged Killer of the President' (Dylan 2012: 85). 'Song and dance man' is familiar to Dylan's audience as the famous quip from his 1965 KQED press conference in San Francisco. The well-known footage of this press conference shows Dylan beautifully exhausted,

---

[2] In the course of Gray's keynote talk, 'Bob Dylan's Affective Symphony', delivered on 4 October 2018.
[3] Footage of the conference is widely available. My source was www.youtube.com/watch?v=OMp8x4SYREI (accessed 1 April 2020).

frail and implacable, responding to the question 'Do you think of yourself primarily as a singer or a poet?' with: 'Oh, I think of myself more as a song and dance man, you know'.[3] The reporters are delighted by what they take to be a moment of witty camaraderie. The quip was subsequently honoured with elevated irony as the title of Michael Gray's vast and commanding analysis of Dylan's work. And now the life of this phrase has passed further from a charged and memorialized public moment signifying Dylan's charisma and his sublime irony to a tawdry wink at Dylan obsessives who fall on this crumb and say we've found him.

A last word on why Bob Dylan and Roland Barthes may be useful at this moment. What gift of composition or performance can Bob Dylan *not* bring to bear on seducing us with his absences and withdrawals? His so-called personae are partly constructed as so many beautiful erasures. And as far as Barthes is concerned, his 'Death of the Author' and *S/Z* help disabuse me of ritual obeisance to meaning fixed in any one author.

Dylan and Barthes in their separate ways are throwbacks. The violating and erasing principles of inscription and personae cannot function freely in contemporary identity culture. Currently, intricate boundaries define subjectivity as regions of birth, or history, or biology, or invention, that are understood as inviolable authenticities always vulnerable to abuse or negation by oppressive convention or agents. The essential self is embedded in a concrete exclusive history and/or is a revealed truth. The essential self signals unassailability and dictates the terms of my engagement with it. I find proscribed appropriation and signalled unassailability the enemies of desire and play in reading art. Barthes's structuralist project may be superannuated for the time being, but when he infiltrates systems of meaning with desire, as in *Lover's Discourse*, he's able to construct love with deeply playful affliction and joy, a project worth keeping alive.

Barthes writes: 'I want to change systems: no longer to unmask, no longer to interpret, but to make consciousness itself a drug, and thereby to accede to the perfect vision of reality, to the great bright dream, to prophetic love' (Barthes 1978: 60). In 'Mississippi', Dylan tries to disillusion us once and for all: 'Got nothing for you, I had nothing before / Don't even have anything for myself anymore' (Dylan 2001). But the voice rises and abrades the listener with its dry old insistent life. Depleted, resistant, or barely there, late Dylan seems to taunt us to keep on inscribing and constructing visions of reality. Some babies never learn.

References

Barthes, R. (1967), 'The Death of the Author', trans. R. Howard, New York: UbuWeb. Available online: www.tbook.constantvzw.org/wp-content/death_authorbarthes.pdf (accessed 5 June 2019).

Barthes, R. (1972), *Mythologies*, trans. A. Lavers, New York: Farrar, Straus and Giroux.

Barthes, R. (1974), *S/Z: An Essay*, trans. R. Miller, New York: Hill and Wang.

Barthes, R. (1977), *Roland Barthes*, trans. R. Howard, Berkeley: University of California Press.

Barthes, R. (1978), *A Lover's Discourse: Fragments*, trans. R. Howard, New York: Farrar, Straus and Giroux.

Dylan, B. (1975), *Blood on the Tracks* [Album], USA: Columbia Records.

Dylan, B. (1989), 'What Was It You Wanted?' [Song], *Oh Mercy*, USA: Columbia Records.

Dylan, B. (1991), 'Eternal Circle' [Song], *The Bootleg Series Vols 1–3 (Rare & Unreleased) 1961–1991*, USA: Columbia Records.

Dylan, B. (2001), 'Mississippi' [Song], *"Love and Theft"*, USA: Columbia Records.

Dylan, B. (2004), *Chronicles, Volume One*, New York: Simon and Schuster.

Dylan, B. (2012), *Revisionist Art: Thirty Works by Bob Dylan*, New York: Gagosian Gallery.

Dylan, B. (2018), 'Buckets of Rain' [Song], *The Bootleg Series Vol. 14: More Blood, More Tracks*, USA: Columbia Records.

Frankfurt, H. (2005), *On Bullshit*, Princeton: Princeton University Press.

Prince, R. (2011), 'Bob Dylan's Fugitive Art', *The New York Review of Books*, 5 October. Available online: www.nybooks.com/daily/2011/10/05/richard-prince-bob-dylan-fugitive-art/ (accessed 18 June 2018).

Ricks, C. ([2003] 2005), *Dylan's Visions of Sin*, New York: Ecco.

Ross, A. (2018), 'Bob Dylan's Masterpiece Is Still Hard to Find', *The New Yorker*, 13 November. Available online: www.newyorker.com/culture/cultural-comment/bob-dylans-masterpiece-is-still-hard-to-find (accessed 14 November 2018).

Said, E. (2007), *On Late Style: Music and Literature against the Grain*, New York: Vintage.

Smith, R. (2012), 'Revisionist Art: Thirty Works by Bob Dylan', *The New York Times*, 13 December. Available online: www.nytimes.com/2012/12/14/arts/design/revisionist-art-thirty-works-by-bob-dylan.html (accessed 16 February 2020).

2

Masked, Anonymized and Chronicled: Dylan's Fatal Auto-Mythos for the New Millennium

Jim Salvucci

Bob Dylan's film *Masked and Anonymous* is an esoteric, idiosyncratic and eccentric offering that, in addition to boasting a future Nobel Laureate as co-screenwriter and lead, features a brilliantly starstudded cast and a maverick director out to compose what he described as 'a great Bob Dylan song' in film (Cameron 2003). Rachel Rubin likewise describes the film as 'a synesthetic's dream: a movie that looks like a Dylan song' (2004: 242). This notion of the film being constructed like a Dylan song may seem a rhetorical embellishment, but the film's peculiar flow is reminiscent of some of Dylan's narrative lyrics that emphasize metaphor and symbol over linear structure. Despite these considerable assets, it proved a critical and commercial disappointment and was largely dismissed as a failed cinematic indulgence. For instance, in his 2003 review, Roger Ebert called *Masked and Anonymous* 'a vanity production beyond all reason' with a screenplay that consists of 'incoherent juvenile ramblings' (Ebert 2003). Ebert's negative assessment, while harsher than most, is representative of many of the film's reviews of the time. *Masked* was filmed over a mere twenty days in 2002 (Williamson 2006: 276) and released in 2003, assuring that its completion either abutted or overlapped with Dylan's work on his memoir, 2004's *Chronicles, Volume One*. Both productions eschew linearity and offer narratives that abound with intertextuality, misdirection, evasion, flat-out deception and bold vision while teeming with odd and larger-than-life characters. The film and the book may be considered together as a sort of trans-genre duology, paired artistic works peculiar to Dylan at a moment of his career and contributing to his lifelong persona-building project. Both lure and repel, intrigue and vex to serve as liminal manifestations of the Dylan myth, wedged as they are between disclosure and deceit. They mask in order to reveal and chronicle to misdirect. Read together, these works manifest a sustained effort in auto-mythmaking, an ongoing and intentional project in artistic mutation and self-performance in which Dylan offers separate but related (re)presentations of himself as a creature of destiny whose life, but for accidents of his origin and early history, might have turned out quite differently. Dylan's agency in creating his auto-mythos is paradoxically offset by the auto-mythos itself in which he cedes control of his artistic progression and attributes his success to an exertion of cosmic destiny, rather than a matter of personal agency and accomplishment.

Decidedly not autobiographical and set in a murky and violent alternate North America, *Masked and Anonymous*'s narrative nonetheless tracks Dylan's life as an artist in both obscure and oblique ways. Most obviously, the character of Jack Fate, played by Dylan, is a Dylan-like musician-songwriter who, unsurprisingly, looks and sounds like Dylan. The songs Fate rehearses and performs, in fact, are mostly Bob Dylan's, such as 'Down in the Flood', 'Cold Irons Bound' and 'Drifter's Escape'. The only songs performed by Dylan and his band in the film and not written by Dylan are renditions of two traditional numbers, 'Diamond Joe' and 'Dixie'. Jack Fate's band, a Jack Fate tribute group cleverly called Simple Twist of Fate – itself the title of a Dylan song – is Dylan's touring band of the time.[1] The image Fate projects, the rugged, world-weary artist who cares little for his audience's bumptious tastes and who throws his all into performing on his terms, is much like that projected by Bob Dylan. In the film, we hear of Fate's musical influences (Blind Lemon Jefferson, Elvis Presley) and of his professional peers (The Rolling Stones, Jimi Hendrix and Janis Joplin), whom Dylan shares. Fate did not appear at Woodstock, which Dylan also famously eschewed. And their fathers, though both domineering, are mirror images: Fate's a ruthless nationalist leader, 'president of this godforsaken nation' (*Masked and Anonymous* 2003), and Dylan's a modest Midwestern shop owner. In a more cryptically allusive mode is a scene of Jack Fate seated on a bus travelling through a war-blighted, dystopian landscape with an unnamed soldier, played by Giovanni Ribisi, who melodramatically recounts his history, his disappointed ideals and his subsequent shifting allegiances from rebel to counter-revolutionary to government loyalist, which he claims, 'No one ever noticed'. His military adventures begin in his mountain village, where he defies his family to join the rebellion, and end in treachery, personal tragedy and regret.

---

[1] Dylan's band both in the film and onstage consisted of Larry Campbell (guitar), Tony Garnier (bass), George Receli (drums) and Charlie Sexton (guitar).

He stumbles over his words: 'And then one day, we wiped out a small village. They – they told us something about . . . that the rebels had it infiltrated. It was a lie. A – all the men were either dead or old. And, uh, there was nothing but women and children left'. The soldier struggles to continue before sobbing, 'It was my village' (*Masked and Anonymous* 2003). The twists and turns of the soldier's tale broadly map the twists and turns of Bob Dylan's artistic personae depicted in *Chronicles* as he navigates churning artistic contexts: from small-town nobody to leader of the folk subculture to rock and roll counter-cultural icon to square conformist and domestic family man and so on. With each new personal/creative transformation, as with the soldier's roving pursuit of political purity, Dylan betrays those who accompanied him before in order to stay true to his artistic ideals. Revealingly, in 'Mississippi', a song from 2001's *"Love and Theft"*, Dylan sings of his forsaken followers while telling those who have travelled with him that he has 'nothin' but affection' for them.

Masked presents a world where a long-time tinpot strongman is dying and war rages continuously – a reality that is 'tawdry and vulgar', as Uncle Sweetheart observes. The country looks and feels postlapsarian – like a nation suffering penance or punishment for an indelible sin – and every character seems to be angling for an advantage in order to survive if not thrive, except Bob Dylan's Jack Fate. The other major characters are played by John Goodman, Jessica Lange, Luke Wilson, Mickey Rourke, Jeff Bridges and Penelope Cruz, and these Hollywood luminaries are joined by an array of big-name actors in bit parts. Despite the stellar cast and some over-the-top characters and performances, Jack Fate is mostly passive in this dystopian alternate reality and is played most passively by Bob Dylan, who never displays the least interest in fully possessing the role. Jack Fate, as his surname suggests, just goes where he is sent and does what he must do. The first time we encounter his name, it is pointedly unspoken and written on a scrap of paper that has been tossed to the ground in mute disgust. It appears upside on the screen. Several scenes later, it is again written, not spoken, and held up so that the camera shows the name through the back of the page and therefore reversed. Finally, it is written once more but upright and forward as Jack Fate himself scribes the Whitman Hotel register. All this visual play with the name, the most literal wordplay, adds to the mystique of Dylan's character.

Strikingly, in *Chronicles, Volume One*, the Bob Dylan who inhabits this version of his life is also a mostly passive creature driven more by kismet than ambition or even intent. He closes the first chapter of his memoir with an exaggeration of his humble origins: 'I'd come from a long ways off and had started from a long ways down. But now destiny was about to manifest itself. I felt like it was looking right at me and nobody else' (Dylan 2004: 22). We are not incorrect to hear in 'destiny … manifest' an echo of 'Manifest Destiny', the American project of westward expansion and colonization, but Dylan's peculiar manifest destiny extends his influence in the opposite direction of the early American empire: west to east, from Minnesota to New York. He offers only one explanation for this migration: his pilgrimage to visit Woody Guthrie, wasting away in a New Jersey hospital. As Daniel Mark Epstein sees it, Dylan's idolization of Woody Guthrie 'and the metropolis combined in his imagination like a king and a kingdom, Guthrie and New York, a single destination, an emblem of the future' (Epstein 2011: 69). Infrequently in *Chronicles*, Dylan's actions suggest proactivity, such as when he first lights out for New York or when he chooses to work with Daniel Lanois to produce the album *Oh Mercy*, or when he boldly attempts a new singing technique. Otherwise, he moves about with little planning or forethought and even in those instances offers minimal explanation of his motives. Larry Charles, *Masked*'s co-writer and director, describes the film's creative process in parallel terms: 'There was no plan. The film began to emerge naturally' (Williamson 2006: 277), which tracks with Dylan's songwriting method as he narrates it throughout the *Chronicles* 'Oh Mercy' chapter.

On those few occasions in *Chronicles* when Dylan does act with agency, though, it is almost always in resistance to the push and pull of the times or of others around him; for instance, in defiance of the liberal counterculture of which he was the purported spokesperson, Dylan states a peculiar predilection for 1964 Republican presidential candidate Barry Goldwater, who he says 'reminded [him] of Tom Mix, and there wasn't any way to explain that to anybody' (Dylan 2004: 283). He also expresses caginess behind his lengthy convalescence after his 1966 motorcycle crash by dispassionately confessing, 'Truth was that I wanted to get out of the rat race' (Dylan 2004: 114). Finally, in these twelve words, Dylan categorically addresses one of his biography's most enigmatic, mystifying, fabled and disputed episodes and its career-changing ramifications. Confoundingly, though, he writes it off as a fortuitous opportunity to take a prudent extended holiday from his relentless touring and recording schedule. The motorcycle crash is generally regarded as a touchstone or crossroads in the life and career of Bob Dylan, and, given *Chronicles*' vexing evasiveness and occasional unreliability, the reader may be forgiven for not taking the author at his word. The crash episode itself has generated many questions. Did Dylan nearly die? Was he faking or exaggerating his injuries? Was he recovering from drug addiction? Did he, indeed, die in the crash to be replaced by a lookalike, as one persistent and unsubstantiated rumour would have it (Bals 2020)? For students and fans of Dylan, the myth surrounding this accident is so pronounced that director Todd Haynes could use it as a framing device in his 2007 meta-biopic, *I'm Not There*, which presents the life of Bob Dylan in thematic/conceptual form with six actors playing Dylan and none of them named 'Bob Dylan'.

Nonetheless, whatever the truth, his subsequent retreat from stardom during the height of the volatile late sixties sees him settle down as a family man: 'Having children changed my life and segregated me from just about everybody and everything that was going on' (Dylan 2004: 114). Moments like these are stunningly human but rare glimpses of Dylan taking charge of his life. Throughout the bulk of *Chronicles*, though, Dylan presents himself more as a weathervane or a leaf on a breeze, not leading or shaping the *Zeitgeist* but simply living in it.

Chronicles abounds with such poignant moments or epiphanies, some equally inscrutable, as when he credits the launch of his career trajectory to a chance encounter with the professional wrestler Gorgeous George (Dylan 2004: 43–4) – an improbable guru even among this memoir's grotesquery of odd characters. In 'The Lost Land' chapter, he describes George entering a Hibbing, Minnesota, arena and strolling past Dylan's teenaged self, who is playing music to warm up the audience. George winks and mouths, 'You're making it come alive'. Dylan concludes, 'Whether he really said it or not, it didn't matter. It's what I thought I heard him say that mattered, and I never forgot it. It was all the recognition and encouragement I would need for years to come' (2004: 44). Dylan's recollection of this incident and many others is thorough and precise, and *Chronicles* is rich with such exacting detail. Similarly, we get minute particulars about the literary contents of an apartment young Dylan stayed at for a bit. He catalogues this household library over several pages even though it has been four decades since he had perused it, a display of recall, among many others, that will cause the cynical reader to suspect the veracity of his recitation (2004: 36–8). To be sure, Dylan is renowned for his ability to recall lyrics and music and may possess or have possessed a photographic memory. Still, as will be noted below, much of *Chronicles*, including his stay in this particular domicile, seems composited or wholesale fabricated. In contrast, he has remarkably few particularities to share regarding his own family. He mentions children with little differentiation, attends a daughter's school play, drops an anecdote about cooking with his 'eldest son' and his son's 'soon-to-be wife' and purchases a suggestive 'WORLD'S GREATEST GRANDPA' sticker (2004: 162, 170 and 209). He also remarks on his wife in the 'New Morning' and 'Oh Mercy' chapters, but you need to have read a separate biography to understand that these are two entirely different women, Sara Dylan and Carolyn Dennis (see Thomas 2017: 97). The former is 'one of the loveliest creatures in the world of women' and the latter 'pretty' and able 'to see a grain of truth in just about anything' (Dylan 2004: 127, 209 and 211). People just seem scattered throughout his world in much the same way as he occupies the world at large. Things happen, and they react. Opportunity appears unexpectedly, and Dylan seizes it.

For instance, he discourses nostalgically on his attraction to his early lovers cum muses: Joan Baez and Suze Rotolo. In Baez's case, he recalls seeing her on television in Hibbing and sensing that they were foreordained to be together; here even his romantic preference seems directed by providence. He expresses profound admiration if not outright affection for her and says, 'The sight of her made me high', and, 'It's like she'd come down from another planet' (Dylan 2004: 254). He describes his connection to her before they ever met in cosmic, almost numinous terms, as his 'counterpart', as 'the one that my voice could find perfect harmony with' (2004: 255). With regard to the seventeen-year-old Rotolo, he voices more affection and even attraction: 'Right from the start I couldn't take my eyes off her. She was the most erotic thing I'd ever seen. She was fair skinned and golden haired, full-blood Italian. The air was suddenly filled with banana leaves' (2004: 265). He talks about being struck by Cupid's arrow and writes, 'Meeting her was like stepping into the tales of 1,001 Arabian nights. She had a smile that could light up a street full of people and was extremely lively, had a particular type of voluptuousness – a Rodin sculpture come to life. She reminded me of a libertine heroine. She was just my type' (2004: 265). As with Baez, Rotolo is a mythical figure, a siren he feels compelled to heed and obligated to pursue, guided as he is by an unseen force. He has no choice.

Much of Dylan's work is populated by such women. For example, a similar muse-like female figure appears in *Masked*: Jack Fate's father's mistress, played by Angela Bassett. A young Jack Fate, in a flashback, risks and loses everything to have her as though he too is guided by an unseen force. It is a puzzling episode until we realize that the impetus for their relationship was his mother, who, in a clumsy attempt at vengeance on her husband, sent Jack to seduce the mistress in view of a cameraman secreted in a closet. Through a voice-over accompanying the seduction flashback, he says: 'I thought I was doing it for my mother. I thought I was doing it for my country. Ultimately, I knew I was doing it for me' (*Masked and Anonymous* 2003). That last statement, albeit unelaborated, is the only expression of Jack's self-interest in the episode or anywhere else in the film for that matter. In a draft screenplay that contains dialogue not included in the film, the mistress makes Jack Fate's motivation clearer: 'Your mama. Jack. You wouldn't have had nothing to do with me if it wasn't for her' (Dylan and Charles 2015: 86). A voice-over from the same draft has Fate conclude about the seduction, 'I guess you could say I was under the spell of my mother' (2015: 84). In a voice-over that is included in both the draft screenplay and the film, he says, 'My mother tried to love me, but I think she was trying to kill me. I don't think she recognized me as her son. It was like I'd become a symbol of everything that had gone wrong in her life, in her world' (2015: 12) – for this very betrayal leads to Jack's final fall from his father's favour and eventually to banishment and prison.

Such outsized characters crowd both *Masked* and *Chronicles*. Jack Fate and Bob Dylan navigate around and with these characters as best they can to varying effects, but neither ever seems the master of his domain. For instance, both Fate and Dylan struggle significantly with their fathers. In *Masked*, Fate's father is a literal tyrant, the nation's dictator, Lear-like and filled with vengeful, filicidal rage, who banishes Jack without regard for the outcome. In *Chronicles*, Dylan portrays Abe Zimmerman as a cold and domineering patriarch, 'plain speaking and straight talking', who sardonically expresses disappointment with his musician son: 'Isn't an artist a fellow who paints?' (Dylan 2004: 107–8). Both are, again, larger than life. The president is a ruthless despot-for-life, brought low by old age and, perhaps, regret. Abe is a hardworking man, a daunting figure, who, as a teenager, rescued a driver from a burning car but was ultimately enfeebled by polio (2004: 229–30).

In the dystopian setting of *Masked*, Fate's estranged father, a military strongman, fades and dies on a bed literally mounted on a stage, which, with Oscar Vogel's Shakespearean echo that 'the whole world's a stage' (*Masked and Anonymous* 2003), projects the theatrical aspects of political power in general. Murray Leeder, in 'Haunting and Minstrelsy in Bob Dylan's *Masked and Anonymous*', extensively documents links between Vogel's blackface apparition and the presidential death scene, and Al Jolson's *The Jazz Singer*, another film featuring blackface and emphasizing tropes of staging and performance as well as instances of pronounced filial defiance (Leeder 2012: 187). In *Masked*, the president is instantly replaced upon his demise by his adopted heir, Edmund, played by Mickey Rourke, the son of the former housemaid who 'asked permission before she did anything' (*Masked and Anonymous* 2003). This turnabout of fortune and authority incites mayhem. The servant's son intends his rule to be permanent and malevolent, an overthrow of the old order symbolized by his tossing aside the podium where he gives his inaugural speech. The transition is swift and sharp and further symbolized by a staticky television broadcast that oscillates between the new president's speech and Jack's final musical performance, and marks the terminal tussle between Fate, the natural-born heir, and his usurper, Edmund. Upon seizing power, Edmund issues the first commands of his new regime:

> We will begin immediately to deploy troops in the southern region. We will resume bombing in the jungle. There will be no more violence from the organized media. Real, actual violence will take the place of manufactured violence. We will empty the prisons, and we will build a football stadium, and the evildoers from the prisons will be trampled by wild elephants, mauled by uncaged bears, and pecked to death by screaming eagles.
>
> *Masked and Anonymous* 2003

Edmund, whose name alludes to the filial usurper and sower of discord in *King Lear*, presents a vision that is brutal and absolute.

Still, in the midst of such political upheaval, Dylan perceives order, recasting lines from the poetic liner notes of his fifth album, *Bringing It All Back Home*, where Dylan paradoxically embraces disorder and turmoil: 'i accept chaos. i am not sure whether / it accepts me' (Dylan 1965: liner notes). In *Chronicles*, Dylan discusses the epochs of history in terms of a rise and fall 'pattern' whereby towards the end of a civilization 'decadence makes things fall apart' (Dylan 2004: 35). With characteristic evasiveness, Dylan adds, 'I had no idea which of these stages America was in. There was nobody to check with' (2004: 35). *Masked and Anonymous* is set in that last period, and Jack Fate utters that same famous phrase from W. B. Yeats in his final monologue: 'Sometimes it's not enough to know the meaning of things, sometimes we have to know what things don't mean as well. Like what does it mean to not know what the person you love is capable of? *Things fall apart*, especially all the neat order of rules and laws' (*Masked and Anonymous* 2003; my emphasis). Dylan's interest in history should be no surprise. As Richard F. Thomas documents in *Why Bob Dylan Matters*, Dylan received a superb education at Hibbing High School (2017: 50–2), and *Chronicles* describes Dylan's ongoing prolific reading, research and cultural immersion in metaphorical terms: 'It seemed like I'd been pulling an empty wagon for a long time and now I was beginning to fill it up and would have to pull harder' (Dylan 2004: 56). Dylan is, in fact, an accomplished autodidact; he is, as in the lyrics of his 1965 song 'Ballad of a Thin Man', 'very well read, it's well known' (Bell 2015: 435). *Masked* is rife with references to literature, film and music, and *Chronicles* is even more so. In fact, Scott Warmuth and other Dylanologists have documented portions of Dylan's memoir that are wholesale lifted from others' writing in every genre to create a distinctive pastiche. In his blog, *Goon Talk*, Warmuth describes the references and copying in *Chronicles* as 'arranged' (Warmuth 2012). For example, in an article called 'Bob Dylan, the Mermaid and the Hemingway Code', Warmuth identifies numerous passages that bear a strong resemblance to lines from Ernest Hemingway and an unremarkable New Orleans guidebook. In an elaborate argument, he identifies various intertexts, borrowings, or imitations with pieces by William S. Burroughs's writing on Hemingway. He then notes references to Burroughs in *Masked and Anonymous*, the first of which appears in the lobby of the Uncle Sweetheart Management office building – the Midas Judas Building – where a directory lists 'DR BENWAY PSYCHIA R', Burroughs's infamous recurring character, as a tenant (Warmuth 2012). The sheer quantity and intricacy of the references Warmuth documents offset their obscurity and reveal an intentionality that is unmistakable. Not surprisingly, this technique of borrowing and pastiche, which winds throughout Dylan's work in the twenty-first century, has origins in his earliest writing, which he describes in *Chronicles*: 'Nothing do or die, nothing really formulated, all major chord stuff, maybe a typical minor key thing, something like "Sixteen Tons." You could write twenty or more songs off ... one melody by slightly altering it. I could slip in verses or lines from old spirituals or blues. That was okay; others did it all the time' (Dylan 2004: 228). Earlier he describes his use of research: 'I crammed my head full of as much of this stuff as I could stand and locked it away in my mind out of sight, left it alone. Figured I could send a truck back for it later' (2004: 86) – which is as fine an analogy for his method as any. In 'Nettie Moore', Dylan sings: 'The world of research has gone berserk / Too much paperwork' (Dylan 2006), a couplet commonly interpreted as a response to the burgeoning field of Bob Dylan scholarship but which could just as easily refer to the far-flung and immersive musical, historical and literary studies that inform Dylan's creative output.

There is a flow of character types through the film, the memoir, Dylan's life and Dylan's lyrics. In *Masked*, Jack Fate's confidant – named Bobby Cupid and played by Luke Wilson – and John Goodman's Uncle Sweetheart argue about the meaning of Dylan's 'Drifter's Escape' while Fate and his band rip through a hard-driving rendition of the song. Pagan Lace, played by Penelope Cruz, comments, 'I love his songs because they are not precise. They are completely open to interpretation' (*Masked and Anonymous* 2003), echoing Joan Baez's sardonic assessment of Dylan in her song 'Diamonds & Rust': 'You who are so good with words / And at keeping things vague' (Baez 1975). Meanwhile, Pagan Lace herself, a woman of mysticism and mystery, resembles Chloe Kiel, a character Dylan describes in *Chronicles* as 'cool as pie, hip from head to toe, a Maltese kitten, a solid viper' (Dylan 2004: 102). Dylan's depictions endow these three women, Baez, Lace and Kiel, with exotic and mystical proportions, and Dylan's ongoing fascination with this interpretative version of woman is pronounced and profound.[2]

The forged aspects of both works warrant elaboration. In describing the book's structure and style, Richard Thomas addresses *Chronicles*' extensive forgeries and undependable narrative with a tact that seems most gentle, given that the book is purportedly a memoir:

> The book covers only a tiny fraction of the enigmatic life of Dylan. In reality, it's more like a play, in five acts, but with constant flashbacks, fast-forwarding, inventions, and falsehoods. The structure is elegant: Chapters 1, 3, and 5 read like the truth, while Chapters 2 and 4 read somewhat like fiction, and as Dylan says, 'that's still well and good.'
>
> Thomas 2017: 96

Ian Bell astutely observes that neither the dust-cover nor the pages of *Chronicles* claim that the book is a memoir or autobiography, and the reader is left with 'only glimpses, as through a dusty window, of an author's thoughts' (2015: 411). Dylan indulges himself with the light forgery of wordplay, which persists as one of his favourite moves. In *Masked and Anonymous,* he displays his fondness for silly puns and jokes, such as when Jack Fate peeks into a tent labelled 'Man Eating Chicken', which turns out to be just a man eating a bucket of fried chicken (2003). He also delivers acrobatic verbal profundities, such as, 'All of us in some way are trying to kill time. When it's all said and done, time ends up killing us' (2003). *Chronicles*, for its part, engages in its own linguistic legerdemain. For instance, Dylan complains that he 'had been anointed as the

---

[2] In Dylan's 1978 film, *Renaldo and Clara*, Baez plays The Woman in White, another siren-like woman with an enigmatic mystique.

Big Bubba of Rebellion, High Priest of Protest, the Czar of Dissent, the Duke of Disobedience, Leader of the Freeloaders, Kaiser of Apostasy, Archbishop of Anarchy, the Big Cheese ... All code words for Outlaw' (Dylan 2004: 120). More craftily, in describing a strange New York apartment, he mixes references to alcoholic beverages with a ghost to create a pun on 'spirit': the place smells of 'gin and tonic' and 'wood alcohol', while nearby there is 'the Bull's Head, a cellar tavern' formerly frequented by John Wilkes Booth, whose ghost Dylan claims to have seen 'in the mirror – an ill spirit' (Dylan 2004: 25). Thomas locates the tavern in question, the Bull's Head, three miles north of where Dylan positions it and himself (Thomas 2017: 103), which indicates that the actuality of the Bull's Head is less significant to Dylan than its symbolic/literary value.

Dylan has populated both *Masked* and *Chronicles* with forged characters. They may be composites or surrogates, to some extent, but they are not real, certainly not in the fictional movie and not always in the quasi-factual memoir. In *Chronicles*, for example, we are introduced to an opium smoker named Ray Gooch, a man Dylan provocatively describes as someone straight out of the songs he had been singing (Dylan 2004: 26). His roommate, Chloe Kiel, has a 'face like a doll and an even better figure' (2004: 26). Dylan claims to have lived with them for an unspecified period at an unspecified time and is not even sure of their relationship, whether they are married, siblings or cousins (2004: 26). Yet, he describes their apartment and them in preternatural detail. Did they ever exist?[3] Richard Thomas calls them Dylan's 'greatest creation in the book, the biggest whopper of them all' (2017: 101). Thomas, though, may be overlooking Dylan's lengthy digressive depiction of Sun Pie and his King Tut's Museum in the 'Oh Mercy' chapter (Dylan 2004: 20–9). Sun Pie is a forlorn eccentric on a lost Louisiana highway, and his singular paranoia has antecedents in *Masked*'s Tom Friend or Nina Veronica, and leaves Dylan equivocating as to whether Sun Pie is talking sense or not in suggesting Elvis Presley was 'an Amazon woman' (2004: 220). Similarly, the conspiracy-prone Friend opines rhetorically to Penelope Lace, 'What if I told you [AIDS] was cooked up by some Mau-Mau men in Africa and they gave it to British sailors?' (*Masked and Anonymous* 2003). For her part, in an early scene, Veronica declares, 'Look, we've got dead aliens stacked up in warehouses. What else do you want to know?' (*Masked and Anonymous* 2003). Later, she is shown transfixed by a lurid radio news report of a giant hole dug by

---

[3] On veracity in *Chronicles*, see McDougal 2014: 51, also Gray 2006: 137. To conclude that *Chronicles, Volume One* is indeed a memoir but one with an unreliable narrator would be close to the mark.

scientists who lower instruments to hear cries of despair, presumably the laments of millions of souls lost in Hell (2003).

What is the function of the desultory Sun Pie episode? There are many other disconnected narrative passages in *Chronicles*, real, imagined and newly reimagined. In *Masked* the fictionalization is more overt: Uncle Sweetheart, Nina Veronica, Tom Friend and Pagan Lace. This is the population of *Masked*'s dystopian reality, and they could find a home in *Chronicles, Volume One*. As actor Val Kilmer's Animal Keeper says in his cameo, 'Human beings, alone with their secrets, masked and anonymous, no one truly knows them' (*Masked and Anonymous* 2003).

Masked and *Chronicles* each present imaginary worlds populated with imaginary people. Within these imaginary settings, nestles Bob Dylan, a Bob Dylan as he wants us to know him. This Bob Dylan, like his alter ego, Jack Fate, is a creature of destiny, not a man of irresistible ambition, but one who rises with the tide while anticipating its ebb. *Masked*'s Jack Fate is a version of Bob Dylan who has receded with the ebb. He only returns to public life briefly because he is summoned from an underground prison cell, which recalls a crypt. His return being a resurrection of sorts, he sports a deathly 'jail pale', as Uncle Sweetheart notes before adding, 'It suits you' (*Masked and Anonymous* 2003). He seems neither enthusiastic nor reluctant. He is simply resigned, as his flat affect suggests throughout. Even as he is marched from the warehouse at the end of the movie, betrayed and arrested for a murder he did not commit, Fate barely blinks at the killing or his arrest as though he expected them both all along. In the final scene, as he is transported back to prison or to execution – his fate – he stares phlegmatically at the camera and muses in voice-over: 'I was always a singer and maybe no more than that. Sometimes it's not enough to know the meaning of things, sometimes we have to know what things don't mean as well' (*Masked and Anonymous* 2003). Jack Fate's fatalism runs as deep as his evasiveness, a fact reflected on the title page of the screenplay draft, which claims its source is an unpublished short story momentously called 'Los Vientos del Destino' ('The Winds of Destiny') by 'Enrique Morales' (Dylan and Charles 2015: 1), thus echoing in theme and phrase Dylan's 'Forever Young', a 1974 song reputedly written for his then-youngest child Jacob, in which Dylan implores, 'May you have a strong foundation / When the winds of changes shift' (Dylan 1974). Unsurprisingly, Morales appears to be a wholly fabricated being himself (Bell 2015: 442).

We have seen the disarray of such outsized characters, named and unnamed, in Dylan's work elsewhere, be it in 'The Lonesome Death of Hattie Carroll',

'Maggie's Farm', 'Desolation Row', 'Lily, Rosemary and the Jack of Hearts', 'Hurricane', the 1978 film *Renaldo and Clara*, 'Highlands', 'Floater' or 'Tin Angel', to name but a few. Dylan clearly returns again and again to the idea of populating his works with a chaos of characters – large, small, real, imagined and borrowed. He does the same with texts and tunes. Sometimes, as in the songs 'Tempest' or even 'Brownsville Girl', their role is less in support of a coherent narrative and more stylistic or symbolic. In other songs, such as 'Joey', the larger-than-life characters operate as figures in a more conventionally linear tale, in this case literally from birth to death.

Dylan writes in his memoir, 'You can say I practiced in public and my whole life was becoming what I practiced' (Dylan 2004: 16). This disclosure helps explain his relentless touring, his haphazard movie career and the liminal nature of *Chronicles*, which oscillates between revelation and deception. What he has practiced his whole life, more, perhaps, than even his music, is the performance of his self-myth. It began when he was young with lies about his origins, lies that early in his memoir he dismisses as 'hophead talk' (2004: 8). It is this practice of auto-mythos that is at work in *Masked*, a film that suggests a version of the artist who makes few choices and whose destiny is disastrous, a what-if alternate reality from that of the artist of *Chronicles*, who again makes few choices, but whose destiny has a far more uplifting outcome. Elizabeth Brake notes *Masked*'s insistence that 'Luck determines our achievement'. She adds, 'But happiness can't even be pursued' and quotes a Fate voice-over: 'It either comes to you, or it [don't]' (Brake 2015: 204).

Chronicles' closing passage is both poignant and instructive as it positions Dylan to face his future in 'a thunderhead of a world' (Dylan 2004: 292–3). The image of a storm-torn world, neither divinely influenced nor diabolical, reverberates with the chaos depicted in the montage of natural and manmade violence – erupting volcanoes and brutal street battles – in *Masked*'s initial title sequence. The ferociousness of the film's opening imagery and *Chronicles*' 'thunderhead of a world' conclusion serve as bookends framing the duology of *Masked and Anonymous* and *Chronicles, Volume One*. Just as the chaos of Jack Fate's world sets his unplanned future, the chaos of Dylan's world sets his. The myth of Bob Dylan and the myth of Jack Fate converge on this point but diverge ever after, with Dylan fulfilling his destiny as a musical and literary star and Fate headed back to incarceration for a crime he did not commit. Bob Dylan's secret, when we view it this way, is that he is just fortunate to be born to a destiny that he did not earn. It's almost an expression of humility, but a dubious humility. As his auto-mythology and the contrast between the film and memoir suggest, his destiny is out of his control and therefore stems from pure happenstance. He may write his own history, but he simultaneously relinquishes dominion over its outcome. His concession to the extraordinary run of luck that constitutes his professional life offers new insight into the opening verse of the song 'Idiot Wind' where he lays out an allegorically autobiographical narrative of paranoia, accusation, deceit and unearned success and then slyly sings, 'I can't help it if I'm lucky' (Dylan 1975). Dylan acknowledges the good fortune of his luminous destiny, but, as luck would have it, with just a twist of fate, it could be all-so different.

References

Baez, J. (1975), 'Diamonds & Rust' [Song], *Diamonds & Rust*, USA: A & M Records.
Bals, F. (2020), 'Let's Go Crazy: 5 of the Weirdest Rock-'n-Roll Conspiracy Theories', *Medium*, 23 February. Available online: https://medium.com/@fredbals/lets-go-crazy-5-of-the-weirdest-rock-n-roll-conspiracy-theories-8194fb8d1899 (accessed 27 February 2020).
Bell, I. (2015), *Time out of Mind: The Lives of Bob Dylan*, New York: Pegasus.
Brake, E. (2009), '"You can always come back, but you can't come back all the way": Freedom and the Past in Dylan's Recent Work', in D. Boucher and G. Browning (eds), *The Political Art of Bob Dylan*, 184–206, Charlottesville: Imprint-Academic.
Cameron, S. (2003), 'Interview with Larry Charles', *Reel Movie Critic* website, July. Available online: https://web.archive.org/web/20090216054600/http://reelmoviecritic.com/20035q/id1996.htm (accessed 7 April 2020).
Dylan, B. (1965), *Bringing It All Back Home* [Album], USA: Columbia Records.
Dylan, B. (1974), *Planet Waves* [Album], USA: Columbia Records.
Dylan, B. (1975), *Blood on the Tracks* [Album], USA: Columbia Records.
Dylan, B. (2001), *"Love and Theft"* [Album], USA: Columbia Records.
Dylan, B. (2004), *Chronicles, Volume One*, New York: Simon and Schuster.
Dylan, B. (2006), *Modern Times* [Album], USA: Columbia Records.
Dylan, B. (S. Petrov, pseudonym) and L. Charles (R. Fontaine, pseudonym) (2015), 'Full Text of "Masked and Anonymous – Bob Dylan"', *Internet Archive*, 24 August. Available online: https://archive.org/stream/MaskedAndAnonymousBobDylan/Masked-and-Anonymous_Bob-Dylan_djvu.txt (accessed 12 February 2020).
Ebert, R. (2003), 'Masked and Anonymous', *Roger Ebert* website, 15 August. Available online: www.rogerebert.com/reviews/masked-and-anonymous-2003 (accessed 12 February 2020).
Epstein, D. (2011), *The Ballad of Bob Dylan: A Portrait*, New York: Harper Collins Press.

Gray, M. (2006), *The Bob Dylan Encyclopaedia*, New York: Continuum.
I'm Not There (2007) [Film], Dir. T. Haynes, USA: The Weinstein Company.
Leeder, M. (2012), 'Haunting and Minstrelsy in Bob Dylan's *Masked and Anonymous*', *Journal of Popular Film and Television*, 40 (4): 181–91. Available online: www.tandfonline.com/doi/full/10.1080/01956051.2012.668577 (accessed 12 February 2020).
Masked and Anonymous (2003) [Film], Dir. B. Dylan (S. Petrov, pseudonym) and L. Charles (R. Fontaine, pseudonym), USA: Sony Pictures.
McDougal, D. (2014), *Dylan: The Biography*, Nashville: Wiley-Turner.
Renaldo and Clara (1978) [Film], Dir. B. Dylan, USA: Circuit Films.
Rubin, R. (2004), 'Roundtable Discussion on Dylan's *Masked and Anonymous*', *Journal of Popular Music Studies*. 16 (3): 242–82. Available online: https://onlinelibrary.wiley.com/doi/10.1111/j.1524-2226.2004.00025.x (accessed 19 February 2020).
Thomas, R. (2017), *Why Bob Dylan Matters*, New York: Dey Street-Harper Collins.
Warmuth, S. (2012), 'Bob Dylan, the Mermaid and the Hemingway Code', *Goon Talk* blog, 16 August. Available online: http://swarmuth.blogspot.com/2012/08/bob-dylan-mermaid-and-hemingway-code.html (accessed 19 February 2020).
Williamson, N. (2006), *The Rough Guide to Bob Dylan*, 2nd edn, London: Rough Guides.

3

Performativity, Subversion and Mask-ulinity: Dylan *on* Screen, Dylan *as* Screen

Sara Martínez

Bob Dylan is one of the dominant figures in post-World War II pop culture: as singer-songwriter, through the release of thirty-nine studio albums, and through his more than five decades of onstage touring all over the world, his chameleonic masculinity – his 'mask-ulinity' – is part of an unfinished, multilayered 'collage' which continues to spur considerable interest among an intergenerational audience. The main aim of this chapter is to examine the musician's response to the projection of his 'persona(e)' inside and outside cinema to highlight the significance of his performativity in offering new possibilities of self-representation that celebrate an inversion of social order and structure by means of a permanent *state of becoming*. Therefore, this chapter will consider Bob Dylan's appearances on screen by rethinking his initial role as 'author' to look at his function as a 'transmitter' upon which the projections of the audience play. I will consider the screen 'persona(e)' inhabited by himself as 'Jack Fate' in Larry Charles' *Masked and Anonymous* (2003), and by other actors in Todd Haynes' *I'm Not There* (2007). The latter movie features six incarnations of Dylan disassembling a linear film-making and narrative structure. The hypotheses of Laura Mulvey, Theodor Adorno and Steven Cohan will be cited as primary sources, in order to demonstrate that Dylan's emergence as pop music icon coincides with the rise of new kinds of screen subjectivity – the dominance of TV, the availability of portable film cameras. These have indeed played a key role in his consolidation as 'screen artist', as well as 'poet' and/or 'musician'.

1. Masculinity as performance

This section will ask the question: How is masculinity impersonated or performed in culture? It will then address Bob Dylan's response to the projection of his persona(e) as a screen in cinema. Critic John Beynon refers to the concept of masculinity as a 'standardised container, fixed by biology, into which all "normal" men are placed, something "natural" that can even be measured in terms of psychological traits and physical attributes' (Beynon 2001: 2). However, other scholars including Steven Cohan argue that masculinity 'does not refer to a male nature but instead imitates a dominant regulatory fiction authorizing the continued representation of certain types of gender performances for men, marginalizing others, and forbidding still others' (Cohan 1997: 24). In short, the term 'masculinity' alludes to an evolving performance which is shaped by factors such as culture, age, ethnicity, belief system, locality, disability, nationality, and sexual orientation, and whose development is directly affected by a series of standards that are already predetermined in society (i.e. social and gender stereotypes that have shaped the individual's will instead of freeing it). Therefore, it can be argued that the concept of 'masculinity' is not biologically but socially, historically and culturally created, as it is not about men, but about images, stereotypes, norms, behaviours, privileges and attitudes. Steven Cohan's *Screening the Male* (1993) is a pivotal work in gender studies and queer theory. Its thirteen essays challenge stereotypical representations of males in classic Hollywood movies, particularly the aesthetics and functions of heterosexual masculinity – dance man, mama's boy, bachelor, muscular men – which are seen as oppressing and undermining the visibility of different, atypical masculinities such as homosexuality or other forms like androgyny. In the eyes of society, men engaging in such practices or identities were counterproductive subjects who did not accomplish their duty as procreators and guardians of the country's morals. The combination of the canonical, restrictive conception of masculinity with a notorious lack of investigation, discussion and visibility of the male condition inside and outside mass media, is precisely what has given rise to a widespread crisis that is still present today.

2. 'He Not Busy Being Born is Busy Dying' ('It's Alright, Ma', Dylan 1965)

One of the main themes that has characterized the evolution of Dylan since his early days in the music industry has been his strong sense of identity and individuality. This distinguishing mark has been underlined in cinema by means of portraying the tension that prevails in the performer–audience relationship both onstage and off. After the release of *The Freewheelin' Bob Dylan* on 27 May 1963, the artist's impact in the music charts meant that, for many devotees, neither listening to the records and attending performances, nor reading or watching public interviews, were enough to satisfy their longings as a public – that is to say, their desire to possess the will of his persona(e) both in musical and private terms. This response became decisive in the intercommunication between audience and performer, since the external demand to obtain much more from him led Dylan to use masks as a self-defence mechanism with which to portray a wide range of facets of his 'self' that did not necessarily correspond to reality. Roland Barthes envisioned the modern writer as a creator who was 'in no way supplied with a being which precede[d] or transcend[ed] his writing, he [was] in no way the subject of which his book [was] the predicate; there [was] no other time than that of the utterance, and every text [was] eternally written here and now' (Barthes 1977: 145). In the same way, Dylan started by reclaiming his role as a mediator who created and interpreted songs without necessarily having a specific political purpose in mind. Steven Cohan's *Masked Men* (1997) examines what he sees as a crisis in post-war masculinity, particularly highlighting the effect of a hegemonic masculine identity where homosexuality and ethnicity were 'either subordinated to the hegemonic authority of the domesticated breadwinner, often in direct opposition to his "tough" conservative partner, or not represented on screen at all' (Cohan 1997: 38). On the whole, these 'lower-rank masculinities' are a series of rebellious performances that coincide with Dylan's varied, controversial roles played over the decades 'as screen' and 'on screen', challenging the norms and rules that shape the status quo – order, stability and obedience. Despite having lived more than five decades under constant press coverage and rigorous study by many critics, the enigma behind Dylan's mysterious multi-layered personality is still alive. Taking this into account, Bob Dylan's performances will be addressed 'as' screen and 'on' screen to the extent that they have revisited and challenged constructions of masculinity, offering new models of male representation in popular culture.

3. Bob Dylan 'as' screen

'The image recognized is conceived as the reflected body of the self, but its misrecognition as superior projects this body outside itself as an ideal ego, the alienated subject, which, re-introjected as an ego ideal, gives rise to the future generation of identification with others' (Mulvey 1999: 60). This quotation is key to comprehending Laura Mulvey's main argument in 'Visual Pleasure and Narrative Cinema' where she argues that the seventh art functions as a vehicle to channel pre-existing representations of masculinity in society. This thesis coincides with Steven Cohan's *Screening the Male* wherein the 'screen' is employed as a metaphor in relation to the construct of masculinity. However, the fact that this mode of narration is created to accomplish specific purposes which are under the authority of influential figures transforms the subject into an object, 'a screen, or an oblique mirror through which the viewer glimpses both the object's creator and other like-minded viewers' (Michasiw 1994: 152), that itself denies room for difference, and hence for individual freedom. Taking this into account, we can say that the release of *The Freewheelin' Bob Dylan* marked a turning point in Bob Dylan's career, since it was the record that consolidated his distinctiveness as songwriter. At the age of twenty-one, the popularization of tracks such as 'Blowin' in the Wind', 'Masters of War' or 'A Hard Rain's A-Gonna Fall' proved his worth not only as a talented interpreter, but also as a unique composer with the ability to capture the spirit of an epoch, and move it forward. That is to say, at the point where Dylan got recognition for renewing the concept of traditional folk music, he passed from talking 'about' a generation, to talking 'to' a generation. Though the launch of his third studio album *The Times They Are A-Changin'* (13 January 1964) constituted Dylan's consolidation as the so-called 'spokesman of a generation' thanks to the socio-political call to action of tracks such as 'The Times They Are A-Changin'', 'Ballad of Hollis Brown' or 'Only A Pawn In Their Game', Dylan felt the need to move forward and experiment with a more personal and interior sound that would differ from the one employed in his previous works. Regarding his portrayal in the public sphere, Dylan developed an entangled relationship with the loyal crowd of journalists, critics, and devotees who, despite belonging to different social, political or religious backgrounds, fused the apparent credo reflected in the artist's song lyrics and their own expectations as 'one'. Such a conflict between reality and interpretation philosopher Theodor Adorno attributes to the difficulty of discerning boundaries in the musical idiom:

> Music suffers from its similarity to language and cannot escape from it. Hence, it cannot stop with the abstract negation of its similarity to language. The fact that music, as language, imitates – that on the strength of its similarity to language it constantly poses a riddle, and yet, as nonsignifying language, never

answers it – must, nevertheless, not mislead us into erasing that element as a mere illusion.

Adorno 2002: 410

This highlights the adverse impact of such a perception of the artist's individuality, since the audience attempts to exercise control over the subject through the meaning of language independently of his identification and commitment to it. As Jeff Taylor notes in relation to the Bob Dylan phenomenon, 'People see characteristics in Dylan that they want him to embody, whether that belief conforms to reality or not' (Taylor 2015: 7). These different stances between the artist and an anxious audience who are never satisfied can lead to unmanageable, annoying situations. When Bob Dylan was interviewed for *Time* magazine at London's Royal Albert Hall, 9 May 1965, both he and the journalist started off amicably enough. But when Horace Judson asked the question, 'What is really the truth?', Dylan became famously irritated and confrontational. In fact, his sarcastic depiction of truth as a 'plain picture of, of, let's say of a tramp, vomiting, man, into the sewer, you know?' (*Dont Look Back* 1967) functions as a constitutional mask working on at least two levels, since besides allowing Dylan to disassociate himself from any kind of constriction, it also converts him into a simple mediator between the material released and the audience who listens to it. This is a key scene in D. A. Pennebaker's documentary *Dont Look Back*, as it succeeds in capturing the controversy surrounding the limitations of art, and the distinction between 'fiction' and 'reality'. This friction, according to Laura Mulvey, leads – in cinematic terms – to 'the birth of the long love affair/despair between image and self-image which has found such intensity of expression in film' (Mulvey 1999: 61). Though events like the well-known altercation with Judson derive from the consequences of being a public figure with whom the audience has created a relationship based on projecting and satisfying inner desires, in some cases unpredictable reactions can have an opposite effect to that initially expected. In Bob Dylan's case, this situation has been recurrent throughout his whole career: that is, though on many occasions the audience's longings have become frustrated, the power, spontaneity and mystery that characterize his performances, added to a defiant and masked attitude against the status quo, have functioned as an attractor and as a screen for them. As Tsioulakis states, 'This level of closeness is not always easy or enjoyable for the performer, since often being accessible to the audience can be straining, resulting in negative feelings' (Tsioulakis 2017: 75). However, Dylan's offstage strategy of physical and emotional estrangement towards the audience, music critics and the press must not be confused with his involvement when he is performing, since such disaffection can lead to misinterpreting his real aim: becoming a transmitter, not an idol to worship. This is a distinctive behaviour that enriches the reliability of Dylan's lyrics, considering that anyone who pays attention to them can recognize the level of emotional involvement and empathy portrayed. As a whole, this strong sensibility is able to evolve depending on the role performed as folk apprentice, rambler or prophet, thus evincing the distinctiveness of a chameleonic-like masculinity which is impossible to imitate. Despite this never-ending performance revealing the inconsistency between Dylan 'the artist' and Dylan 'the citizen' whose deeds contradicted both themselves and his songs, his consolidation as 'the voice of a generation' and 'the prophet' in the early sixties was not affected by it. This is an issue which was directly related to the musician's gender, considering that although Joan Baez's songs were tremendously political and matched her involvement with humanitarian causes, her impact as a protest artist in the folk sphere was to some extent overshadowed by his.

4. Bob Dylan 'on' screen

The concept of masculinity is performed on the big screen as a mirrored illusion which is empowered by the use of cinematic effects – dolly zoom, bullet time, digital compositing – the main aim of which is to satisfy a series of repressed desires that evince a clear tension between ideal models of manhood and a crisis of self-determination. This quandary is explored in Steven Cohan's *Screening the Male* (1993), whose essays dispel the representations of men as strong, authoritative figures in classic titles such as Alfred Hitchcock's *North by Northwest* (1959), Howard Hawks's *Red River* (1949) and Michael Gordon's *Pillow Talk* (1959). The direct consequences of these veiled boundaries mean that any remaining enactments that differ from the norm – homosexuals, black men, drug addicts, misfits – become condemned and excluded. Although in post-war American mass-media representation, males stand out for their physical strength and leadership at work, this outward appearance is in reality a fallacy considering the subjects' inability to accomplish fully their personal and professional development as beings. It is precisely this fragility and lack of agency in refusing society's desires which turns them into passive objects, as Kim Michasiw points out in 'Camp, Masculinity, Masquerade': 'The recognized object offers no resistance to having been engulfed in projective fantasy and turned into a relay point linking a network of looks' (Michasiw 1994: 12). By contrast, the main feature that characterizes Bob Dylan's masculinity is the chameleon-like state of becoming that turns his presence into a living organism made up of a great number of layers which are constantly evolving, in particular using masks as a self-defence mechanism that, besides allowing him to portray a wide range of faces, has succeeded in captivating a diverse audience to this day. As will be explored in the following section, despite constant scrutiny from press and critics alike, the enigma behind Dylan's persona(e) is still in debate when adapted to the big screen.

5. Bob Dylan's performativity in Larry Charles' *Masked and Anonymous*

Larry Charles' *Masked and Anonymous* is a drama written by Bob Dylan and starring him as Jack Fate, a convict folk singer who is taken out of prison to perform at a benefit concert. Following a non-normative methodology that differs from popular cinema's standard structure, the movie includes some dialogues full of imagery and symbolism, such as the one between Jack Fate and the Animal Wrangler next to the corrals – a dialogue which, instead of clarifying the enigmas presented, strengthens them (*Masked and Anonymous* 2003). This is a strategy that can be addressed from theorist Laura Mulvey's perspective. Mulvey points to the anomaly of a movie script that frustrates the 'normal pleasurable expectations and pleasures in order to conceive a new language of desire' (Mulvey 1999: 59), thus confirming that such a distinctive mode of narration is the best vehicle to demolish the portrayal of gender stereotypes in cinema. One of the biggest achievements of *Masked and Anonymous* is the depiction of the dangers entailed in being a profitable artist whose self-determination is constricted by marketing strategies. Considering this, it is imperative to analyse Tom Friend and Jack Fate's encounter in the dressing room. In this scene, Dylan inhabits a 'screen' persona that recreates in detail the turbulent relationship he has always maintained with the press. Though there exists an incipient tension between both characters from the moment they start speaking, Tom Friend attempts to reconcile with Jack Fate: 'You've been avoiding me, man. You don't need to avoid me. I just want to know a few things.

I want to ask you some questions' (*Masked and Anonymous* 2003). However, after a few minutes of one-way communication, the artist's impassivity pushes the journalist to strengthen his dominant position with some aggressive speech: 'What about the king of the sexual revolutionaries? Hefner, that son of a Bible thumping Baptist. Huh? How does that guy figure into this? You're supposed to have all the answers. Come on. Huh? Sexuality is, er . . . more revolutionary than any ideology, and you know it' (*Masked and Anonymous* 2003). This is a significant scene that, besides functioning as a reversal of the aforementioned encounter between Dylan and journalist Horace Judson at London's Royal Albert Hall, recalls the objectification Dylan suffered after being labelled a 1960s 'male icon', as reported in *GQ Style* magazine some decades later ('Indomitable Style' 2016). With this action, Tom Friend tries to put on the same level Fate's impact as 'prophet' or 'voice of a generation', and Hugh Hefner's influence as founder of the erotic magazine *Playboy*. The connection between iconic pop star and sexual desire is analysed by Kenneth MacKinnon thus: 'The fetishisation of the pop star [occurs] in the double sense of making him an object of the erotic gaze at the same time that the gaze is denied through such alibis as his connoted innocence or wholesomeness' (MacKinnon 1997: 95). Actually, this is a remark that coincides with the conceptualization of the musician's aesthetics on the covers of *Bob Dylan* (1962) and *The Freewheelin' Bob Dylan* (1963), where the image/look that reads as 'be authentic, say something significant, and leave a mark' (Rotolo 2009: 10) was conceived to highlight the principles of musical integrity and authenticity so characteristic of the folk genre. In *The Image or What Happened to the American Dream* (1962), Daniel Boorstin argues that the concept of reality during the Cold War era was personified by pseudo-events characterized by their artificiality (Boorstin 1962). One direct consequence of this was that the lives of many Americans became inauthentic. In Dylan's particular case, his mannerisms, gestures and clothes, representative of the beatnik Bohemian style, indicate that his image was itself fabricated. Indeed, though performing the role of the outsider, he kept returning to his rural roots in pursuance of the inspiration he needed to create a distinctive performance on stage – that is, by having as a major reference the figure of Woody Guthrie, but developing his own identity through a process of assimilation, imitation and performance.

In *Masked and Anonymous*, Larry Charles' use of portable film cameras is quite effective at capturing Fate's threatening look and deafening silence: gestures which, besides operating as a defiant response towards the journalist, reproduce the behaviour that Dylan adopted after being praised as a countercultural icon. Unlike most conventional artists for whom interaction with the press was decisive in the promotion of their work, for Dylan it was the opposite: in the same way as Jack Fate avoids being emotionally involved with the many characters that populate *Masked and Anonymous*, Dylan has always been characterized for marking a clear barrier with the outside world. Although in Jack Fate and Tom Friend's scene both seem quite uncomfortable, the journalist keeps interfering in the artist's private life by asking: 'Who's your true companion? What makes your life easier? Can you answer that? I'm on your side, OK? I want to put your story on the cover of the London *Times*, man. You . . . you need the publicity. You know that. You've been to England lately? It ain't so English any more' (*Masked and Anonymous* 2003). This attitude reproduces the interaction that has prevailed between Dylan and the media, since the music business and pressmen's primary goals have been focused on profiting from his success as an artist, promising access to the 'real' Dylan without any official consent, just like finding the degree of truth that exists between his most important masks in the professional field – 'the prophet' or 'Judas' – and those he employed for the preservation of his private side as Robert Allen Zimmerman. After the interlude, the character of Oscar Vogel appears on stage. With his face painted black like a minstrel, and dressed in an impeccable dinner suit, this banjo-player introduces Jack Fate as 'the star of the show here. One of the biggest stars. I was one of your father's favorite performers once. Everything was going great as long as you kept your mouth shut' (*Masked and Anonymous* 2003). This is an allusion to the musician's father, pointing to the entanglement that characterized Bob Dylan and Abe Zimmerman's relationship in real life, where the father's lack of support for the professional career of his eldest son created an emotional and physical distance between them that was never overcome. The fact that this unpleasant situation keeps being recalled throughout Vogel's whole speech suggests that one of Dylan's main goals when developing the script of *Masked and Anonymous* was to liberate an emotional burden he had kept inside for a long time.

Jack Fate and Oscar Vogel highlight the Shakespearean idea of the world as stage and the importance of performance: '"My name is Oscar Vogel." "Oscar Vogel. Well, I got to get back to the stage." "The stage? Ah, yes. The stage. The whole world is a stage"' (*Masked and Anonymous* 2003). By taking as a reference point Jaques's words from *As You Like It* (II vii 139ff), the combination of these three sentences evokes Dylan's conception of art as a fluid, changeable process ruled by a permanent state of reinvention that resembles theatre-making; that is to say, as a performance where actors focus on a concrete narration that functions as a catalyst for social and cultural change. Likewise, the audience's comprehension of it as a collaborative experience based on the lack of restraint, and in which the main player acts as a mediator, when not an idol of the masses, has a positive effect on the subject, since by the time he is done with the interpretation onstage he is allowed to be freed from the mask worn, thus enacting a different character.

6. Bob Dylan's non-performativity in Todd Haynes' *I'm Not There*

I'm Not There (2007) recreates several chapters in Bob Dylan's life and music by featuring six incarnations of his self that break with the narrative structure that prevails in filmmaking – introduction, rising action, climax, falling action, and resolution – thus coinciding with the non-normative methodology that characterizes Larry Charles' *Masked and Anonymous* (2003). As director Todd Haynes suggests, this is a challenging format that, far from constraining the actors' performances, encourages the viewer to become aware of the everlasting tension that exists between the use of masks and the 'collaged' Dylan: 'But what's so amazing about Dylan is that each of those transitions from character to character or self to self, which come with a death – the death is built-in – is also a liberation into a new self, a new identity' (Marcus 2007). The movie's opening scene gives the audience the chance to feel as if they were Dylan himself on his way to the stage, a brief illusion which is followed by the presence of a motorbike: a detail that alludes to the motorcycle crash the musician suffered at Woodstock on 29 July 1966, an event that enabled Dylan to step out of the limelight and accomplish his role as husband and father. Certainly, this was a mysterious incident which led to all kinds of speculation, some crash theories even questioning the veracity of the event itself. As expected, Dylan did not address such conjectures in *Chronicles, Volume One (2005)*, where he simply acknowledges that he had a motorbike accident but had got over it, and that this was an opportunity to leave the rat-race (Dylan 2004: 114). Accordingly, the motif of the road can be addressed as a metaphor of 'speed, change and fluidity' that enabled Dylan to undergo a chameleon-like transformation into a bucolic performer that corroborated the fact that he is never the same thing twice. The film's following sequence makes use of Kris Kristofferson's voice-over to introduce the six characters to be examined throughout the film.

The cadaver we see in the coffin is actress Cate Blanchett playing Dylan's archetype of rebellious singer-songwriter that prevailed throughout the 1960s: in this regard, a performance that disrupted and challenged the understanding of masculinity as an illusory construct that lacked the complexities involved in being male. In fact, a key feature of *I'm Not There* that deserves particular consideration is Cate Blanchett's role as Bob Dylan, since her androgynous acting constitutes a powerful method of deconstructing the stereotypes and constraints entailed in a musical or dramatic performance through an aesthetic act of subversion. On the premise that 'it has become the norm for actresses to prove dedication to the craft of roles that require a compromise of their glamorous looks [while] few have embraced androgyny by crossing the gender divide' (O'Meara 2014), Blanchett's corpse in the coffin constitutes a direct parallel between Haynes' murder of Bob Dylan as a skilled musician who is adored or hated by the audience – depending on his ability to satisfy their own needs – and Roland Barthes's depiction of the initial role of the artist in 'The Death of the Author' (1968). Barthes conceives the artist as 'a modern figure, produced no doubt by our society insofar as, at the end of the middle ages, it discovered the prestige of the individual, or, to put it more nobly, of the "human person"' (Barthes 1977: 143). Thus Bob Dylan's role as a chameleonic, defiant and contradictory performer can be addressed as his way of refusing to be objectified either by music critics or journalists, or by his public across the decades. Concerning Cate Blanchett's impersonation of Bob Dylan, her cross-gender acting draws the spectator's attention to three aspects of the film: how director Todd Haynes attempts to overcome the barriers and societal prejudices that have conditioned women's ability to perform on stage since the Renaissance; the confirmation that gender 'is continually negotiated, continually in the act of becoming ... Gender performances mark not only private but also cultural constructs of power and powerlessness, frequently reveal[ing] individual and collective anxieties about identity boundaries' (Millar-Heggie 2004: 1); and the vindication of the fact that *I'm Not There* is an unconventional movie ahead of its time for it does not hesitate to take risks at narrative, aesthetic and performative levels. Considering that the 'critical reception of the film praised Blanchett's performance with several reviewers rating her embodiment of Dylan as the most convincing' (O'Meara 2014), it is worth noting the conceptualization of gender as a continuous performance that allows the subject to wear a mask which may or may not alter the reproduction of a socio-cultural archetype in people's minds. In this respect, in the same way as Blanchett's performance of Jude in *I'm Not There* strengthens the concept of ambiguity in the sequence where he angrily acknowledges to a journalist that 'I don't owe you the truth, and anyway the truth is a static thing' (Barkham 2007), the reality behind Bob Dylan's persona(e) is an enigma motivated by a series of incongruities around a specific fiction. The use of masks keeps that multiple fiction constantly alive.

7. Conclusion

'Writing can no longer designate an operation of recording, notation, representation, "depiction" (as the Classics would say)', wrote Roland Barthes. '[R]ather, it designates exactly what linguists, referring to Oxford Philosophy, call a performative, a rare verbal form (exclusively given in the first person and in the present tense) in which the enunciation has no other content (contains no other proposition) than the act by which it is uttered' (Barthes 1977: 146). Bob Dylan's understanding of the creative process as a series of actions which are ruled by the principles of immediacy, fluidity and change, has played a key role in his rejection of being reduced to a mere cliché, a rationale the musician brought to light in Martin Scorsese's *No Direction Home* (2005): 'An artist has got to be careful never really to arrive at a place where he thinks he is at somewhere. You always have to realize that you're constantly in the state of becoming, you know? And, as long you can stay in that realm, you'll sort of be alright' (*No Direction Home* 2005). This statement can be considered as one of Dylan's most sincere insights ever, as it can explain the reasons why he has never stopped using masks throughout his whole career. But most importantly, it is a reflection that turns him into the vivid incarnation of the modern writer, in particular as an experimental artist whose power of resistance – against the limitations of language – depends on reclaiming his self-individuality as persona(e) at odds with public expectations. In this regard, Bob Dylan's early subversion of the hegemonic models of performativity that prevailed in early post-war America – images of 'the breadwinner' and 'the warrior' – can be addressed as a departure point in a series of radical acts whose strength resides in never being the same thing twice, a procedure which has been constant right up to the release of Larry Charles' *Masked and Anonymous* and Todd Haynes'

I'm Not There – two films that show he has never, is not, and will never be present, either *as* screen or *on* screen.

References

Adorno, T. (2002), *Essays on Music*, Berkeley: University of California Press.
Barkham, P. (2007), 'Cate Blanchett: The power and the glory'. Available online: www.theguardian.com/culture/2007/oct/26/awardsandprizes (accessed 12 April 2020).
Barthes, R. (1977), *The Death of the Author*, trans. S. Heath, New York: Hill & Wang.
Beynon, J. (2002), *Masculinities and Culture*, Buckingham: Open University Press.
Boorstin, D. (1962), *The Image or What Happened to the American Dream*, New York: Vintage Books.
Cohan, S. (1993), *Screening the Male: Exploring Masculinities in the Hollywood Cinema*, London: Routledge.
Cohan, S. (1997), *Masked Men: Masculinity and the Movies in the Fifties*, Bloomington: Indiana University Press.
Dont Look Back (1967) [Film], Dir. D. A. Pennebaker, USA: Leacock-Pennebaker.
Dylan, B. (1962), *Bob Dylan* [Album], USA: Columbia Records.
Dylan, B. (1963), *The Freewheelin' Bob Dylan* [Album], USA: Columbia Records.
Dylan, B. (1965), *Bringing It All Back Home* [Album], USA: Columbia Records.
Dylan, B. (2004), *Chronicles, Volume One*, London: Simon and Schuster.
I'm Not There (2007) [Film], Dir. T. Haynes, USA: The Weinstein Company.
'The Indomitable Style of Bob Dylan' (2016), *GQ Style*, 13 October. Available online: www.gq.com/story/bob-dylan-style (accessed 25 March 2020).
MacKinnon, K. (1997), *Uneasy Pleasures*, London: Cygnus Arts.
Marcus, G. (2007), 'Bob Dylan Times Six: An Interview with "I'm Not There" Director Todd Haynes', *Rolling Stone*, 29 November. Available online: www.rollingstone.com/movies/movie-news/bob-dylan-times-six-an-interview-with-im-not-there-director-todd-haynes-67251/ (accessed 26 February 2018).
Masked and Anonymous (2003) [Film], Dir. L. Charles, USA and UK: Sony Pictures.
Michasiw, K. (1994), 'Camp, Masculinity, Masquerade', *A Journal of Feminist Cultural Studies*, 6 (2–3): 146–73.
Millar-Heggie, B. (2004), 'The Performance of Masculinity and Femininity'. Available online: www.glossa.fi/mirator/pdf/Millar-Heggie.pdf (accessed 11 April 2020).
Mulvey, L. (1999), 'Visual Pleasure and Narrative Cinema', in L. Braudy and M. Cohen (eds), *Film Theory and Criticism: Introductory Readings*, 833–44, Oxford: Oxford University Press.
No Direction Home (2005) [Film], Dir. M. Scorsese, USA: Paramount Pictures.

O'Meara, J. (2014), 'Cate Blanchett's Deconstruction of Performance Through Performance', *The Cine-Files* website. Available online: www.thecine-files.com/cate-blanchetts-deconstruction-of-performance-through-performance/ (accessed 12 April 2020).

Rotolo, S. (2009), *A Freewheelin' Time*, London: Aurum Press.

Taylor, J. (2015), *The Political World of Bob Dylan: Freedom and Justice, Power and Sin*, London: Palgrave Macmillan.

Tsioulakis, I. (2016), *Musicians and Their Audiences: Performance, Speech and Mediation*, New York: Routledge.

4

No Direction Home: When Dylan Does Look Back

Charles Bonnot

When asked about Martin Scorsese's *No Direction Home* (2005), rock critic and Dylan expert Greil Marcus gave the following answer: 'I was one of the people who were interviewed but not included in the film … It is overwhelming, it has a great complexity, it leaves things unresolved, which is very rare in a documentary, and it has Bob Dylan as a guide with a great sense of paradox and lucidity.'[1]

The complexity of Martin Scorsese's portrait of Bob Dylan can be contrasted with the simple aim and construction of *Dont Look Back*, D. A. Pennebaker's 1967 film which has become the emblem of *cinéma vérité*. Indeed, while *Dont Look Back* is a chronological 'musical travelogue' (Chanan 2013: 341) following Bob Dylan during a week-long European tour in 1965, the construction of *No Direction Home* is more complex: it recounts Dylan's life and career from his childhood in Hibbing to the famous motorcycle accident of 1966, although the film is not strictly speaking chronological, as the years 1965 and 1966, with Dylan's decision to 'go electric', play an important role in both parts of the film.

The most obvious connection between these films is the presence of *Dont Look Back* within *No Direction Home*, through different scenes, arguably the most iconic, being included in the final editing: conversations with British fans, a party in a hotel room with Donovan, the famous argument with the *Time* reporter, different songs performed onstage and the very last moments backstage before a concert. Moreover, D. A. Pennebaker was actually interviewed for *No Direction Home*, and he provides context to the project and describes his relation to Bob Dylan at the time. His observations seem relevant when examining the

---

[1] 'The Doors. Une vie à l'écoute de cinq années d'enfer', talk at the Maison de la Poésie, Paris, 12 May 2015.

importance of *Dont Look Back* in the construction of *No Direction Home* and the evolution of Dylan's personae between these two cinematographic portrayals. Pennebaker appears in three different sequences:

> It interested me just to watch Dylan. I could sort of see that things that he did and said were interesting to me. And I didn't know why, and so that got me hooked on making a movie.
>
> …
>
> When we'd go into a town, there would be no sign and there would be people, kind of, just hanging out at the steps waiting for him to … and not waiting to crowd around or see him or get his autograph. Just waiting for him. And it gave you a feeling that there was some substance that you had to really see through, that you weren't going to find out about this quickly. But you had to kind of see it the way they did.
>
> …
>
> We showed him the first rough cut. What he saw must have made him look like he was bare bones and I think that was a big shock to him. But then he saw, I think the second night, he saw that it was total theater. It didn't matter. He was like an actor, and he suddenly had reinvented himself as the actor within this movie, and then it was okay. That's what he's good at, is getting used to the way things are, I mean, he understands that time changes everything.
>
> Pennebaker quoted in *No Direction Home* 2005

Relying on the theoretical frameworks of film studies, rock studies and discourse analysis, this chapter will take these quotations as a starting point for its argument. Indeed, D. A. Pennebaker's presence in *No Direction Home* and his remarks encapsulate the evolution of the claim to truth (Plantinga 1997: 37) at work in rockumentaries over the last fifty years, from an ideal of transparency to the construction of a situated and polyphonic form of truth (Nichols 1991: 21). The claim to truth has a strong influence on the structural, temporal and narrative differences between each film, and this evolution parallels that of the issue of authenticity, a question which has often been raised during Bob Dylan's career.

No Direction Home can therefore be read as a continuation of the project initiated by *Dont Look Back*, since it takes over some of its ideological aims, while overcoming some of its shortcomings, notably through the use of polyphony. It is also an opportunity for Bob Dylan, who was involved in this twenty-first-century portrait of his 1960s persona, to show how much he understands that 'time changes everything'.

1. *Dont Look Back*: a 'paradigmatic film' of the 1960s

The importance of *Dont Look Back* in the history of documentary cinema should not be overlooked as it was one of the first major documentaries to adopt the style of *cinéma vérité*, and defined some of its main technical, editorial and ideological characteristics. According to Michael Chanan's comparative analysis of *Dont Look Back* and *Charlie Is My Darling* (a 1965 documentary by Peter Whitehead of a two-day Irish tour by the Rolling Stones), the narrative designs of these 'paradigmatic films' share a certain simplicity: 'musical numbers are interspersed by travelogue observation and other verbal sequences' (Chanan 2013: 341).

Another comparison, suggested by Jeanne Hall, casts an interesting light on this construction and on the technical aspect of *cinémavérité*, and makes for a good working definition of the genre. She remarks that both *Dont Look Back* and *Primary* (a 1960 documentary by Richard Drew about the Democratic primary of the same year) aim at 'record[ing] the exploits of celebrities and stars in "crisis moments" and subordinating them to the real star' (Hall 1998: 223). Because of the importance given to this 'crisis moment', the technical style of *cinéma vérité* is very easily recognizable: the restless and wandering movement of lightweight, hand-held cameras; the blurred, grainy images of fast monochrome film; the synchronous sound rather than voice-over narration; the ubiquity of preoccupied subjects (Hall 1998: 223).

These technical choices also point towards an ideological and epistemic stance. It could be best summed up by one of its critics, T. F. Cohen, as he tries to defend the value of musical performance onstage (Cohen 2012: 9): these films are based on the claim to go beneath the surface, behind the scenes in order to see the 'real person' behind the star. The notion of an authentic private person who needs to be found behind the necessarily artificial mask of the star could echo what D. A. Pennebaker describes when he mentions 'a substance' (*No Direction Home* 2005) through which one needs to see, though the specific nature of said substance remains elusive in his remark. The idea that the most interesting part in the life of a musician is any moment when they are not playing music remains somewhat paradoxical. When taking into account the sheer volume of each activity in the final version of the film, one is left with the impression that 'talking is deemed superior to playing music', as it reveals an interiority which is essential 'to invest the person as the protagonist of their own story' (Cohen 2012: 16).

Interestingly, this dimension is in keeping with two values identified as essential to folk music – authenticity and transparency – as expressed by musicians and fans heard in *Dont Look Back* and *No Direction Home* (for instance John Cohen) and by scholars working on the topic such as Simon Frith:

> What Dylan and his successors brought into pop, then, was the concept of authenticity. Folk singers had always been contrasted to pop singers because they wrote and sang about the 'real' world ... and it was this convention of reality that singer-songwriters brought to rock ... Musicians were judged for their openness, honesty, their sensitivity, were judged, that is, as real, knowable people.
>
> Frith 1984: 66–7

The transfer of these values from folk to rock ideology by Bob Dylan is part of what is at stake in *No Direction Home*. Still, it could be argued that the project of continuously filming Bob Dylan onstage and off in *Dont Look Back* was part of that glorification of transparency, and that a form of continuity, or a very high compatibility, could be established between the ideological bases of the folk revival and the birth of *cinéma vérité*, despite the inherent shortcomings of the project, on which Pennebaker has always been 'maddeningly equivocal' (Hall 1998: 227). Indeed, what is the meaning of transparency or the benefit of continuously filming 'a guy acting out his life' (Hall 1998: 227)?

The importance of the film also comes from its contribution to the definition of Bob Dylan's public persona, especially through his critical relation to the media at the time. Jeanne Hall makes a very convincing case when showing that D. A. Pennebaker's project and Bob Dylan's vision concur in 'a systematic critique of traditional newsgathering and reporting practices' (Hall 1998: 224), with the film trying to establish itself as a superior alternative. She underlines four different methods used by Pennebaker:

1. 'let Dylan do it directly' – notably in his argument with the journalist from *Time* magazine;
2. 'let Dylan do it indirectly' – when he reads the tabloids and mocks the use of the term 'anarchist' to describe him;
3. 'show the opposite of what Dylan says or what the press reports about him' (e.g. his claim of not writing when he is on tour being belied by the footage of Dylan typing on a typewriter); and finally
4. 'abort or omit potentially productive interviews' (Hall 1998: 224), the reference here being the sequence showing the preparation of the interview with a journalist from BBC Africa.

It can be argued that *No Direction Home* is to a large extent a re-reading of these elements, seen through the prism of Bob Dylan's rock career and his electric shift. Similarly to what Bob Dylan describes in *No Direction Home* as 'channelling Woody Guthrie' (2005) when he began writing his own material, it seems interesting to see how *Dont Look Back* is channelled in Martin Scorsese's documentary on visual, narrative and ideological levels.

2. Channelling *Dont Look Back* in *No Direction Home*

In his reflection on the centrality of authenticity in the folk revival, Simon Frith remarks that the notion was both taken as a musical value and a form of class consciousness, with an emphasis on the collectivity of the musical experience. Both dimensions were rejected simultaneously by Dylan who, according to Frith, 'didn't represent anyone but himself', though the notion of truth was kept, this truth becoming a truth to self (Frith 2007: 35). Nonetheless, the choice of leaving the folk community was synonymous with rootlessness and estrangement and a feeling of betrayal on the part of fans, the sentimental framing of the break-up being encapsulated by Simon Frith: 'For Bob Dylan's folk-club followers musical taste was a key to the way they differentiated themselves from the mainstream of commercial pop consumers. Dylan going pop thus had for his folk fans something of the same emotional impact as betrayal by a lover' (Frith 2007: 330).

The intensity of the break-up is reflected in the very construction of *No Direction Home*, which seems to stage this movement of entering and leaving a community as the framework for the construction and affirmation of Bob Dylan's artistic identity. The movement can be linked to Christine Delory-Momberger's concept of a metanarrative, that is to say the culturally shared narrative template through which life stories are told in formal and informal contexts (Delory-Momberger 2010: 98). The overall narrative line of the film should be recalled at this point, while highlighting the presence of sequences which encapsulate leaving at very salient moments of the film. The first musical sequence of the film is the famous live performance of 'Like a Rolling Stone' during the 1966 English tour – a strong and vocal symbol of Dylan's confrontation with his audience after his choice to go electric. The first part of the film, presented as such thanks to an inscription on screen in the first few seconds, then follows a rather linear timeline: Bob Dylan growing up in Hibbing and discovering music before leaving town to go to college in Minneapolis, hitchhiking to New York after hearing Woody Guthrie's record, meeting Joan Baez, Woody Guthrie and other musicians playing in clubs, finding a manager and making a record, writing his own material, becoming the heir of the folk revival and being anointed at the Newport Festival (*No Direction Home* 2005). The second part focuses on the years 1965 and 1966, the recording of *Bringing It All Back Home* and *Highway 61 Revisited*, the chaotic concerts and tours (Newport, Forrest Hill, Royal Albert Hall), and ends with the motorcycle accident.

While, according to Pennebaker, *Dont Look Back* originated from Dylan's encounter with fans, making it a fairly peaceful film, the motif of Bob Dylan's leaving makes *No Direction Home* quite bitter and angry, especially in the second half. This can be accounted for by the well-known reactions to his decision by infuriated fans, included in both parts of the film, one of them famously accusing Dylan of 'prostituting himself'. Yet the issue is also discussed by different witnesses and figures of the folk scene, their observations being interpretations of symbolic events embodying the schism and usually followed by Bob Dylan's comment or justification. The most interesting take on Bob Dylan's estrangement from the folk scene is that of Joan Baez, as the musical and political break-up entailed by his giving up folk music was synonymous with the end of their romantic relationship:

> But then . . . he wanted to do his music and I wanted to do all this other stuff and he said he didn't want to do all that other stuff, so that was pretty clear. And yeah, I was disappointed. I mean, he'd given us, by that point, the greatest songs in our anti-war, civil rights arsenals . . . But I think that he didn't want to have to be the guy people were going to go to. I mean, the times then were cut and dry . . . And you were forced to take a side.
>
> *No Direction Home* 2005

The editing mirrors the abruptness of the break-up, as Joan Baez's remark on Dylan giving up topical song is immediately followed by the electric intro and cue-cards video of 'Subterranean Homesick Blues', a song which epitomizes Dylan's exploration of nonsense and absurd imagery as opposed to more explicit 'protest songs'. The various figures of the folk scene gradually disappear from the film after the Newport Festival of 1965, probably because their opinions and testimonies are less relevant for this period, yet it also mirrors Bob Dylan's movement away from them.

The motif of estrangement as the radical choice of a wandering individual, a more positive variation on what is otherwise presented as a betrayal, also frames the film. Two techniques can be mentioned here, in the manner of Jeanne Hall: let Dylan do it directly and let Dylan do it indirectly. Dylan does it directly in his remark chosen as the opening of the film, an answer given in the context of a profilmic interview, that is to say an interview conducted in order to be integrated into the documentary (Lioult 2004: 41). This remark, a contemporary reading of his career and personal story, becomes key in a film aiming at retracing his life:

> I had ambitions to set out and find, like an odyssey of going home somewhere. I set out to find this home that I'd left a while back and I couldn't remember exactly where it was, but I was on my way there … I didn't really have any ambition at all. I was born very far from where I'm supposed to be and so I'm on my way home, you know.
>
> *No Direction Home* 2005

The reference to an 'odyssey', a glorified wandering, works as a suggested metanarrative for the film, the interpretation being offered by its protagonist.[2] The way in which Martin Scorsese allows Dylan to frame his narrative indirectly can be seen in this sequence and it has to do with the recurrence of 'Like a Rolling Stone', which intrudes in the film in a direct cut right after Dylan has pronounced the words 'I'm on my way home' (*No Direction Home* 2005). Making one of the most famous songs of an artist the cornerstone of their filmic biography does make sense, of course, but the lyrics of the song and its narrative (the snarl of an unknown persona mocking a fallen heiress as she has to live on the street on her own, 'with no direction home') are naturally significant, all the more so as they are taken up in the title of the film. The writing of the song and the audience's reaction to it are also discussed, and an interpretation of the song as a statement directed towards the folk audience is suggested in the film by Paul Nelson who describes it as 'a slap in the face to everything that the topical song represented' and a 'very selfish statement' (*No Direction Home* 2005).

Despite their differences, it would seem excessive to see *No Direction Home* as a mere negative of *Dont Look Back*, thinking of Pennebaker's film as showing mostly harmonious encounters of a folkie with his fans and Scorsese's project as

---

[2] Various examples of the centrality of leaving and wandering in the metanarrative framing rock portraits can be found in my analysis of the depiction of the road (Bonnot 2018) and cities (Bonnot 2019) in these films.

the story of a necessarily lonesome rock star drifting afar, away from the crowd (Chastagner 2011: 243). However, interesting visual contrasts are exploited within *No Direction Home*. Indeed, the film includes a large quantity of archival footage, quoting Lerner's *Festival* (1967), *Dont Look Back* and *Eat the Document*, the failed project of Dylan and Pennebaker on the 1965-6 tour.

The presence of similar settings and situations, and the filming by the same crew, led to radically opposed results, especially in the recording of live performance. *Festival* and *Dont Look Back*, mostly quoted in the first part of the film, were shot in black and white with a focus on Bob Dylan and his shadow in the light on an otherwise dark stage (*Dont Look Back*) or accompanied by other folk singers (*Festival*), in front of a silent and captivated audience left in the dark (*Dont Look Back*) or sitting very close to him. On the other hand, the footage of *Eat the Document* conveys a sense of chaos: the stage is crowded by the Band and by amplifiers, the sequences include askew close-ups of Bob Dylan and various shots in which a musician crosses the frame, and the aggressive reactions of the audience and the booing make up an important part of the soundtrack. All these contrasts, because they are based on common characteristics – the venues in which Dylan plays for instance – make the turning-point of the electric shift even more blatant.

Still, an ideological continuity can be established between *Dont Look Back* and *No Direction Home*, as the latter takes up the former's critique of the media. Bob Dylan is more directly involved since he participates in profilmic interviews in *No Direction Home*, while interaction with the film crew is not part of the method of *cinéma vérité*. A number of elements that were not necessarily alluded to in *Dont Look Back* are also present in *No Direction Home*, a result of the time gap between the period at stake in the film and its actual making.

Recurrent remarks made about labels and generalizations are part of the explicit critique of the media. The use of words, mostly by the media and the general public, is questioned throughout the film by Dylan and other witnesses, with Dylan claiming that he 'didn't care what kinds of label were put on [him]' (*No Direction Home* 2005). Problematic terms and concepts associated with his early career – such as 'topical song', 'protest song' or poetry – are discussed. Another explicit method, which aims at establishing the film as a superior form of information gathering, a method also used in *Dont Look Back*, is counter-discourses (Bonnot 2015), that is to say, profilmic interviews that are used to correct widely shared assumptions shown in multiple archives.

Counter-discourses can question the use of a word but they can also aim at correcting facts and opinions, as can be seen in this remark by Dave Van Ronk: 'Bobby was not really a political person. He was thought of as being a political person and a man of the Left. And in, you know, in a general sort of way, yes, he was. But he was not interested in the true nature of the Soviet Union or any of that crap' (*No Direction Home* 2005).

A more implicit critique of the media is the motif of the press conference. Numerous press conferences are shown in the film, the date and city in which they were organized being indicated onscreen. Their repetitiveness becomes all the more blatant as the tour goes on, and Bob Dylan's irritation with the questions about his art, the Vietnam war or artistic and political labels, is easily perceivable. The physical presence of the press also becomes more and more stifling toward the end of the film, as press conferences in which journalists seem to sit closer and closer to the singer (especially in Paris in 1966) come in succession and are not interrupted by any profilmic interview. The physical exhaustion culminates with a nonsensical interview with a troubled and obviously drugged Bob Dylan talking with an Italian journalist about his desire to 'just go home' (*No Direction Home* 2005). This sequence, which echoes the title and Dylan's opening remark, is the last of the succession of interviews referred to above, and leads to the actual ending of the film – composed of archives – though a profilmic remark by Dylan comes in between.

The ending of *No Direction Home* is actually quite similar to that of *Dont Look Back* in terms of visual composition and editing. The frames shared by both films are numerous: shots taken within a leaving car giving a feeling of entrapment and illustrating the separation of the singer from the crowd; tracking shots taken from a car as Bob Dylan flees in *Dont Look Back* and showing the endless waiting line for the concert in *No Direction Home*; the final steps backstage before the concert begins, and a movement upwards from the stage towards the lights of the concert venue. Yet, a contrast exists, as *No Direction Home* ends with Dylan's performance of 'Like a Rolling Stone' after his famous exchange with a member of the audience 'Judas' and his order to 'play it fucking loud' addressed to his band (*No Direction Home* 2005), while *Dont Look Back* ends on the quiet introspection of 'the wandering American' mocking the British press (1967). Pennebaker's film also ends with the title of the movie appearing onscreen, which can be read as an injunction to look towards the future. On the other hand, *No Direction Home*'s written conclusion is a reminder of the motorcycle accident and a non-opening towards the rest of his career, focusing on touring and live performance (or lack thereof): 'he would not go back on the road for eight years' (*No Direction Home* 2005).³

3. *No Direction Home:* a paradigmatic rock portrait

In order to understand what makes *No Direction Home* a paradigmatic rock portrait, we can go back to Greil Marcus's remark on Bob Dylan acting as a guide through an open-ended, paradoxical and very lucid film. The narrative construction of the film as a macro-discourse and its epistemic stance have come to define the genre of the rock portrait, in Martin Scorsese's work and for other contemporary directors, in the same way *Dont Look Back* was established as the template of *cinéma vérité*. Though this very complex construction could be discussed at length,⁴ we will focus here on three major aspects: time frame, narrative and reflexivity.

No Direction Home is a deliberately incomplete biography, as opposed to *Dont Look Back* which presented itself as a week-long snapshot capturing a very specific moment in the life of the artist. Besides, Martin Scorsese's film pivots around a moment of crisis – Dylan's choice to go electric – and uses it to establish the division between its two parts. He made the same choice in his portrait of George Harrison, *Living in the Material World* (2011), the construction of which is very similar to that of *No Direction Home* (mostly through the weaving together of profilmic interviews and archives), though a major difference stems from the fact that he made his film after Harrison's death. The pivotal moment is another key episode in the history of rock music, the separation of the Beatles in 1969, giving the film a focus on the Beatles in its first part and on George Harrison's solo career in the second half (*Living* 2011). Going back to *No Direction Home*, one also notices a gradual reduction of profilmic interviews in the second part, up to the final sequences that have already been described. One of the effects of this editing is to give a minimal opening towards the future and the time frame in which the film was made.

Overall, an impression of circularity prevails both from a filmic and a linguistic perspective. The overall editing of the film is circular, as its opening

---

³ It is telling that Martin Scorsese did not do another film about Bob Dylan for fourteen years, until *Rolling Thunder Revue: A Bob Dylan Story by Martin Scorsese* in 2019, namely a film about Bob Dylan going back on tour.
⁴ See Bonnot 2015 for a more detailed study of rock portraits.

and ending are made of the same footage, namely 'Like a Rolling Stone' being played onstage. Moreover, sequences of the 1966 tour pop up regularly during the first half of the film, disrupting an otherwise mostly chronological timeline. These interruptions, in which the audience boos and insults Dylan, have the haunting quality of a nightmare which seems to frame them as traumatic experience, until they are explained and put in perspective in the second part.

On a smaller scale, we may also notice that both parts are constructed as flashbacks leading back to 1965–6. In the first part, right after the images of 'Like a Rolling Stone', an intertitle appears over Bob Dylan's childhood home, reading 'Many years before'. In the second part, the opening footage is that of Bob Dylan playing with the words written on signboards outside a British shop during the 1966 tour, followed by the intertitle 'Three years before', taking the audience back to the March on Washington (*No Direction Home* 2005). It can therefore be argued that the macro-discourse of the film is explicitly circular and the same could be said of the micro-discourses that compose it. Indeed, the temporal construction also works around the contrast between archives and profilmic interviews that look back on the period. The audience is taken back and forth in time, yet the main point remains to look backwards, as the succession of archives and contemporary interviews also enables the audience to read the passing of time on the faces of Dylan and other witnesses. Finally, it should be added that time is discussed as a topic in the film, mostly by Dylan. His remarks are included in a rather playful montage that establishes a form of dialogue between the present of the filmmaking and the archive of the period discussed by the witnesses, a very common technique in contemporary rockumentaries:

> **Bob Dylan**   'Time, you know, time kind of obliterated the past that was around when I was growing up. Just time and progress, really.' [cut to archive]
>
> **British Fans**   'He's just changed altogether. He's changed from what he was. He's not the same as what he was at first.'
>
> No Direction Home 2005

The temporal construction of the film also has to do with the fact that it relies on narratives to construct truth. The stance is therefore in stark contrast to that of *Dont Look Back*, whose claim to truth had to do with minimal intervention on the part of the director and direct or bare editing. *No Direction Home* works with a different, perhaps more modern, approach, in keeping with the ideology of rock as described by Pouivet (2010) and Chastagner (1998, 2011). Indeed, they argue that rock culture is founded on a principle of accumulation and contradiction (Chastagner) and artificiality (Pouivet), as exemplified by the importance of recording technology. They attempt to account for the complexity of the phenomenon and to go beyond the alleged superiority of the live experience of a concert. On the contrary, rock is fundamentally linked to the mass production of records. The centrality of the record, as an object and an artefact, enabled rock music to become a global culture and most records are fundamentally a cut-up, a montage of different takes.

While *Dont Look Back* tried to capture the truth of a fleeting moment on the basis of authenticity and transparency, in keeping with the ideology of folk music, *No Direction Home* explicitly reconstructs and narrativizes its topic through accumulation and montage, thereby placing itself in continuity with both Dylan's prose and songwriting, and with rock culture in general. The consequence of this artistic and epistemic stance is the complex editing we have analysed, with sequences echoing one another, and a rather wordy film. Since access to truth comes from recollections, truth therefore becomes a situated kind of truth based on the accumulation of points of view, even when contradictory. At several points, there is clearly no will to decide what actually happened, the best example of this ambiguity being the description of Newport 1965 and the episode in which Pete Seeger allegedly tried to chop through the amplifier cables. Five protagonists of the scene are heard (Pete Seeger, Maria Muldaur, Paul Nelson, John Cohen and Bob Dylan) and different versions of the story are told: Seeger actually tried to cut the cables and had to be subdued; he only said he wished he could if he had had an axe; he was upset because his father Charlie Seeger couldn't hear properly (*No Direction Home* 2005). The audience is left with no conclusion as to what really happened. Martin Scorsese seems to be interested in the obvious symbolism of Dylan cutting himself off from the folk scene and in the reaction of one of its towering figures, and in seeing how the myth of his persona is constructed through narratives, rather than trying to narrow down possible interpretations.

The film also relies on narrativity on a macroscopic level, as it is framed by metadiscursive remarks, a technique which is frequently found in subsequent rock portraits, such as Julien Temple's *Joe Strummer* (2007). Indeed, *No Direction Home* opens with Dylan's suggestion that his life was an odyssey and a quest and, after the interview with the Italian journalist about 'going home' and before the full rendition of 'Like a Rolling Stone', it ends with the following exchange – the only instance in which the profilmic interviewer is heard:

Bob Dylan   'And I'd just about had it, though. I'd had it with the ... with the whole scene. And I was ... Whether I knew it or didn't know it, I was looking to ... just quit for a while.'

Interviewer   'What about the scene? What had you had it with? What about the scene were you sick of?'

Bob Dylan   'Well, you know, people like you. People like [chuckles], you know like, just, you know, like just being pressed and hammered and, you know, expected to answer questions, you know. What can I ... You know, like ... It is enough to make anybody sick, really.'

No Direction Home 2005

This exchange illustrates the importance of reflexivity, as the very activity of pressing Dylan is questioned by Dylan himself in an interview focusing on his weariness of journalists' persistent questioning in the 1960s. This amusing re-enactment of the situation, while seeming to establish the superiority of the documentary as a format in which the interviewer is able to take a perspective – both humorous and temporal – that journalists seemed to lack, does raise a troubling question: could it be that profilmic interviews are as flawed here as those of the 1960s? In other words, if *Dont Look Back* is a documentary about 'a guy acting out his life', could *No Direction Home* be a portrait composed of interviews of a man refusing to be labelled in interviews? As Bob Dylan constantly oscillates between clarification, contextualization, justification on the one hand and deconstruction through cryptic remarks on the other, one could take Martin Scorsese's film as yet another opportunity for Dylan to 'reinvent himself' and to offer a contradictory and complex portrait of the persona of his best-known years.

*

By focusing on the heyday of Bob Dylan, *No Direction Home* offers a portrait of the artist as a young man, as a loner, as a man 'constantly reinventing himself' but it also paves the way for subsequent rock portraits by Martin Scorsese and other directors in terms of motifs, editing, epistemic basis and ideological construction. Scorsese's recent choice to make another movie about Dylan (*Rolling Thunder Revue*), several years after what was supposed to be the 'definitive portrait' of the artist (according to the summary of the film on the DVD case), shows that he followed the advice given by Dylan himself in *No Direction Home*: 'An artist has got to be careful never really to arrive at a place where he thinks he's "at" somewhere. You always have to realize that you're constantly in the state of becoming, you know? And, as long as you can stay in that realm, you'll sort of be all right' (*No Direction Home* 2005).

References

Bonnot, C. (2015), 'Le discours des documentaires musicaux – de Robert Johnson à LCD Soundsystem', PhD diss., Études Anglophones, Université Paris-Diderot, Paris.

Bonnot, C. (2018), 'Mythique et mortifère: la route comme métonymie dans les documentaires rock', in B. Bernard, J. Michot and I. Schmitt (eds), *Sur la route . . . Quand le cinéma franchit les frontières*, 159–73, Dijon: Éditions Universitaires de Dijon.

Bonnot, C. (2019), 'Construction biographique de la ville dans les documentaires rock', in S. Béligon and R. Digonnet (eds), *Manifestations sensorielles des urbanités contemporaines*, 197–216, Brussels: Peter Lang.

Chanan, M. (2013) 'Music, Documentary, Music Documentary', in B. Winston (ed.), *The Documentary Film Book*, 337–44, Basingstoke: Palgrave Macmillan.

Chastagner, C. (1998), *La loi du rock: ambivalence et sacrifice dans la musique populaire anglo-américaine*, Castelnau-le-Lez: Climats.

Chastagner, C. (2011), *De la culture rock*, Paris: Presses Universitaires de France.

Cohen, T. F. (2012), *Playing to the Camera: Musicians and Musical Performance in Documentary Cinema*, London: Wallflower.

Delory-Momberger, C. (2010), *La condition biographique: essai sur le récit de soi dans la modernité avancée*, Paris: Téraèdre.

Dont Look Back (1967) [Film], Dir. D. A. Pennebaker, USA: Leacock-Pennebaker.

Festival (1967) [Film], Dir. M. Lerner, USA: Peppercorn-Wormser.

Frith, S. ([2004] 2007), 'What is Bad Music?', in S. Frith, *Taking Popular Music Seriously: Selected Essays*, 313–34, Aldershot: Ashgate.

Frith, S. (1984), 'Rock and the Politics of Memory', in S. Sayres, A. Stephanson, S. Aronowitz and F. Jameson (eds), *The 60s without Apology*, 59–69, Minneapolis: University of Minnesota Press.

Hall, J. (1998), '"Don't You Ever Just Watch?" American Cinema Vérité and *Dont Look Back*', in B. K. Grant and J. Sloniowski (eds), *Documenting the Documentary: Close Readings of Documentary Film and Video*, 223–37, Detroit: Wayne State University Press.

Lioult, J.-L. (2004), *À l'enseigne du réel: penser le documentaire*, Aix-en-Provence: Publications de l'Université de Provence.

Living in the Material World (2011) [Film], Dir. M. Scorsese, USA: Spitfire Pictures.

Nichols, B. (1991), *Representing Reality: Issues and Concepts in Documentary*, Bloomington: Indiana University Press.

No Direction Home (2005) [Film], Dir. M. Scorsese, USA: Spitfire Pictures.

Plantinga, C. (1997), *Rhetoric and Representation in Nonfiction Film*, Cambridge: Cambridge University Press.

Pouivet, R. (2010), *Philosophie du rock: une ontologie des artefacts et des enregistrements*, Paris: Presses Universitaires de France.

Rolling Thunder Revue: A Bob Dylan Story (2019) [Film], Dir. M. Scorsese, USA: Netflix.

5

Dylan Does Adverts. Surely Not? Surely?

Andrew McKeown

In April 2004 Bob Dylan appeared in a Victoria's Secret promotional film (Victoria's Secret 2004). He was wearing a cowboy hat and something of a leer while Adriana Lima modelled underwear and a pair of wings. The scene was shot in a Venetian palace and was set to extracts from Dylan's 1997 track 'Love Sick'. The question at the time seemed to be: why did he do it? Seth Stephenson, writing in *Slate* in a piece entitled 'Tangled up in Boobs', suggested Dylan's motivation was that shared by other oldsters looking for exposure in a music market where they are heard less and less:

> It's a real struggle for older rockers to remind the world that they still exist. Their music's not played on the radio, and their videos (if they even make them) aren't in heavy rotation on VH1. Thus you see the Jaguar ads with Sting, or the MCI ads with James Taylor and Michael McDonald – all of them prominently featuring the artist's song. It's essentially a way to put a video on the major networks, where an older audience might see it. Yes, in exchange for publicizing their art they sacrifice some integrity, but this is basically an understandable tradeoff. And Dylan even gets, in the terms of his deal, a mix CD of his songs sold at Victoria's Secret stores.
>
> Stephenson 2004

So, Bob did it because he needs a showcase. Looking at the then sixty-something musician and bearing in mind the idea of selling underwear, perhaps it is less obvious why Victoria's Secret did it. For Ed Razek, head of marketing at LBrands where Victoria's Secret is stabled, the reason is simple: Dylan is 'so iconic, and so arresting' (Steinberg 2004). Dylan is a selling point irrespective of the product he endorses? The mechanics of association whereby Dylan entices you to buy lingerie for yourself, or as a gift for someone else, tests this reviewer's suspension of disbelief. Perhaps another way to make sense of the pants and bra story, and one which fits more easily into the accepted Dylansphere, is to recall the answer he gave in 1965 when, at a press call in San Francisco, Dylan was asked: 'If you were going to sell out to a commercial interest, which one would you choose?' 'Ladies' garments', came the reply (Gleason 1967). Seen in this light, the Victoria's Secret ad is a decades-in-the-making private joke being played out. Dylan playing with us and the persona we make of him: a familiar pitch.

If it is a joke, then it's a big one, for Dylan has endorsed all manner of products: yoghurt (Chobani 2014), Christmas decorations (Target 2017), the Co-op (2009), Google (2010), IBM (2015), Apple (iPod 2006), sundry businesses (BOM 1996, Kohl's 2013, WGU 2018[1]) and, what appears to be his favourite, the good old horseless carriage. Let's look more closely at one of his car ads: the 2014 Super Bowl Fiat Chrysler film (Chrysler 2014). Dylan's two-minute slice of Super Bowl history continues to divide opinion among YouTubers, where the film is regularly taken down and re-uploaded. There are compliments: 'Please! someone give this man the Nobel prize. If only the likes of Thomas Pynchon, Don DeLillo and Ursula K. Le Guin could do something like this.'[2] And there are others: 'That was not Dylan – that was a salesman prostituting for money.'[3] Or 'What the f***? So sad.'[4] Here is a reaction from another critical quarter, the Rochester Institute of Pop Music, whose John Covach, cited by Brian Steinberg in *Variety*, has this to say:

> Having earned his stripes resisting 'the man', he has now become a cultural icon representing unqualified authenticity. Partly because his music is no longer current pop, there is no risk of fans perceiving him of being co-opted by big business. His position in music history assured, Dylan stands as an image of integrity, independence, and authenticity in a way that only a person with a long and established presence in pop culture can. I think fans will love seeing him. There will be no question of sell out, as there was at the Newport Folk Festival in 1965, for instance. Dylan means quality.
>
> Steinberg 2014

Covach sees Dylan as elder statesman, his credibility is already banked, so, the idea goes, he can do as he pleases. I would like to focus on two points that Covach makes and which Razek also pointed to (and which are implied in the YouTube

---

[1] My thanks to Erin C. Callahan, San Jacinto College, Houston, for bringing this commercial to my attention.
[2] Demfrabanken, YouTube, 23 November 2018.
[3] Brien Doyle, YouTube, 23 November 2018.
[4] Ryan Leone, YouTube, 23 November 2018.

comments): first, the iconic status and second, the insistence that Dylan is (and forever shall be) authentic.

*

In modern usage people and things get called 'iconic' when it is deemed they have transcended the everyday/random/contingent paradigm and have achieved exemplary/venerable/idol status. In addition to that, and perhaps less welcome, icons are also easily dispossessed and transformed by their idolaters. Let me bring in Philip Larkin's 'An Arundel Tomb', a poem that has no direct dealing with Dylan but which describes the process of 'iconification' quite admirably. Larkin's poem is about the carved sarcophagus of the Earl and Countess of Arundel to be found in Chichester Cathedral in England. 'Only an attitude remains', says the poet of the stone effigy of the couple. 'Time has transfigured them into / Untruth', he goes on, adding, in reference to the Latin inscription at the base of the tomb, 'people stop reading and look' (Larkin 1964: 45–6). Larkin's poem is an interesting take on objects in the public eye: what starts out as original and relevant becomes a shrine, transfigured by the devotion of the pilgrims, coming to pay homage endlessly, washing like waves at their feet. Somehow, something becomes 'untrue' in the process. So being an icon is no sinecure and, in Bob's case, the transfigurations that go on allow for some crazy paradoxes to take place. Such as: 100 million US citizens can watch the Super Bowl, guzzle their way through 1 billion chicken wings, washed down with 325.5 million gallons of beer, and still feel endorsed by the man who once said 'all is phoney'.[5]

Dylan's attitude/attiude to being an icon is famously grumpy, as seen in the honorary degree episode at Princeton in July 1970. Dylan turned up with his wife Sara, David Crosby and what gets known as an 'aide' in show business ('Dylan Receives Degree' 1970). After handing over the customary parchment and scroll, the following, less formal citation was read out: '[T]hough he is approaching the perilous age of thirty, he remains the authentic expression of the disturbed and concerned conscience of Young America' (Dylan 2004: 133). This is how Dylan felt about that:

> Oh Sweet Jesus! It was like a jolt. I shuddered and trembled but remained expressionless. The disturbed conscience of Young America! There it was again. I couldn't believe it. Tricked once more. The speaker could have said many

[5] Statistics from: https://pursuitist.com/how-much-food-will-be-consumed-during-the-super-bowl/ (accessed 8 April 2020).

things, he could have emphasized a few things about my music. When he said to the crowd that I preferred isolation from the world, it was like he told them that I preferred being in an iron tomb with my food shoved in on a tray.

Dylan 2004: 133

An Arundel iron tomb, of course. Time had already transfigured him, apparently, and what he had been turned into was not to his liking. Which is the point with icons: they have greatness thrust upon them, like it or not. Dylan gives the parting shot about the afternoon in Princeton to David Crosby, who, sucking orange pith throughout the award ceremony, was on top form: 'Bunch of dickheads on auto-stroke' (Dylan 2004: 134). Clearly it isn't easy being a university professor. Not easy being Bob Dylan either. At the tender age of almost thirty, people were already saying of him, 'only an attitude remains'.

Not that Dylan took this lying down. In Scorsese's biopic *No Direction Home*, Dylan states his case unequivocally: 'an artist has got to be constantly in a state of becoming' (*No Direction Home* 2005). In one sense his forays into advertising films are exactly that: an attempt at becoming something else, something other than the folkster conscience of a nation. Or, put differently, an attempt at throwing off the icon/iron mask. Part of the problem with the reinvention angle is the material you choose. With ladies' garments Dylan was asking a lot. When he pitched for commercial radio with his *Theme Time Radio Hour* adverts he was on safer ground. Dylan made two commercial films for the radio show which ran from 2006 to 2009. Both appeared in 2007. The first combined a plug for his show with a pitch for the Cadillac Escalade, to a tune called 'Held', from a band named 'Smog' (Dylan, with his connoisseur of ironies hat on, no doubt enjoyed that one) (Cadillac 2007a). The second commercial was a full two-minute slot, again plugging Cadillac cars and XM radio, where Dylan's show could be heard, all of which to the tune of Les Paul and Mary Ford's distinctly fifties-sounding 'Sweet and Lovely', and this time with a Bob voice-over extolling the virtues of radio and the open road (Cadillac 2007b).

Dylan's radio show pitches, like the radio show itself, are all about Dylan going back to his roots: the USA of the 1940s and 1950s that he grew up in, the radio stations he listened to, the source of his musical inspiration. And of course the radio shows the young Bobby Allen tuned in to were commercial shows, such as the now famous WDSM, broadcasting out of Duluth and hosted by DJ Pat 'The Cat' Cadigan (Heylin 2001: 14). So Dylan doing adverts for radio can be seen as just a matter of completing the circle. No need to be an icon here. *Theme Time Radio* was Bob meets Bob. What greater authenticity can there be?

True, authenticity does mean original and the 2007 radio films work a rootsy vein. But authenticity also means honesty and sincerity – another greatness that Dylan has had thrust upon him, recalled by David Bowie in his 1971 track 'Song for Bob Dylan': 'His words of truthful vengeance / They could pin us to the floor' (Bowie 1971). 'Words of truthful vengeance', that is, that sense of (self?-) righteous indignation that Dylan's listeners find in his songs, and what Christopher Ricks has called his 'unpropitiatory words' (Ricks 2003: 11). The acoustic/folk footing on which Dylan began was by implication a stand for truth, belief and integrity, against the pomp and pompadour of commercial music, which Dylan described as 'lame as hell and a big trick' (Dylan 2004: 35), whereas 'Folk songs transcended the immediate culture' (2004: 27). But were things really so simple, even then? *Chronicles* relates the story of when Bob met talent scout John Hammond at Columbia Records. 'I understand sincerity', said John to Bob (Dylan 2004: 45). Hammond's remark, maybe with its own flip sincerity, points to figures, sales, openings: 'I see how this is going to work.'[6] And of course Hammond was speaking just as the folk sincerity thing was about to become big business, with major labels like Columbia signing what they saw as being the next big names. Big like Bob Dylan. Moreover, Hammond's understanding embraces Dylan's own. They both saw openings in sincerity: Hammond saw returns, Dylan saw himself as the next Woody Guthrie. The point being that authenticity is something that can be construed and acted on, and acted out on the marketplace.

In his essay '"Authenticity", or the lesson of Little Tree', Henry Louis Gates Jr. examines how our ideas about authenticity inform the way we respond to texts, basing his discussion on the 'fake' First Nations story *The Education of Little Tree* which was in fact written by the very un-First Nations Asa Earl Carter, the man who also wrote the infamous 'Segregation now, segregation tomorrow, segregation forever' speech for Governor George Wallace of Alabama. Gates's point is simple: 'all writers are "cultural impersonators"' (Gates 1991: 29), meaning white separatists *can* impersonate Native Americans, and do so quite convincingly. If we translate this through to Bob Dylan, the point is also simple: Dylan's folk sincerity was only as sincere as any act of performance can be, that is to say, convincing so long as we're convinced – no more, no less. Or, put

---

[6] Or am I being cynical? In his MusiCares speech, 6 February 2015, Dylan declared John Hammond to be a talent scout not interested in commercial artists: 'Trends did not interest John, and I was very noncommercial but he stayed with me' (Dylan 2015). I will leave it to the reader's discretion to decide how far a talent scout is or isn't interested in the sales appeal of the talents he signs.

differently, folk authenticity is neither realer, nor truer than, say, glam rock's camp exuberance, or trad jazz's Storyville snazz.

In 1965 Marianne Faithfull called in on Dylan's 'at home' (cum Mad Hatter's tea party) in London's Savoy Hotel, upsetting Mr Dylan by being pregnant and unable to resume an earlier sentimental near encounter. The chatter turned on folk music, which apparently was on its way out. She remembers: 'Aside from Joan Baez, nobody really sang folk songs around the hotel room. Country music was the latest rage with Dylan and Neuwirth. As Neuwirth so charmingly put it: "Country music's the last authentic goddam shit left for us to rip off"' (Faithfull 1995: 69–70). Joking aside, the other Bob's glib remark is telling: musical styles have a prompt book and they can be learned and exploited. They can be conned and they can con us. Marianne Faithfull was possibly taken aback by Neuwirth's candour because she had fallen for the image as truth. Someone who hadn't was Harry Jackson. 'He's so goddamned real it's unbelievable!', joked the painter and sometime singer, as reported by Nat Hentoff in his album notes for *The Freewheelin' Bob Dylan* (Dylan 1963). Jackson's quipping paradox is a tribute to Dylan's diligence in learning his part: heir to Woody Guthrie and poster boy for the folk boom as it came to the boil in and around Greenwich Village circa 1963. But it also reminds us – as does Neuwirth's throwaway line – that Dylan's workshirt authenticity can only be construed so far. Take it too seriously and it unravels, like any act of performance or entertainment. The difficulty with the folk movement was that its pitch was authenticity itself. Here was a musical form which set up shop as counter to commercial musical interests. Bob signing for Columbia, getting taken on by Albert Grossman, were signs that he was not prepared to subscribe to the folk orthodoxy, as he not so indirectly informed us when he gave his electric/electrifying performance of 'Maggie's Farm' at Newport in 1965. What's more, folk worked on the assumption that artists, that is, humble troubadours, only reinterpreted standards, contributing to a great, nay greater circle of music. Dylan's early recordings did indeed borrow liberally from others, but did not (always or directly) acknowledge hereditary authorship: it's 'Dylan', not 'Traditional' who gets the song credits. In other words, Dylan never was 'folk', in the way others such as Pete Seeger understood the term. Nor was – or is – he 'authentic' in the way others would like to believe.

*

So is Bob just toying with us? Let's go back to the 2014 Super Bowl. Is this Dylan playing with a celluloid cut-out Dylan, teasing us with blind alleys of identification? A game of phoney association we could call 'tangled up in truth'? Well, yes and no. Some of the commercial rings true: the road as metaphor/emblem/direction is certainly home ground. But parts of it sound hollow: the globalization pitch – 'let Asia assemble your phone . . . we will build your car' – is surely ersatz Dylan, and, if we care to look at the facts, hardly true. We remember Philip Larkin's remark about 'only an attitude remains', and it feels like it's only Dylan's attitude, a little petrified, a little botoxed, that has endured, while all around him has changed. To bring in another poet, is it then a case of 'Look on my Works, ye Mighty, and despair!'?[7]

A way out of this (possibly only rhetorical) impasse, is to recall that Dylan's adverts are first and foremost in a visual medium: they are films. And Bob's thing is arguably centred on words, as David Bowie pointed out in his 'Song for Bob Dylan'. Let's go back to the 2014 Super Bowl and dig out the words. The ad itself was the work of the Detroit-based marketing company GlobalHue and the final pitch of the voice-over for the Chrysler 200, 'America's Import', was part of a strategy to reboot the motor industry out of its original downtown production plants, like the infamously crumbling Packard factory, into the suburban production sites such as Sterling Heights. New for old. In fact, the only authentic Dylan contribution in terms of words comes just as the film is closing where we get the tail end of 'Things Have Changed'. 'I used to care', go the lyrics from the track recorded in 1999 (Dylan 2000). Is that Dylan being cynical? I used to care about what advertising does to people – 'Advertising signs they con / You into thinking you're the one' (Dylan 1965) – but things have changed and now I don't. Is that the idea?

Not exactly. 'Things Have Changed' flashes up word pictures of a life less deceived: a woman with assassin's eyes, losing hands at cards, Bibles telling of apocalypse, and a man who hurts easy but with a clear eye on what's in store: the last train, the hangman's noose, etc. Pick your own metaphor. As a tagline for selling cars, it's not a great fit. It's also a dubious way to sign off a spiel on American originality and legacy. A rug puller, not a plug? For GlobalHue and their client the idea is a good one. 'Things have changed' means 'Detroit has changed, we're back on track (thank you 2008 Federal bailout), we make the best'. But for Dylan, or Dylan's fans who would be familiar with the Dylan context and the lyrics as a whole, the sign-off is definitely a twist, not a taster.

[7] Percy Bysshe Shelley, 'Ozymandias' (1818).

I am focusing on words with what could be kindly called an academic's attention to detail – not something we have time to do with adverts. Maybe my approach is eccentric, because it's logocentric, but it is an approach that Dylan endorses. Let's go back to the *Theme Time Radio Hour* film: 'nothing goes better with a Cadillac than a long ride to nowhere full of the right music. It can be rock and roll, jazz, jump, jive, punk, folk or hip-hop, it could be calypso or the blues, doesn't matter what you listen to as long as you listen' (Cadillac 2007b). Listen to the music, listen to the words: a rare moment of candid pedagogy from Bob. Let me return to ladies' garments and see if this helps us out. The lyrics to the Victoria's Secret film are a cut and paste from *Time Out of Mind*'s opening track 'Love Sick', where Dylan watches lovers, in pastoral settings or indoors, moving behind windows. Like them, he has experienced love's ambiguities, its turn-ons and its turn-offs (Dylan 1997). I'm sick of love, says the song, its illusions and frustrations, but I'd do anything for another fix. Perhaps on this occasion the lyrics are better fitted to the apparent, that is visual, purpose of the film: I want it even if I know in the end it isn't good for me. Or, also possible: I like it because it hurts. One thing that can't be finessed away here is that the words have to share the space with close-ups of Bob, in a way they don't in the Super Bowl film, and I wonder if we see more of him than the model, Adriana Lima. The pairing is a jarring one. Witness the following YouTuber's reaction: 'I remember seeing this commercial as a kid and I had no idea who Bob Dylan was at the time and I was just thinking "why is that creepy old man in this lingerie commercial?" Now that I'm older and know who he is I think "why is that creepy old man in this lingerie commercial?"'[8] Sick of love? Or sick of Bob Dylan? Maybe the point is another level in the elaborate joke about lingerie set in motion back in 1965. Maybe the point is a serious one, too. The British art critic John Berger sees lingerie advertising as the modern-day heir to the nude in Western art. In Berger's analysis, the nude, like the semi-nude bra and panty advert, enacts women's entrapped exposure to the male gaze, the image industry (art or advertising) creating unwinnable versions of sexuality for the gratification of the male/buyer/viewer, at the expense of the female/buyee/viewee (Berger 1972: 35–64). This film is love that is sick, or, to bring it back to Berger's frame of reference, it's Dylan and Adriana Lima acting out a twenty-first-century version of 'Susanna and the Elders' brought to you courtesy of LBrands and Madison Avenue. And I'm sick of the whole thing, says Bob?

---

[8] Ash A, YouTube, 23 November 2018.

*

Let me try and draw all these threads together. At the centre of this discussion has been the question – Why? Why did he do these adverts? The short answer to our musing comes from an anecdote in Boblore, the one where a journalist asks him, after the 1965 Newport Folk Festival, 'why did you go electric?' Bob's answer has become legend: 'Why did *you* go electric?'[9] Quite so. And if we asked Dylan why he went commercial, we would, dare I say *should*, get a similar reply.

In responding to his forays into marketing it might help to recall another Bob anecdote, recorded by Ian MacDonald in an essay marking Dylan's sixtieth birthday on 24 May 2001. MacDonald relates how a certain A. J. Weberman had got into an altercation with Dylan on Manhattan's Lower East Side, outside a neighbourhood store some time in 1972. Weberman had been going through Dylan's dustbins, so the story goes, in search of proof that the star was a sell-out, a 'singing real-estate agent', and, for good measure, a Zionist (MacDonald 2003: 1). Dylan tried reason, but ended up resorting to fists and slamming the head of the self-styled 'garbologist' into the pavement. In an unlikely setting, Dylan broke out of his Arundel Tomb. Or, in the terms of this discussion, Dylan showed he is authentic in a way that his performances – songs, films, paintings, commercials – are not. It may well be that the adverts are less convincing than the stage performances, or the studio albums, and maybe the covers albums (especially the Christmas LP?) are only just a short head in front of them in the authenticity stakes, but all of Dylan's pitches *are* pitches. As MacDonald says, it is possible to see Dylan as a performance, not a performing, artist (2003: 2).

Maybe the problem of Dylan's commercial films, if it is a problem at all, is a symptom of a bigger issue: the death of rock and roll, or, if it isn't quite dead yet, and to borrow from Frank Zappa, the fact that it is starting to smell a little funny. Aren't Dylan's adverts a part of a picture where the music industry has simply moved on? What place for Dylan in the infosphere? Now that rock and roll has grown old maybe its authenticity can only be seen in a rearview mirror, while the new authenticity (memes, vlogs, gifs?) is taking shape in ways that we are as yet unable to recognize, precisely because it is new, and we, that is critics and Dylan fans, are not? If Bob's road to the 2014 Super Bowl is a lost highway, then it's ours too.

---

[9] I have been unable to trace the origin of this anecdote. Even if the story is apocryphal, the light it sheds on my discussion here is no less telling.

Then again, maybe the whole thing is better seen in inverted commas, just a postmodern game of genres, is that it? I'll see your hegemony and raise you a cultural syncretism? Or, money where our mouth is, maybe music in the end *really is* just a tie-in for other stuff, like chicken wings or sex?

Maybe. True and false are still ideas that matter, though. They haven't been outmoded by the digital age, even if they have mutated (fake news? fake muse?). They are concepts very close to Bob Dylan's heart – not the one in his wallet, the one on his sleeve. Cut to another line from 'Things Have Changed', one that didn't make it into the Chrysler film, but that is there by dint of being in the same song: 'All the truth in the world adds up to one big lie' (Dylan 2000). To end, I suggest we switch the variables around in that equation and watch one final advert, a plug for Bob Dylan's Subterranean Home-Style Blues Buffet, conveniently located on Highway 61, just past the Positively 4th Street Exit ('Dylan's Latest Ad' 2006). What 'big truth' such 'lies' add up to, I leave to the imagination of the viewer.

References

Berger, J. (1972), *Ways of Seeing*, Harmondsworth: Penguin.
'Bob Dylan + IBM Watson' (2015) [Commercial], *YouTube*. Available online: https://youtu.be/8xYvwcnHn9k (accessed 6 April 2020).
'Bob Dylan Receives Honorary Princeton Degree' (1970), *Rolling Stone*, Available online: www.rollingstone.com/music/music-news/bob-dylan-receives-honorary-princeton-degree-187265/ (accessed 8 April 2020).
'Bob Dylan's Latest Ad' (2006), *YouTube*. Available online: www.youtube.com/watch?v=6gro3Fga11k (accessed 6 April 2020).
'BOM – Bank of Montreal: "The Times They Are A-Changin"' (1996) [Commercial], *YouTube*. Available online: https://youtu.be/9z0tNUxjZmE (accessed 8 April 2020).
Bowie, D. (1971), 'Song for Bob Dylan' [Song], *Hunky Dory*, UK: RCA Records.
'Cadillac Escalade / XM Radio' (2007) [Commercial], *DailyMotion*. Available online: https://dai.ly/x32u0ij (accessed 6 April 2020).
'Cadillac Escalade / XM Radio' (2007) [Commercial], *YouTube*. Available online: www.youtube.com/watch?v=YRkch5FcN-8 (accessed 16 October 2018).
'Chobani Greek Yogurt' (2014) [Commercial], *YouTube*. Available online: https://youtu.be/P9GZrVxIIbU (accessed 6 April 2020).
'Chrysler and Bob Dylan: America's Import' (2014) [Commercial], *YouTube*. Available online: www.youtube.com/watch?v=qOotVKvKrdk (accessed 16 September 2018).

'Co-op: "Blowin' in the Wind"' (2009) [Commercial], *YouTube*. Available online: https://youtu.be/YHzBltFKHAw (accessed 8 April 2020).

Dylan, B. (1963), Album Notes, *The Freewheelin' Bob Dylan* [Album], USA: Columbia Records.

Dylan, B. (1965), 'It's Alright, Ma (I'm Only Bleeding)' [Song], *Bringing It All Back Home*, USA: Columbia Records.

Dylan, B. (1997), 'Love Sick' [Song], *Time Out of Mind*, USA: Columbia Records.

Dylan, B. (2000), 'Things Have Changed' [Music single], USA: Columbia Records.

Dylan, B. (2004), *Chronicles, Volume One*, New York: Simon and Schuster.

Dylan, B. (2015), 'Read Bob Dylan's Complete, Riveting MusiCares Speech', *Rolling Stone*, 9 February. Available online: www.rollingstone.com/music/music-news/read-bob-dylans-complete-riveting-musicares-speech-240728/ (accessed 3 April 2020).

Faithfull, M. (1995), *Faithfull*, Harmondsworth: Penguin.

Gates Jr., H. L. (1991), '"Authenticity", or the Lesson of Little Tree', *New York Times Book Review*, 24 November. Available online: www.nytimes.com/1991/11/24/books/authenticity-or-the-lesson-of-little-tree.html (accessed 3 April 2020).

Gleason, R. J. (1967), 'Bob Dylan Gives Press Conference in San Francisco: Part I of the interview Dylan gave in 1965 at KQED', *Rolling Stone*, 14 December. Available online: www.rollingstone.com/music/music-news/bob-dylan-gives-press-conference-in-san-francisco-246805/ (accessed 8 April 2020).

'Google Instant: "Subterranean Homesick Blues"' (2010) [Commercial], *YouTube*. Available online: https://youtu.be/qcm0rG8EKXI (accessed 3 April 2020).

Heylin, C. ([1991] 2001), *Bob Dylan: Behind the Shades Revisited*, New York: HarperCollins.

'iPod + iTunes: Bob Dylan Modern Times' (2006) [Commercial], *YouTube*. Available online: https://youtu.be/TvJ-f4ykvBE (accessed 6 April 2020).

'Jeep Cherokee: "Built Free"' (2014) [Commercial], *iSpot.tv*. Available online: www.ispot.tv/ad/71cA/2014-jeep-cherokee-built-free (accessed 3 April 2020).

'Kohl's: Holiday Surprise' (2013) [Commercial], *iSpot.tv*. Available online: www.ispot.tv/ad/75Ds/kohls-holiday-surprise (accessed 3 April 2020).

Larkin, P. (1964), 'An Arundel Tomb', *The Whitsun Weddings*, London: Faber and Faber.

MacDonald, I. (2003), *The People's Music*, London: Pimlico.

No Direction Home (2005) [Film], Dir. M. Scorsese, USA: Spitfire Pictures.

Ricks, C. (2003), *Dylan's Visions of Sin*, New York: HarperCollins.

Steinberg, B. (2004), 'Bob Dylan Gets Tangled up in Pink: Victoria's Secret Campaign Drafts Counterculture Hero', *The Wall Street Journal*, 2 April. Available online: www.wsj.com/articles/SB108086174426172226 (accessed 3 April 2020).

Steinberg, B. (2014), 'Super Bowl: How Bob Dylan Jumped from Counterculture Icon to Car Salesman', *Variety*, 2 February. Available online: https://variety.com/2014/tv/news/super-bowl-how-bob-dylan-jumped-from-counterculture-icon-to-car-salesman-1201083508/ (accessed 3 April 2020).

Stephenson, S. (2004), 'Tangled up in Boobs', *Slate*, 12 April. Available online: https://slate.com/business/2004/04/bob-dylan-shills-for-victoria-s-secret.html (accessed 3 April 2020).

'Target: "Must Be Santa"' (2017) [Commercial], *Music Mill* website. Available online: www.musicmill.com.au/portfolio/target-artist-bob-dylan-track-must-be-santa/ (accessed 8 April 2020).

'Victoria's Secret: Angels in Venice' (2004) [Commercial], *YouTube*. Available online: www.youtube.com/watch?v=QsFrFQ-F64Y (accessed 5 October 2018).

'WGU – Western Governor's University: The Times They Are a-Changing' (2018) [Commercial], *YouTube*. Available online: https://youtu.be/72c8zVCn73o (accessed 6 April 2020).

6

Bringing the Margin to the Centre: Dylan's Visible Republic

Erin C. Callahan

Dylan's ascent to folk music fame began with his interest in experiences beyond the middle-class, mid-century American pop culture in which he grew up. In *No Direction Home*, Dylan explains his hometown of Hibbing, Minnesota was a replica of most rural American towns with very little interest in, or room for, rebellion or alternative ideologies. However, the eccentric performances of travelling carnivals and late-night radio stations that played country, bluegrass and blues piqued Dylan's interest in people and experiences underrepresented in American life and media. This is what Greil Marcus called 'the invisible republic', an altered state of reality featuring marginalized characters and experiences that Dylan communicates through highly skilled poetry revealing fundamental truths (Marcus 1997: 20–7). Dylan's works penetrate the diluted, superficial content of prime-time network sitcoms and top forty radio stations in favour of songs that pull back the surface of American society to expose and promote the full spectrum of American pluralism.

The conformity and consumerism of post-war mid-twentieth-century America, when the country rose to world superpower status, provided the conditions for the development of the New Left, with Dylan as its anointed spokesperson. However, the commodification of American culture and increased mass media also signalled the near impossibility of keeping artistic creation separate from the artefacts becoming products bought and sold for profit. In this way, Dylan and his songs have always been commodities, even in the most nascent stages of his career. Initially, he was able to mask this practice by appropriating folk conventions. Dylan's early identity was a *bricolage* of previous folk tropes, a consciously constructed identity in response to pop culture he disliked because he found it to be false (Dylan 2004: 35). Andrea Svedberg's 1963 *Newsweek* article exposed Dylan's orphan vagabond identity as a fraud, noting:

'the ironic thing is that Bob Dylan, too, grew up in a conventional home and went to conventional schools' (Svedberg 1963). However, Dylan's violation of folk authenticity did not affect his image, popularity or commercial success because his music and lyrics reflected values in the musical tradition of Woody Guthrie and the poetic tradition of Walt Whitman. Joan Baez told Svedberg: 'There's a lot about Bobby I don't understand ... But I don't care. I understand his words. That's all that matters' (Svedberg 1963). That's what the first generation of Dylan fans responded to: someone in their generation articulating a vision of an idealized democratic America.

This vision, which Dylan represented, countered mainstream consumer culture that had quickly become both lucrative and ubiquitous. Film, radio, television and mass media dominated the American cultural landscape, reinforcing the values of the hegemony. In *Chronicles,* Dylan reflects on this, saying that when he listened to the radio he wanted to hear contemporary 'Jekyll and Hyde themes', not characterless schmaltz, and current ideas he found in Kerouac and the Beats but which were not reflected on the radio (Dylan 2004: 34). The works Dylan refers to are examples of the 'invisible republic' that fascinated him in his youth, experiences subversive to the homogenized and sanitized America projected in blockbuster movies and popular television and music. However, as Herbert Marcuse argues in *One Dimensional Man,* in industrial consumer culture, even counterculture ideas are eventually consumed into the hegemony, marketed and sold for profit (Marcuse 1991: 1–4). Marcuse explains a distinction between earlier periods of human artistic creation and creation in the post-industrial period. He explains that '[w]hat has changed in the contemporary period is the difference between the two orders and their truths. The absorbent power of society depletes the artistic dimension by assimilating its antagonistic contents' (Marcuse 1991: 61). Understanding that concept allows artists the better to control the extent to which their art is 'absorbed' and 'depleted' through commodification and mass distribution (Marcuse 1991: 61). Dylan acknowledges the subversive nature of his songs would probably limit their commercial success. They reflected that 'new type of human experience', through lyrics about 'debauched bootleggers, mothers that drowned their children, Cadillacs that only got five miles to the gallon, floods, union hall fires, darkness and cadavers at the bottom of rivers' (Dylan 2004: 34). However, through his partnership with Albert Grossman, Dylan married the authenticity of his songs with the American consumer capitalist economy. Describing this, journalist Michael Verity critiques: 'Dylan's alliance with

Grossman was dissolved in the early '70s . . . . But, 40 years hence, Dylan still finds meaning in the capitalistic Gospel of Grossman' (Verity 2018). Verity focuses on Dylan's business practices, not the authenticity or merit of his art. Once Dylan breaks the final barrier of commodification of his work by appearing in commercials, he uses his performed and perceived authenticity to promote the 'invisible republic', increasing the visibility of its themes and characters through mass media and advancing technology.

Dylan's original technological sin occurred when he performed an electric set with his makeshift band at the 1965 Newport Folk Festival. This seminal event in Dylan's mythology has been widely sensationalized and was so traumatic to audience members that Todd Haynes represented it in his film, *I'm Not There*, as Dylan opening machine-gun fire on the crowd. That trauma was born from Dylan violating expectations fans had of him and of his performance. Folk music is traditional, populist and anti-commercial. Conversely, Dylan's electric music was loud, popular and overly produced. Most audience members responded by booing Dylan's new music. In *No Direction Home: The Life and Music of Bob Dylan*, Robert Shelton recalls: 'From the moment the group swung into a rocking electric version of "Maggie's Farm", the Newport audience registered hostility' (Shelton 1986: 348). Whether it was a response to Dylan playing electric music or the volume of the PA system, the audience's reactions signalled their rejection of Dylan abandoning folk traditions. That was confirmed by the audience's cheers when he returned to play an acoustic set.

Contemporaneously, the folk establishment was equally divided in its reactions. Some decried Dylan as a traitor to folk authenticity by capitulating to the consumerism of mainstream popular music. Folk purists like Alan Lomax expressed hostility to Dylan's new style similar to that of the Newport audience (Shelton 1986: 348; Heylin 2003: 206–11). When Shelton asked George Wein, technical production manager at Newport, what he resented about Dylan's performance and folk-rock, he responded: 'You've been brainwashed by the recording industry' (Shelton 1986: 349). Others defended Dylan, lauding him for creating electric folk-rock, presaging the movement away from traditional folk music. In the *Village Voice*, Phil Ochs addressed festival directors, writing, 'I think the best way to judge for yourself who was making the most valid musical point is to listen to a couple of Newport records of previous years and then listen to Dylan's new single, "Like a Rolling Stone"' (Heylin 2003: 215). Paul Nelson echoed Ochs's support and 'in a strong defense of Dylan, Nelson described Newport '65 as "a sad parting of the ways for many, myself included. I choose

Dylan. I choose art"' (Heylin 2003: 216). Newport 1965 was not the first time Dylan leveraged technology to further his career and reach a broader audience, nor was it the first time Dylan profited from the establishment against which he rebelled. It would also not be the last time Dylan's actions, behaviour or performance would elicit conflicting responses. Throughout his career, Dylan has been able to resist the subversive elements of his songs being absorbed by and assimilated into the mainstream.

At the same time Dylan was writing anti-establishment songs capturing the *zeitgeist* of the early 1960s, he signed a management deal with Albert Grossman and learned business practices he would follow throughout his career. Grossman's questionable ethics made him a divisive figure among the folk community, although he was admired for his business acumen (Spitz 1991: 176–8). Biographer Bob Spitz notes that once Dylan generated interest among the Greenwich Village community as the next major folk singer, Grossman focused intently on managing Dylan, and by '[h]arnessing Bob's sense of inspiration, rebellion, exaggeration, peculiarity, posturing, and conceit, Grossman intended to create a legend' (Spitz 1991: 180). In Dylan, Grossman found a willing partner. Under Grossman's management, Dylan first violated folk authenticity and conventions. Michael Verity argues that '[t]he truth is: Bob Dylan's never hesitated to take a payment from the very establishment against which he has railed' (Verity 2018). While singing about the injustices of American capitalism, Dylan enriched himself as a willing participant in the marketplace without adulterating the subversive elements of his works. Early in his career, Dylan sold the rights to his songs for other artists to record, thus using his songs for profit beyond his recordings of them. Even the commercially successful versions, like recordings by the Byrds and Peter Paul and Mary, did not diminish the original compositions' artistic quality. Traditionally, folk song authorship remained uncredited or in the public domain. Recording, rerecording, and alteration of songs by various artists across genres and time, sanctified their content. Dylan profiting from the publishing rights of his songs indicated a departure from this practice, commodifying his compositions for commercial use.

During this time, Dylan also followed other artists like Elvis and the Beatles by expanding his performance into film. He appeared in two documentaries chronicling his 1965 and 1966 tours in England in which he allowed a film crew access to concert performances, impromptu and scripted material. The behind-the-scenes footage intended to provide an 'authentic' or private view of Dylan on tour, through which his performance, lyrics and cast of characters presented the 'invisible republic' to broader audiences. The scripted or planned scenes highlighted Dylan's wit and charm as he interacted with fans, friends and others. Through the films, Dylan used the technology of the film industry to broaden his audience and further market himself. Of Pennebaker's film, released in 1967, Richard Goldstein wrote in his *New York Times* column entitled 'Dylan: We Trust What He Tells Us': '*Dont Look Back* shows us Bob Dylan as a young performer feeling around the edges of fame ... He is no visionary here but an entertainer, deeply concerned with pleasing audiences through his songs and a bit unsure of his power as a pop conquistador' (Goldstein 1967). As early as the 1960s, many recognized the dominant commercial ethos of Dylan's performance. The implicit titular 'trust' the audience has in what Dylan tells them, through his lyrics and performance, is unmarred by the film's capacity to reveal the intersection between Dylan's art and his capitalist practices.

As noted, 1965 proves a pivotal year for Dylan due to his Newport performance and films, but also because he revealed how he would eventually appear in commercials. During a press conference in December, he fielded a question about how he would 'sell out to a consumer interest' should he decide to do so (Dylan 1965). Dylan's response, notably part of his mythology, was he would sell 'ladies' garments' (Dylan 1965). Thirty-nine years later, when Dylan appeared in the 'Angels in Venice' campaign for Victoria's Secret, he fulfilled his prediction, eliciting a similar response his performance in Newport had. Again, he was met with criticism that he had violated his authenticity as a serious artist. Outraged journalists, fans and scholars denounced him as a creepy old man stalking after a woman one-third his age while his song 'Love Sick' played in the background (Victoria's Secret 2004). The advertisement contains no discernable message or motivation for Dylan's participation, causing many to condemn it as the final step towards his complete commodification. Conversely, other commenters felt it was just another one of Dylan's put-ons, one that furthered his relevance in pop culture. Not only had Dylan told the press on a lark how he would 'sell out' and fulfilled it, he potentially introduced himself to a new audience as the commercial aired during the popular talent show *American Idol*. Brandon Gaille reports: 'For eight consecutive years beginning in 2003–2004, [*American Idol*] was ranked #1 in US television ratings' (Gaille 2015). Additionally, the target demographic for the show was viewers between the ages of eighteen and forty-four, all of whom were outside Dylan's original Baby Boomer fan base (Gaille 2015). Dylan appears to capitalize on the show's cult-like viewership to sell himself. It is clear he's not selling or promoting an album. *Time Out of Mind,* on which 'Love Sick' appears, was released in 1997. Few people believed Dylan was genuinely peddling 'ladies' garments'. It is reasonable to conclude that the ad's placement during a popular prime-time television show signals Dylan's promotion of himself and the New Left ideas associated with him.

Further demonstrating his use of developing technology and American consumer culture to promote those ideas, Dylan next appeared in ads for iTunes and Cadillac. Just as he had done in Newport when he 'went electric', and when he appeared in the 'Angels in Venice' ad, Dylan's partnership with new distribution formats grows his audience beyond his Baby Boomer base. The 2006 iTunes commercial depicts Dylan against a white backdrop performing 'Someday Baby' cross-cut with images of people wearing Apple iPods, dancing and listening to music. The commercial then cuts to a black background with the words 'Bob Dylan Modern Times' appearing in white, signalling a pairing of Dylan's product, his music, with Apple's product, the mode by which the music could be purchased and consumed (iTunes 2006). Not only does Dylan appear in the commercial before an image of the iPod does, his album is advertised before iTunes and iPods are. It is essentially a commercial for the release of *Modern Times*, which tells the viewer the album can be immediately purchased on iTunes. At only three years old, iTunes was still new technology, but monopolized the digital music market.

In the ad, Dylan did not seem to sell iTunes or iPods; he was selling his album and *Modern Times* is an appropriate pairing for Apple's new platform. The album's title suggests Dylan's movement away from his nostalgic folk identity into something current, vital and relevant. Still able to reflect the *zeitgeist* of the country, *Modern Times* marries traditional music like blues, rock and roll and folk with lyrics communicating post-industrial concerns facing the United States. *Rolling Stone*'s Joe Levy notes, 'Almost every song retraces the American journey from the country to the city, when folkways were giving way to modern times. The mood is America on the brink – of mechanization, of war, of domestic tranquility, of fulfilling its promise and of selling its dreams one by one for cash on the barrelhead' (Levy 2018). *Modern Times* suggests America is in a metaphase, between old and new, traditional and modern, but is rapidly moving forward paced by technological development.

Dylan's appearance in a 2007 Cadillac Escalade commercial provides a romanticized and nostalgic view of America's open road and highlights Dylan's *Theme Time Radio Hour* on XM Radio more than it sells the car Dylan is driving (Cadillac 2007). The opening shot shows a Cadillac Escalade zooming through the frame with guitar accompaniment as the audio. The ad jump-cuts to shots of desert roads and rural western landscapes. As the guitar music continues softly in the background, Dylan's voice-over is introduced. It is a mock-up of his newly launched radio show including some ad copy promoting Cadillac, the product featured in the commercial and the sponsor of Dylan's show. Similar to the Apple commercial, viewers see the marriage of nostalgia – Dylan, the format of the radio hour and the car – with developing technology – satellite radio.

The voice-over of Dylan's *Theme Time Radio Hour*, reminiscent of shows he listened to as a teen in Hibbing, pairs with images of Dylan in America's rural west signalling the connection between them. Dylan standing at a crossroads alludes to the Robert Johnson myth, often appropriated by or ascribed to him in his mythology. His key line in the commercial poses the question: 'What's life without the occasional detour?' (Cadillac 2007). Alluding to the American *Declaration of Independence*, the words 'life, liberty, and the pursuit' appear superimposed over Dylan before the background fades to black (Cadillac 2007). Pairing Dylan's image with the allusion reinforces his connection to ideals of American democracy and the New Left and his antipathy toward mainstream pop culture, even as he appears in a commercial for a luxury car, or what Verity called 'a markedly more bourgeoisie brand than Chrysler' (Verity 2017). The next image, white text on a black background, encourages viewers to 'Listen to "Bob Dylan's Theme Time Radio Hour" exclusively on XM' (Cadillac 2007). 'Bob Dylan's Theme Time Radio Hour' is in a larger font than the other text, except the XM logo, making both the focal points of the ad. The commercial cuts to another title card reading 'XM standard on all Cadillacs', placing the car and radio service secondary to promoting Dylan's show (Cadillac 2007). Although a natural platform for him, the radio show signalled Dylan's entry into a new media outlet, providing him the opportunity to perform for and interact directly with listeners through scripted material and answering phone calls. The commercial is the vehicle to promote his latest project – a radio show through which he explores some of the altered or parallel reality of his 'invisible republic'. Satellite radio provided hosts with agency over content and fewer commercial interruptions. Therefore, Dylan had complete artistic control over his playlist, format and guests. In the ad, he does not simply use his image to sell the car or the radio service. He sells his radio show as the viewers' experience of authentic American music and culture.

In addition to using his image to promote his radio show in this commercial, Dylan also dictated the way he appeared in it. Control over how the artist's image or work is used, represented and distributed helps mediate the exploitation of the art and artist in this arrangement. Dylan's status as a cultural icon allowed him control over how he and his music appeared in commercials. In his *Rolling Stone* review of the ad, Evan Serpick noted, 'When Cadillac's ad agency, Modernista, heard Dylan was also willing to appear in a TV ad, it constructed a simple script, Dylan had requirements: He wouldn't speak on camera, he would wear his own clothes, and he didn't want his music to be used' (Serpick 2018). With the exception of the script copy, Dylan had full control over his participation in the commercial. In his article 'Hey, Mr. Escalade Man', Andrew Adam Newman suggests corporate and ad execs treated Dylan with reverence, and quotes Liz Vanzura, global marketing director for Cadillac, as saying: 'We tried to be very respectful of the fact that he's a legend. He's not talking about the fact that we've got the biggest navigation screens' (Newman 2007). Even Cadillac's executives recognized Dylan's appearance extended beyond the role of a traditional celebrity spokesperson.

Until the 2014 Super Bowl Chrysler ad, Dylan's appearances in commercials included him licensing his songs and image or appearing briefly as he did for iTunes and Cadillac. His licensed image in the 2009 Super Bowl commercial for Pepsi again depicted nostalgic and sentimental Americana, set alongside similar contemporary representations of it. Dylan's song 'Forever Young' serves as the backdrop for these parallel experiences of American youth and is performed by both Dylan and Black Eyed Peas frontman Will.I.Am to reinforce the contrast and congruity (Pepsi 2009). The opening shot of a mid-1960s Dylan framed in a doorway cuts to him looking at and through Ray-Ban sunglasses. The younger Dylan represents youth and the rebellion and protest of the New Left. The jump-cut editing of the next images suggests the 1960s Dylan passes those sunglasses to Will.I.Am. The shot then jumps to a split screen of Dylan and Will.I.Am in perfectly matched profile wearing the sunglasses, a symbolic 'passing of the torch' from Dylan's generation to Will.I.Am's. Other images in the ad include a soldier returning home from the Vietnam War cutting to a soldier returning from the Iraq conflict, video of the March on Washington jumping to video from Grant Park on election night 2008, Gumby juxtaposed with Shrek, and concert footage of Dylan cutting to concert footage of Will.I.Am. Each contemporary representation is faster, more colourful and more dynamic than its counterpart to signify each generation builds upon and gives energy to what the previous generation started. The concluding voice-over, 'Every generation refreshes the world', reinforces the message that Pepsi is the soft drink of young people (Pepsi 2009).

Dylan's approval of the use of his image in this campaign capitalizes on the nostalgia it elicits for a more hopeful period, but parallels the hope created by the election of Barack Obama the previous November. It's doubtful the Pepsi Corporation is making an overt political statement outside the commercial benefit of doing so. However, Dylan's participation in the ad that debuted to an audience of 98.7 million Super Bowl viewers can be interpreted as his support of nostalgia for the liberal ideals the ad engenders (Rovell 2018). In June 2008, he recognized America was in a 'state of upheaval' and tacitly endorsed Barack Obama for president of the United States saying Obama was 'redefining the nature of politics from the ground up' ('Dylan Hopeful' 2008). It was the first time Dylan spoke publicly about a candidate. Aside from some mixed accounts of Dylan's live performance on election night 2008, Dylan has not commented about presidential politics since. With that large a viewing audience during the ad's Super Bowl premiere, Dylan isn't just selling the Pepsi product, but also the ideologies of youthful protest, civic participation, and the hope and change his 1960s image represents. These images paralleled with contemporary versions of them suggest each new generation will reinvigorate the world with progressive ideals and action.

In the 2014 Super Bowl ad for Chrysler, Dylan not only appears via voice-over and while driving a Chrysler, he also addresses the camera – and therefore the audience – with a direct message (Chrysler 2014). Evoking similar nostalgia to the previous ads that use young Dylan's image, the commercial begins with a black and white shot of Dylan in concert in the 1960s looking out over the audience. While the opening of 'Things Have Changed' plays, the image cuts to an older Dylan filmed from behind while he looks through blinds out a window. The shot jumps to Dylan's eyes peering through the blinds. On the next cut, viewers see what Dylan sees: a montage of sentimental Americana. The images jump from cowboys and horses, to cheerleaders, to a woman wrapped in a flag. The commercial continues with Dylan's voice-over asking, 'Is there anything more American than America?' (Chrysler 2014). Though the redundant question arguably communicates a nationalistic message the younger Dylan in the opening seconds would reject, posing the question with a pastiche of mainstream mid-century American cultural images of muscle cars, American flags, baseball, Marilyn Monroe, James Dean, diners, young Dylan and all he represents, cheerleaders and 'creatures of the open road', elicits both nostalgia for the era of a booming American labour economy and appeals to the general audience of 112.2 million Super Bowl viewers who likely responded positively to the ad's message (Sandomir 2016). Further, pairing of images of young and old Dylan and marginalized figures with mainstream Americana positions Dylan as part of that nostalgia and an authentic representative of it. Dylan's voice-over includes descriptors of American identity such as 'original' and 'cool', and credits Detroit as innovator, inspiration, and the heart of the car industry that revolutionized America.

When Dylan steps off the elevator, he looks directly at the camera, addresses the audience and endorses the struggling city and its working-class community by saying, 'Yeah, Detroit made cars and cars made America' (Chrysler 2014). Here, Dylan uses 'Detroit' as synonymous with the people who work in the auto industry as well as a synecdoche for the entire American auto industry. His repetitive use of the verb 'made' assumes two meanings. In the first clause, 'made' literally means cars were built or assembled in Detroit by the people who lived in Detroit. The second clause is more abstract as Dylan alludes to the auto industry, labour and unions as the foundation of America's mid-century middle-class economy. The succeeding montage depicts auto workers getting ready for work and at work at the plant as Dylan says, 'And you can't import the heart and soul of every man and woman working on the line' (Chrysler 2014). The commercial continues with juxtaposed images of iconic figures of American identity, like cowboys and American labour, solidifying a sense of unity among America's diversity. Dylan's voice-over idealizes 'American pride' as the one thing that can't be imported. These overly sentimentalized figures and 'creatures of the open road' are members of Dylan's 'invisible republic', brought together in this commercial to illustrate strength in American unity, diversity and labour.

The pro-labour message echoes Dylan's folk, New Left and Whitmanesque origins recognizing the dignity of labour as foundational to the American republic, its identity and strength. In contrast with his previous appearances in commercials, Dylan is the spokesman for these ideals, using his performance to sell the cars in the ad and the people who make them. This is overtly clear when he tells viewers to 'search the world over for the finer things' and names products associated with countries and continents that best produce them (Chrysler 2014). Over a montage of beer being brewed and poured, watches being built and cell phones being assembled, Dylan says, 'Let Germany brew your beer. Let Switzerland make your watch. Let Asia assemble your phone' (Chrysler 2014). The camera then follows Dylan as he walks through a pool hall and shoots pool. The penultimate shot of the commercial is a medium-wide view of Dylan at the end of a pool table surrounded by auto workers and pushes in to a close-up on his face as he looks at the camera to emphasize the next line and says, 'We will build your car' (Chrysler 2014). Dylan's use of the first-person plural pronoun 'we' in this scene creates a feeling of community with the auto workers who build the cars featured in the commercial. Further, it associates the cars with the authenticity of that labour rather than the corporation that owns and controls the modes of production and employs those labourers.

Dylan's 2015 pairing with IBM's Watson highlighted the expediency of data analytics, particularly in the study of Dylan's lyrics (IBM 2015). In the same way Dylan appeared in ads for iTunes and Cadillac, he does not directly endorse the product in the commercial. Dylan's self-promotion is a tongue-in-cheek homage to the entire field of Dylanology and those who analyse his lyrics and music. The commercial also illustrates the advantages and limits of artificial intelligence (AI). Sitting opposite IBM's AI computer, Watson, a much more personable and social Dylan than viewers have seen in previous commercials engages the computer in a dialogue. Just as many scholars, critics and fans have, Watson, who has the impressive ability to read and analyse data at 800,000,000 pages per second, has read through and analysed all of Dylan's lyrics. The AI's analysis echoes Dylan's words to Joan Baez in the 1960s: in *No Direction Home*, Baez shares that when Dylan asked her what she thought of his lyrics, he told her even he didn't know what they meant, but people would study them for years (*No Direction Home* 2005). Dylan was accurate about the mystery, merit and academic interest in his lyrics as poetry as Watson engages in the same exercise to learn more about language and improve his language skills. The computer concludes the primary themes of Dylan's songs are 'that time passes and love fades', two very human concerns (IBM 2015). Dylan agrees with Watson's assessment and suggests they write a song together. However, Watson confesses he has never experienced true love, thus reinforcing the limits of AI's human capabilities. In the commercial, Dylan does not overtly endorse IBM computers or the merits of data analytics in the way he does cars for Chrysler. However, Dylan's appearance with Watson further promotes the relevance of his work and the study of it using the new technology of data analytics.

In addition to appearing in commercials, Dylan continues to license his image and songs for a multitude of ads ranging from Jeep to Chobani Greek yogurt to online courses at Western Governor's University. As Kory Grow notes, the ad for Chobani, which aired during the same Super Bowl as the Chrysler ad, 'uses the folk-rock icon's harmonica-powered 1966 hit "I Want You" as the soundtrack to a very hairy scene' (Grow 2014). A bear is ransacking a rural town and terrorizing its residents (Chobani 2014). Grow further describes the marriage of song and images: 'Eventually, it [the bear] finds what it's looking for (it's easy to guess what it is) and the vocal line of the *Blonde on Blonde* track plays to narrate just what the bear is thinking' (Grow 2014). The pairing of 'The Times They Are A-Changin'' with images of people bettering their lives through education in commercials for Western Governor's University's online courses features the chorus to depict adult learners improving their lives through education (WGU 2018). What changes for the people in the ads is their ability to achieve success in a career that allows them a stable and liveable income. Both ads maintain the artistic integrity of the original songs despite their commercial use. Through the lyrics and images, the Chobani commercial exchanges one sensual desire for another, while the ad for Western Governor's University depicts education as a catalyst for change.

Instead of signalling his selling out to consumer interests, Dylan's appearance in commercials is an extended performance providing new avenues of interpretation, thus keeping him relevant in the sixth decade of his career. As the twentieth century progressed into the twenty-first and technology altered the mediation between art and artist, and the public, the rules governing art's authenticity and purpose and its separation from consumer culture have collapsed. Part of this is based on fundamental changes to the music industry that forced artists to find other revenue streams and outlets for their work. Over the course of Dylan's career, he went from selling vinyl, to eight-tracks, to cassette tapes, to CDs, and ultimately MP3s and iTunes. The digital age eliminated the established recording industry distribution model and allowed artists to distribute their work directly. It also allowed for bootleggers and file sharing that essentially robbed artists of payment. Services such as iTunes have corrected that issue, but the shifts in American consumer culture have made it more acceptable for artists to license their music for commercial use. This is similar to Dylan's use of social media outlets such as Facebook, Instagram and Twitter. As many celebrities do, Dylan uses these platforms to communicate with the public directly, controlling his image and message outside the apparatus of management and public relations representatives. In this way, he continues to remain relevant and challenge mainstream culture with the technology used to promote it.

Regardless of the platform he uses to distribute his songs, the personae and themes they communicate remain constant representations of the 'invisible republic', the underrepresented people and ideas in American culture that occupy spaces outside the margins of the hegemony. These personae are fragmentations of Dylan's identity, including the Emersonian poet and troubadour in the IBM and iTunes commercials, the hobo, outlaw, and cowboy from the Victoria's Secret, Cadillac and Chrysler ads, and the romantic in the Victoria's Secret ad. Images of young Dylan evoke democratic ideals of the New Left associated with his early career. In the Pepsi commercial, they represent youthful protest of the Civil Rights and Vietnam War era. This depiction is repeated several times in the opening and the montage of the Chrysler commercial, signifying the ad's pro-labour message. The themes of love fading, time passing, the dignity of labour and the allure of the open road and the 'creatures' one will find on it remain vital components of Dylan's songs and commercial work.

It is irrelevant how many commercials Dylan appears in or how many times he sells his songs for commercial use, thus violating the artistry and authenticity Dylan purists ascribe to them – he and his works remain generally untainted by consumerism *en masse*. Rather, they have been institutionalized, normalized and consumed by the hegemony as essential American folk art. Since the airing of his first commercial, Dylan's work has been sanctified for its artistic merit through numerous awards, by both governments and arts organizations. In 2012, President Obama awarded Dylan the Presidential Medal of Freedom for his contributions to American art and culture. His introduction during the ceremony read, 'More than fifty years after his career began, Bob Dylan remains an eminent voice in our national conversation and around the world' (Obama 2012). In the following years, he was awarded the Order of the Légion d'Honneur and the Nobel Prize in Literature. These awards may signify Dylan's acceptance into the mainstream culture which he rejected, from which he felt alienated and which he has critiqued throughout his career, but through that process he infiltrated the mechanisms of post-industrial consumer culture to give voice to and represent a segment of American culture and society beyond the superficial Disney World, top 40, suburban experience. As a result, commercials, which formerly signified selling out to consumer interests or a bastardization of artistic integrity, have been appropriated as a tool to further one's artistic performance. By the time Dylan appeared in his first commercial in 2004, he had already established post-industrial capitalist practices through publishing rights sales of his early songs and going electric in 1965. As technology has developed, Dylan has been able to partner with the modes of distribution increasingly to bring his themes, stories and personae from the margins into the centre of culture, making the invisible republic more visible.

References

'Bob Dylan + IBM Watson' (2015) [Commercial], *YouTube*. Available online: https://youtu.be/8xYvwcnHn9k (accessed 6 April 2020).

'Cadillac Escalade / XM Radio' (2007) [Commercial], *YouTube*. Available online: www.youtube.com/watch?v=YRkch5FcN-8 (accessed 16 October 2018).

'Chobani Greek Yogurt' (2014) [Commercial], *YouTube*. Available online: https://youtu.be/P9GZrVxIIbU (accessed 6 April 2020).

'Chrysler and Bob Dylan: America's Import' (2014) [Commercial], *YouTube*. Available online: www.youtube.com/watch?v=qOotVKvKrdk (accessed 16 September 2018).

Dont Look Back (1967) [Film], Dir. D. A. Pennebaker, USA: Leacock-Pennebaker.

'Dylan "Hopeful" over Barack Obama' (2008), *BBC News*, 7 June. Available online: http://news.bbc.co.uk/1/hi/entertainment/7441708.stm (accessed 6 April 2020).

Dylan, B. (1965), KQED Television Press Conference, San Francisco, 3 December, *YouTube*. Available online: www.youtube.com/watch?v=m68JY-7LfpQ (accessed 3 April 2020).

Dylan, B. (2004), *Chronicles, Volume One,* New York: Simon and Schuster.

Gaille, B. (2015), '17 Amazing American Idol Demographics', *Brandon Gaille: Small Business and Marketing Advice* website, 12 October. Available online: brandongaille.com/17-american-idol-demographics (accessed 3 October 2018).

Goldstein, R. (1967), 'Dylan: "We Trust What He Tells Us"', *The New York Times*, 22 October. Available online: www.nytimes.com/1967/10/22/archives/dylan-we-trust-what-he-tells-us.html (accessed 7 October 2018).

Grow, K. (2014), 'Bob Dylan Will Be a-Changin' Super Bowl Ads This Weekend', *Rolling Stone*, 29 January. Available online: www.rollingstone.com/movies/movie-news/bob-dylan-will-be-a-changin-super-bowl-ads-this-weekend-195973/ (accessed 6 April 2020).

Heylin, C. ([1991] 2003), *Bob Dylan: Behind the Shades*, 20th Anniversary Edn, London: Faber & Faber.

I'm Not There (2007) [Film], Dir. Todd Haynes, USA: The Weinstein Company.

'iPod + iTunes: Bob Dylan Modern Times' (2006) [Commercial], *YouTube*. Available online: https://youtu.be/TvJ-f4ykvBE (accessed 6 April 2020).

Levy, J. (2018), 'Modern Times', *Rolling Stone*, 25 June. Available online: www.rollingstone.com/music/music-album-reviews/modern-times-115063/ (accessed 4 November 2018).

Marcus, G. (1997), *Invisible Republic: Bob Dylan's Basement Tapes*, New York: Henry Holt & Co.

Marcuse, H. (1991), *One Dimensional Man,* 2nd edn, Boston: Beacon.

Newman, A. (2007), 'Hey, Mr. Escalade Man', *The New York Times*, 4 November. Available online: www.nytimes.com/2007/11/04/automobiles/04DYLAN.html (accessed 14 October 2018).

No Direction Home: Bob Dylan (2005) [Film], Dir. Martin Scorsese, USA: Paramount Pictures.

Obama, B. (2012), 'Remarks by the President at Presidential Medal of Freedom Ceremony', *Obama White House Archives* website, 29 May. Available online: https://obamawhitehouse.archives.gov/the-press-office/2012/05/29/remarks-president-presidential-medal-freedom-ceremony (accessed 26 September 2018).

'Pepsi: Forever Young' (2009) [Commercial], *YouTube*. Available online: www.youtube.com/watch?v=ommfjkIqDRs (accessed 6 April 2020).

Rovell, D. (2018), 'Eagles-Patriots Super Bowl Watched by Fewer People', *ESPN*, 5 February. Available online: www.espn.com/nfl/story/_/id/22336786/viewership-super-bowl-lii-patriots-eagles-down (accessed 26 September 2018).

Sandomir, R. (2016), 'Viewership of Super Bowl Falls Short of Record', *The New York Times*, 9 February. Available online: www.nytimes.com/2016/02/09/sports/football/viewership-of-super-bowl-falls-short-of-record.html (accessed 8 October 2018).

Serpick, E. (2018), 'Bob Dylan's New Ride', *Rolling Stone*, 25 June. Available online: www.rollingstone.com/music/music-news/bob-dylans-new-ride-69676/ (accessed 7 October 2018).

Shelton, R. (1986), *No Direction Home: The Life and Music of Bob Dylan,* New York: Ballantine.

Spitz, M. (1991), *Dylan: A Biography,* New York: W. W. Norton & Company.

Svedberg, A. (1963), 'I Am My Words', *Newsweek*, 4 November, in E. Coleman, 'Revisit Our Infamous 1963 Profile of Bob Dylan', *Newsweek*, 24 May. Available online: www.newsweek.com/bob-dylans-75th-birthday-revisit-our-infamous-1963-profile-462801 (accessed 6 April 2020).

Verity, M. (2017), 'The Paycheck is Blowin' in the Wind: A Brief History of Bob Dylan in Commercials', *The Bluegrass Situation* website, 18 January. Available online: https://thebluegrasssituation.com/read/the-paycheck-is-blowin-in-the-wind-a-brief-history-of-bob-dylan-in-commercials/ (accessed 6 April 2020).

'Victoria's Secret: Angels in Venice' (2004) [Commercial], *YouTube*. Available online: www.youtube.com/watch?v=QsFrFQ-F64Y (accessed 5 October 2018).

'Western Governor's University: The Times They Are a-Changing' (2018) [Commercial], *YouTube*. Available online: https://youtu.be/72c8zVCn73o (accessed 6 April 2020).

7

Creation and Re-Creation in Dylan's Performances of 'Blowin' in the Wind' (1963–2016)

Julie Mansion-Vaquié

Dylan is often portrayed as a performing artist reshaping his songs for his concerts. It is in musicological and performing arts terms that this idea of the performing artist will be analysed. 'Blowin' in the Wind' is certainly an old song from Dylan's repertoire, but it has a unique history and a cultural and societal impact: it was the hymn of a movement and a generation. The aim of this chapter is, first, to examine briefly Dylan's approach to recording what we consider here as the template of the song, and then, in detail, to compare several stage versions in order to measure the musical re-creation of this successful song as well as to evaluate the evolution of the artist's stage performances.

1. From disc to stage: methods and concepts

Popular music has a multiple mode of existence, a specific ontology, due to its link with recording. This phonographic character implies that, at several levels of musical creation, the recording comes into play. Indeed, the studio makes it possible to create arrangements, to use effects that cannot be reproduced in concert situations, and to deploy the artist's creativity free from certain technical and acoustic limitations. According to Keith Negus, Dylan's creative approach in the studio is an element little addressed by musicologists for a number of reasons: the attachment to the study of lyrics; critics, especially Paul Williams, focusing on demonstrating that concert versions are more interesting than recorded versions; or even some anecdotes about protagonists working with Dylan (Negus 2010). In this regard, Colin Irwin, in his 2007 book, quotes bassist Harvey

Brooks citing Dylan's spontaneity during recording sessions (Irwin 2007: 165). His spontaneity in the studio and readiness to try different arrangements of any one song means that it is unsurprising that over the years he has often entirely reworked the arrangements of his songs.

1.1 Approach

The type of approach proposed here mainly takes into account three concepts related to the transition from one medium to another: performance, interpretation (to which I prefer the term *intrapretation*, as shall be explained) and scenic re-creation.

Like other musicologists,[1] I consider the work recorded on disc as the original work. It is indeed a kind of finished product offered to the listener where the essential characteristics are thought out during the mixing (number of musicians, effects, spatialization, volume, etc.). The lack of interest in Bob Dylan's studio-recorded versions pointed out by Negus seems unjustified. He says that the artist devoted a lot of time to them in order to obtain the sound he wanted throughout his career:

> Dylan has entered studios with a very clear purpose, his work guided by clear sonic intentions, even if the songs have initially been 'unfinished' and the final musical arrangement and full text of lyrics completed during the process of recording. The fact that Dylan has frequently rewritten songs in the studio as arrangements have coalesced and suggested new angles is itself an indication of the importance of the studio in shaping and extending his songwriting... While Dylan has challenged the ethos of perfectionism inherent in these aesthetic values and technological practices, he has also selectively employed them as he has used the studio, often in subtle unacknowledged ways, as an integral part of the process of composition – as a means through which the possibilities of songs are explored and realized.
>
> Negus 2010: 135

This approach is all the more interesting when we look at Dylan's influences on phrasing and rhythm. For Negus, in fact, the singer's first albums are full of rhythmic irregularities (see Ford 2012), variations in tempo, starting a verse or

---

[1] Richard Middleton, Allan F. Moore, Erik Clarke, Serge Lacasse, Theodore Gracyk, Keith Negus, to name but a few.

chorus slightly early (not quite on time), signs that betray the influence of blues singers such as Robert Johnson. Moreover, when Dylan took a position on his records during various interviews, he considered the recordings of his works to be less important than the concerts, stating in 1978:

> An album for me isn't anything more than a collection of songs... written to be sung from the stage... It's always been that way for me... songs aren't any good unless they can be sung on stage. They're meant to be sung to people, not to microphones in a recording studio.
>
> Heylin 2009: 19

But as Steven Rings points out, the studio version is often the listener's first contact with the song, and is also the best known by fans and listeners (Rings 2013). For Lubet, 'If one is to find a song, which seems a necessary part of enjoying a concert, it needs to be identified with some normative performance to form comparisons' (Lubet 2012: 51; on the concept of 'finding' a song, see 3.5 below). Furthermore, for this author, Dylan himself has a definite interest in recording:

> That this [*sc.* the normative performance] would be a familiar studio recording is reinforced by Dylan's practice since 1990 of only premiering new songs on legit record releases on his label and never in concert... He has stated that he does this expressly because his concerts are bootlegged... That is hardly the practice of someone who considers his albums insignificant.
>
> Lubet 2012: 51

1.2 Concepts

The notion of interpretation in contemporary music seems problematic because it only partially corresponds to the reality of the types of music it encompasses. Indeed, the notion of interpretation refers to written music in which the artist acts as a mediator between the composer and the listener. However, in popular music the performer is often the composer, so he does not intervene between the two protagonists to convey a message (the work), hence my preference for the prefix 'intra'. This question of vocabulary is not without consequences for the meaning of the song. Indeed, it is arguable that when you are the creator of a work yourself, the way you interpret it is specific. The cover of a song allows a re-reading of the original meaning, but probably this is never entirely complete, because the performer is not the creator. One may legitimately wonder, however, whether a meaning is immutable even for the creator of a song.

Performance is the implementation of all levels of expression (musical, scenic, gestural, contextual), used, consciously or unconsciously, by an artist or group of contemporary musicians in the creation and re-creation of a work. Both interpretation and intrapretation are part of the performance and its analysis includes musical, scenic, gestural and other analyses as well as elements relating to the presence of an audience.

This concept of scenic re-creation refers to an artefact comparable to an existing one (the created work), but produced differently. That is to say, an object is created (the work, the song) and by a process that brings into play the tools of creation, this object will be transformed without deviating from the essence of the piece (without still being a recognizable version of the original). The purpose here is therefore to analyse several versions of the same song in order to highlight their differences and common points on the one hand and, on the other, to compare their levels of re-creation.

2. 'Blowin' in the Wind': the original and its versions

> *I didn't know if it was a good song . . . it sounded right. But I didn't know it had this quality of anthem.*
>
> Dylan quoted in *No Direction Home* 2005

2.1 General presentation

'Blowin' in the Wind' is a song written by Bob Dylan in 1962, in his Greenwich Village period. As a true artistic centre, Greenwich Village offered places to perform and many artists rubbed shoulders with each other. Folk had an important place and Bob Dylan developed his original persona there.

The song lyric was first published in the late May 1962 issue of *Broadside* magazine (*Broadside* 1962). Recorded on 9 July 1962 at Columbia Records studio (see Bjorner n.d.), it was first released as a single and then as part of Dylan's second album, *The Freewheelin' Bob Dylan*, from 1963. However, it had already been recorded live at Gerde's Folk City on 16 April 1962 and for the Broadside Show at WBAI studio in May 1962 (Bjorner n.d.).

From a harmonic and melodic point of view, 'Blowin' in the Wind' is largely inspired by the spiritual 'No More Auction Block'. Dylan played this song at the Gaslight Café in 1962. It was performed by several other singers; the version by singer Odetta Holmes (known as Odetta) would have particularly marked Dylan.

The lyrics of this song are based on a blues model in which questions (three in this case) are followed by an answer. The latter remains enigmatic, and this is undoubtedly what makes it so strong. Dylan does not give a ready-made answer, but encourages the listener to find it. The overall form of the lyrics would therefore be as follows: AAAB, with part B acting as a 'chorus'. The content of the text allows everyone to project their own reading into it. Thus certain references, such as the freedom of peoples, war or slavery, could resonate with the struggles of the folk movement of the time and the tradition of protest songs,[2] as well as with African-American communities, as Mavis Staples pointed out (*No Direction Home* 2005). Extremely metaphorical, this very generalist text then finds a particular echo and is transformed into a true hymn, and probably this process enables the song to survive through time.

2.2 'Live' versions: from 1963 to 2016

The choice of these stage versions was made thanks to several criteria, the first of which was to have sufficient audio and video quality to be able to work on both aspects. Most of the concert versions that can be found are bootlegs, recorded by fans with equipment that creates an increasingly global vision of the show. The second criterion was that of the orchestration and the protagonists present onstage with Dylan. Finally, the last criterion was the more contextual one of different types of staging.

The first stage version chosen (VS1; Folk Songs 1963) is a television appearance in the programme produced by Westinghouse Studios in New York, *Folk Songs and More Folk Songs*, recorded on 3 March 1963 and broadcast in May by stations owned by Westinghouse. Presented by John Henry Faulk, it traced the history of America through its popular songs. Other guest performers included the Brothers Four, Barbara Dane, the Staples Singers and Carolyn Hester. Dylan was

---

[2] This period corresponds to a process of aesthetic and artistic recognition through admired mentors such as Seeger or Guthrie. However, Dylan has always denied being an activist or protest singer.

accompanied by the Brothers Four's double bass player (Bob Flick) and banjo player (Mark Pearson).

The second version (VS1b; Newport 1963) is still dated 1963 and took place during concerts at the Newport Festival. Dylan appears on stage with such renowned singers as Joan Baez, Peter, Paul & Mary, and The Freedom Singers, among others. In 1963, the Newport Festival was produced by the Newport Folk Foundation (an artist-run non-profit organization).[3] Evening concerts by well-known folk artists were the most important features to bring in audiences. In that period, the festival also included an extended day programme with workshops, informal concerts and non-musical sessions such as debates or walks (Brauner 1983). What is important to remember is that folk music and the Newport Festival at the same time symbolized a 'pure' and 'authentic' alternative to rock music then tarnished by payola. 'Payola in radio and television broadcasting may be defined as undisclosed payments (or other inducements) which are given to bring about the inclusion of material in broadcast programs' (Coase 1979: 269). Following numerous scandals involving entertainers and DJs (like Alan Freed), this practice was outlawed in 1960 and particularly impacted rock 'n' roll music.

The third version chosen (VS2; Bangladesh 1971) was the result of the charity concert 'The Concert for Bangladesh', initiated by ex-Beatle George Harrison and held on 1 August 1971 at Madison Square Garden in New York. The event had been organized to raise awareness in the international community and to fund relief efforts for refugees from East Pakistan (now Bangladesh), following the genocide linked to the Bangladesh Liberation War. The concerts were followed by a live album, a three-record set and a documentary of the concert, distributed by Apple Films and released in the spring of 1972 in cinemas. The concerts took place at 2.30 pm and 6 pm. Bob Dylan did not offer exactly the same set list for the two concerts, but 'Blowin' in the Wind' appeared in both.

The last version chosen (VS3; Berkeley 2016) is taken from the concert given in Berkeley on 10 June 2016 at the Greek Theater. The concert was part of the 'Never Ending Tour' initiated in 1988, with the 2016 leg of the tour running from 4 April 2016 to 23 November 2016. 'Blowin' in The Wind' was played as an

---

[3] Originally established as a commercial company in 1958 by George Wein and Dylan's future manager, Albert Grossman, the Newport Folk Festival came to be managed by the foundation following a commercial bankruptcy in 1960.

encore during this concert. Dylan was accompanied by the following five instrumentalists: Donnie Herron (violin), Tony Garnier (double bass), George Receli (drums), Stu Kimball (rhythm guitar, acoustic guitar) and Charlie Sexton (electric guitar).

3. Musical analyses of the different versions

In the context of a comparative analysis between different versions (whatever the medium), taking into account multiple parameters will make it possible to target the elements that have been transferred, changed, or adapted. These will then enable us to establish the degree of re-creation in the different versions.

3.1 Duration/tempo

The first parameter taken into account concerns the duration of the songs and their tempi.

With regard to Table 7.1, there does not seem to be a direct link between the duration of a version and the tempo at which it is performed. This is interesting, because it seems logical that a version should be longer if, for example, the tempo is slower. It is therefore necessary to look at the structure to see if any changes may explain this discrepancy.

Table 7.1 Duration and tempo according to the studied versions of the song 'Blowin' in the Wind'

Versions	Duration (mn)	Tempo
VP	2.45	83
VS1	2.53	94
VS1b	3.25	71
VS2	3.32	100
VS3	5.43	75

3.2 Structure

The studio version, released on the album *The Freewheelin' Bob Dylan* (Dylan 1963) has the structure shown in Table 7.2.

Table 7.2 Structure of the song 'Blowin' in The Wind' – the *Freewheelin'* album version

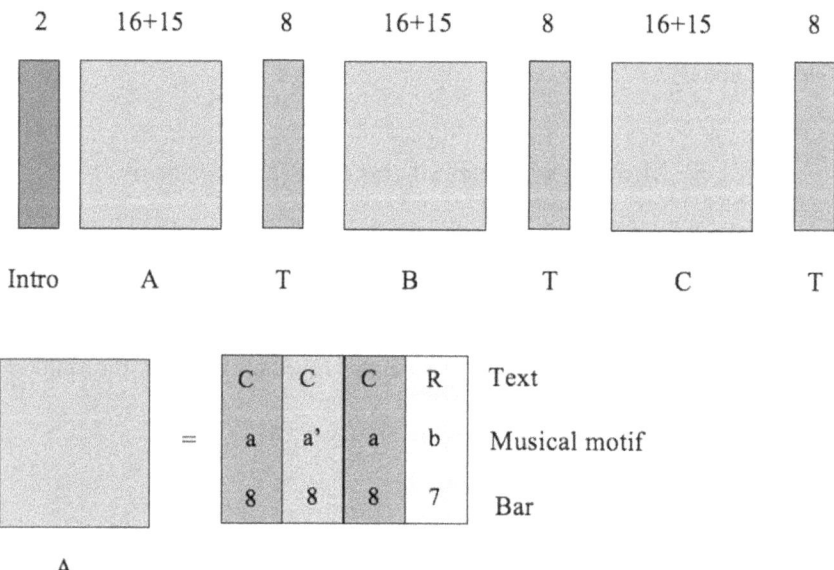

Two remarks should be made about this relatively simple structure. First, the construction of the text and its melody are very strongly based on a blues tradition; the latter's primitive versification is elaborated on the AAB model and the first lines often ask a question, as in 'Sweet Home Chicago' by Robert Johnson. Here, we have three questions supported by a slightly varied melodic pattern on the second question, and, if not the answer, in any case an affirmative sentence built on a different melodic pattern.

Second, the overall structure remains traditional and repetitive. We can also expect that the various parts here are mainly the introductory and instrumental transition parts (here, the one played by the harmonica). The listener's attention is drawn to an unusual or out-of-place element: if Dylan refers directly to the blues in this song, in its construction, but also – and this is what we will see later – in its intrapretation, the internal structure of the parts should be 32 bars, or a multiple of 2 or 8. However, here, it is clear that the 'answer' line has only seven bars, maybe with the idea of enhancing it.

By offering a comparison of the different versions proposed here from a structural perspective, Table 7.3 shows several relevant elements.

Table 7.3 Structures of the five versions of 'Blowin' in The Wind' studied

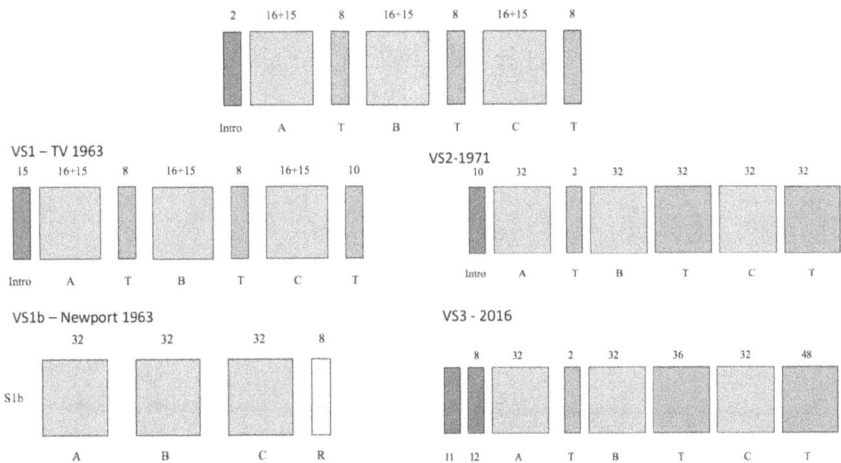

First, as expected, some parts are, in a more or less equal way, either deleted (introduction and instrumental transition in the VS1b version, or a VS3 transition), or elongated (the same parts); or, more rarely, added (last B text repeated, VS1b). For example, in VS2, the first transition lasts two bars and is extended in the next two transitions to thirty-two bars.

Another very interesting aspect is that only the VS1, recorded for TV in March 1963, has a close bar/structure breakdown – that is, it takes up the previously mentioned 8+7. However, we notice that since the July 1963 versions, all sections have been multiples of 8 (or almost). The most likely hypothesis for this series of bars is that the atypical form is too disconcerting for the musicians who accompany Dylan.

3.3 Instrumentation

To explain these changes and see what is happening in more detail, let us first look at the relationship between instrumentation choices and structural and musical choices (Table 7.4). The evolution of the instrumentation is particularly remarkable between the VS1b and VS3 versions, which have one thing in common: the absence of a harmonica.

Several remarks can be made on structural choice and orchestration. On the one hand, the textual parts are never changed: they form an indivisible entity.

Table 7.4 Instrumentation of the five versions of 'Blowin' in the Wind' studied

Versions	Instrumentation
VP	Acoustic guitar Voice Harmonica
VS1	Acoustic guitar Voice Harmonica Double bass Banjo
VS1b	Acoustic guitar Voice Backing Singers
VS2	Acoustic guitar Voice Electric bass Electric guitar Percussion
VS3	Voice Piano Violin Double bass Acoustic guitar Electric guitar Percussion

The one and only time that part of the text is repeated occurs in the concert at Newport where Dylan, accompanied by other singers, repeats the last verse as a chorus. I also hypothesize here that context influences the choice not to include an introduction or a harmonica solo. Indeed, this hymn song, within the context of the 1963 Newport Festival with all the representatives of the folk movement and their commitments, carries a collective symbolism and sense of union, which the solo parts would probably have diminished. The same is true of the repetition of this textual part, which reinforces the communion of the different protagonists within the festival (actors and audience).

On the other hand, the versions with the most developments in the transition parts are VS2 and VS3. This is not surprising since these are sections subject to improvisation by Dylan himself and/or the musicians surrounding him. Moreover, it is interesting to note that in VS2 (1971), only Dylan occupies these passages, while in VS3 (2016) other instrumentalists are allowed to take part in the musical development. In other words, the moments when other instrumentalists are foregrounded become more important.

Finally, VS1 (TV version) seems to have a somewhat different status. Indeed, as it is part of a television programme, everything is staged so that attention is focused on Dylan (camera shot, staging . . .). And yet he is accompanied by two instrumentalists who are never seen!

3.4 Music

This musical approach is divided into three relevant points: tonality, harmonica use and accompaniment. Particular attention will be given to VS3 (2016).

Table 7.5 allows us to observe changes in tonality concerning what are called related keys. The main impact, apart from key change – which is actually not very problematic for the instruments – is perceived in the voice itself. Indeed, Dylan, for example, has to sing a fourth just above the original melodic line (1971 version).

When the harmonica is used by Dylan, he does not improvise but plays the melodies of the song (a, a', b) using ornamentations close to a rhythmic and slow trill. Table 7.6 shows the use of these models in the different versions. It is interesting to note that the 1971 version uses all the melodic phrases of the song and leaves no room for other instruments in the instrumental parts.

In each of the chosen versions, Dylan is accompanied by various musicians. Depending on the version, this musical support changes.

In VS1, the double bass accentuates the bass on all the beats and the mandolin follows the guitar chords. They are not very noticeable and seem to be somewhat lost especially in the sequences between chorus and verse, which could be explained by the unusual structure of the chorus (seven bars).

In VS1b, the backing singers support the sung part in two ways and with progressive additions. Table 7.7 shows that the only words sung by the backing singers are the chorus and then progressively all the verses. In the rest, the accompaniment sung by the backing singers is the onomatopoeia 'ooh'. It should be noted that sometimes Joan Baez's voice takes over and she even allows herself a counterpoint (2'18–2'28).

Table 7.5 Keys used in the five versions of 'Blowin' in the Wind' studied

Version	VP	VS1	VS1b	VS2	VS3
Key	D	G	G	G	A

Table 7.6 Harmonica playing in three versions of 'Blowin' in the Wind'

VP	VS1	VS2
b	(intro = a) b	a + a' + b

Table 7.7 Distribution of lyrics between Dylan and backing singers in the 1963 Newport version of 'Blowin' in the Wind'

Lines	Lyrics
L1	How many roads must . . .
L2	
L3	
L4	
L5	
L6	
L7	The answer, my friend . . .
L8	
L9	How many years . . .
L10	
L11	
L12	
L13	Yes, 'n' how many times . . .
L14	
L15	
L16	
L17	How many times . . .
L18	
L19	Yes, 'n' how many ears . . .
L20	
L21	
L22	
L23	
L24	
L25	
L26	

In VS2, the electric bass produces the same kind of accompaniment as in VS1, providing the fundamentals, with some adornments. The electric guitar follows the chords of the folk guitar by adding some melodic patterns, and a cymbal tambourine provides a repetitive rhythmic accompaniment. The whole thing has a definite 'country' sound.

The Berkeley version is different for several reasons: first, the number of people accompanying Dylan; second, because the only thing that allows you to recognize the song is the lyrics. Indeed, the musical accompaniment is completely different. The only thing that is similar is the melodic change between the verse and the chorus. Finally, the instrumentalists can enjoy improvisation sections, which until then, for this song, were relatively absent.

3.5 What about the intrapretation?

The disc version of 'Blowin' in The Wind' has recurring rhythmic variations: most lines start before the first beat of the bar. This is one of the blues elements pointed out by Keith Negus. This variation is highlighted by the 'yes and' before the 'how many'. In addition, the last verse is much more irregular, highlighting the word 'times' and the line 'That too many people have died'. The lyrics are sung with a slight vibrato on the held notes, with a relatively restricted ambitus.

The 1963 television version is mainly sung using the melodies of the original version, but the *sostenutos* are less extended. In addition, stresses are marked on certain words ('call', 'just', 'died', etc.), thus highlighting them.

In the Newport version, Dylan adopts a higher volume level than in the other versions, perhaps to ensure his role as leader. The rhythmic variations are less rich than in the phonographic version. The repeated 'yes and' is no longer so systematic, the voice starting in time with the words 'how many'. The 'how' that follows 'Yes and' is quite sustained. This intrapretation is probably informed by the accompaniment from other singers, allowing for a synchronized pronunciation of the words.

In 1971, Dylan's voice was similar to that of country singers: the vocal placement was more nasal and some vowels had *glissandi* vocal effects or pitch variations. In addition, the vibrato of the disc version disappeared, and the held notes were shorter. Anacruses (or rhythmic variations) were also much less numerous.

The latest version marks a turning point in Dylan's intrapretation. His voice is less powerful, more breathy, and his timbre has, as it were, deteriorated. His vocal play alternates between spoken and sung, delivering certain lyrics to a significant rhythm and dragging on certain sung words. This approach seems to allow greater freedom of intrapretation of the text (acceleration, slowing down, speaking, ambitus, sound level, etc.).

Steven Rings has worked on different versions of the song 'It's Alright, Ma (I'm Only Bleeding)'. He states that 'Lyrics, melody, harmony, rhythm, tempo, form, and genre all contribute more fundamentally [than the song's key] to this process of categorization ...; in the case of "It's Alright, Ma", all but the first vary in remarkable ways from the song's inception in 1964 to its most recent iterations' (Rings 2013: 12; the 'process of categorization' to which Rings refers is a method for linking a first, or studio, version of a song to subsequent versions). It thus seems that what has been pointed out in this study is not an isolated case of how Dylan has approached his songs in recent decades.

Furthermore, for Rings, Dylan challenges listeners, especially Never Ending Tour audiences: 'Indeed, most attendees at Dylan shows in recent decades ... have to exert considerable effort to recognize the songs, a fact that is borne out by belated cheers when a recognizable line emerges clearly' (Rings 2013: 20). This is corroborated by Alex Lubet's research on Dylan.[4] Lubet calls this the process of 'song finding' – a very difficult process: 'This requires listening to two works at once, one virtual – that is, remembered – and one actually being performed' (Lubet 2012: 53).

3.6 What's going on on stage?

This part of the analysis is directly linked to the context of the song's production. It should also be noted that most videos of Dylan's concerts are amateur recordings, so they enable us to perceive certain elements of the stage (placement, light, sometimes musicians playing their instruments, movements), but often focus on Dylan.

VS1: TV show (Folk Songs 1963)

Stage version 1, recorded and broadcast on television, has a carefully thought-out scenography. Against a drawn background that appears to depict symbols of American culture such as the Statue of Liberty, host John Henry Faulk introduces the singer for almost fifty seconds without ever naming him or the title of the song. The elongated introduction of the song is played while the presenter is speaking, but the main shot shifts as soon as the first words are sung (Table 7.8).

Table 7.8 shows close-ups on Dylan during the major structural parts, that is, A, B, C, with a slight backward change to medium close-up (shot c) to allow for the singer's final movement to be filmed. The transitions during which Dylan plays the harmonica are filmed in close-up from the left side of Dylan's face. This treatment of the performance creates a focus on the singer, because we

---

[4] Lubet describes an experiment on some of Dylan's songs played by changing components of them. Changing the melody of 'Blowin' in The Wind' would seem to make his own recognition of it extremely complex, because, for him, it appears as the foundation of the song.

Table 7.8 Separate shots from 1963 TV version of 'Blowin' in the Wind' (VS1; video stills)

Shot 1	Part A
Shot 1b	Part B
Shot 1c	Part C
Shot 2	Transitions
Shot 2b	Final Transition

never see the double bassist and the banjoist. The staging is refined: Dylan is static and performs a semicircle backwards while playing his last instrumental transition as a coda.

It is interesting to note Dylan mostly glances towards his left: perhaps because the other musicians are there. When he sings, he leans his head backwards to look beyond his harmonica. Otherwise, he mainly looks at his guitar neck.

VS1b: Newport, communion (Newport 1963)

This performance seems to be filmed from the right side of the audience. It is not known whether someone from the audience or a professional filmed it. That said, given the time, and the zoom used, we can imagine that it is indeed a professional recording. Strictly speaking, no scenography is initiated by the video: the long shots and close-ups on Dylan or Baez do not seem to follow any particular logic.

In this diagram, we can see the positioning of the different protagonists. Bob Dylan is in front of the microphone, in front of the other singers who form a semi-circle behind him. The main reason seems to be the position of the microphones above them. The scene is not very bright: a spotlight in front of the stage illuminates Dylan and to a lesser extent the backing singers, with another spotlight behind him. What is interesting here is that as the song progresses, Dylan moves away from the main microphone gradually to get closer to the backing singers. In addition, the backing singers sway in rhythm from left to right together, without Dylan joining in with this movement.

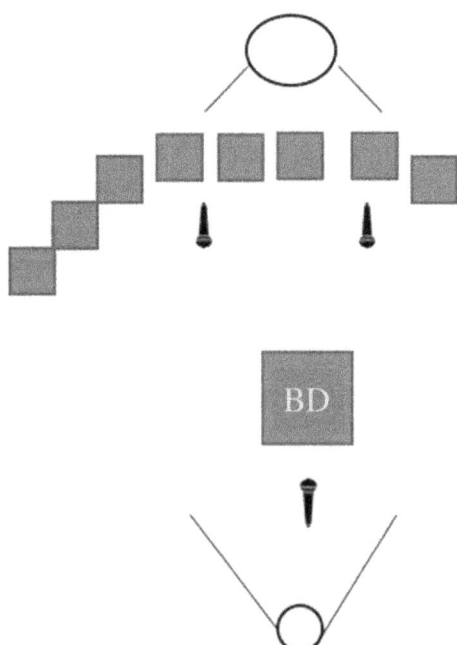

Figure 7.1 Stage plan of 1963 Newport version of 'Blowin' in the Wind' (VS1b)

This performance and what happens in it accentuate the symbolism of a certain common fraternity around a song but, more broadly, an idea and a position, in a time of protest.

VS2: Madison Square Garden (Bangladesh 1971)

The camerawork clearly highlights Dylan. We can imagine that this is a professional shot in view of the time and the camera's zooming capabilities. If we perceive the other protagonists (guitarist, percussionist, bassist), it is only because of the wide-angle shot used at the beginning of the song allowing us to see the stage almost entirely. This shot focuses extremely quickly on the singer and from the second verse on, it focuses on his face.

This image processing is made possible by the fact that Dylan remains relatively static in front of his microphone (for voice or harmonica). Finally, he never looks at the other musicians at any time, but focuses his attention on the audience or his guitar.

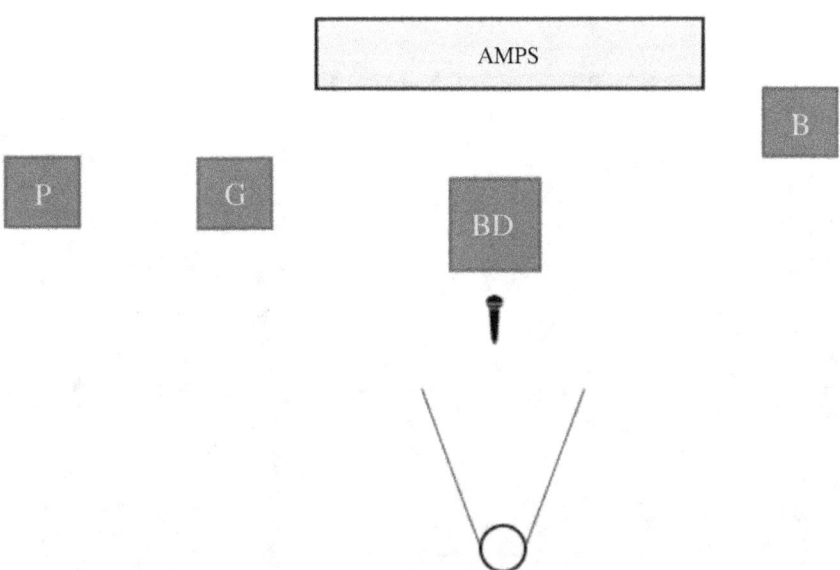

Figure 7.2 Stage plan of 1971 Madison Square Garden version of 'Blowin' in the Wind' (VS2)

VS3: Rehearsal at Berkeley (Berkeley 2016)

This version is filmed by a spectator from within the audience, which explains the static point of view as well as the wide view of the stage.

The placing of the musicians is here particular since they are in a semicircle almost excluding the violinist. The latter is placed slightly raised behind one of the guitarists (electric guitar) and behind the piano (Bob Dylan). Dylan stands closest to the stage front with his profile to the audience. In reality, he almost turns his back on the latter, in an inclusive movement towards the band. Indeed, this version shows a certain equality between the musicians (in terms of solos, for example). The stage layout reinforces the idea that the musicians are amongst themselves, almost as in a rehearsal. What's more, Dylan never looks at the audience.

The scenic evolution of this song seems to indicate increasing inclusion of other instrumentalists who become, in the last version, more than mere accompanists. Dylan's stage positioning and looks are relevant in this respect. From a dominant and (self-)centred position, undoubtedly supported by the media emphasis of his persona, Dylan becomes slightly more integrated into a whole, to the point of turning his back on part of his audience without looking at it (VS3; Berkeley 2016).

Figure 7.3 Video still from 2016 Berkeley version of 'Blowin' in the Wind' (VS3)

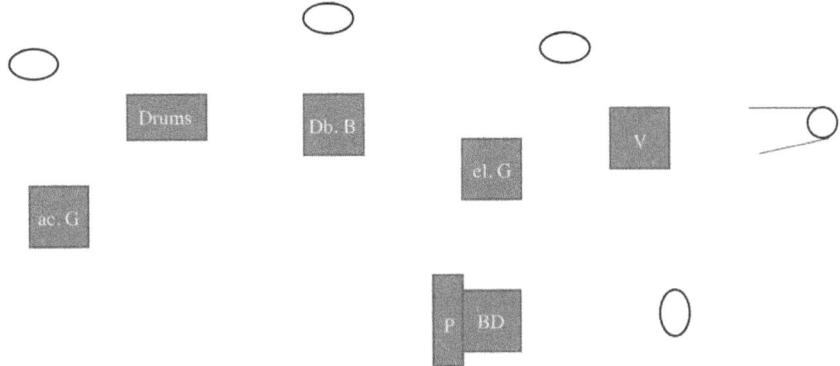

Figure 7.4 Stage plan of 2016 Berkeley version of 'Blowin' in the Wind' (VS3)

4. Conclusion

Our comparative analytical study reveals several points. First, of all the versions presented, the one closest to the phonographic version is the television version. It can be assumed that this is due to the fact that it is also the closest in time to the creation of the recorded work. On the other hand, the most distant is the Berkeley version (2016) where, apart from the words and the reference to the blues structure, everything has changed (harmony, melody, instrumentation, place of the other musicians, improvisations etc.). This version is also the furthest chronologically from the creation of the song. It would be necessary to check with the study of other Dylan songs from the same period, to see whether a song written a long time before is more subject to re-creation – which, according to Rings' study, seems to be the case. But this version of 'Blowin' in The Wind' also questions the definition of a song. For indeed, it can be recognized by the words. However, a song is usually defined by the intrinsic link it creates between a piece of music and a set of words that are inseparable from it.

Second, in all versions, the place of improvisation is increasingly important, or at least, the 'instrumental' parts are more and more important. Moreover, significant room is provided for the other musicians present on stage in 2016, as if we were observing an opening-up, a sharing on Dylan's part, with the other instrumentalists.

Third, the context influences the version. It seems clear that the Newport version, for example, was conceived in connection with Dylan's 'choral' interpretation, thus involving a lighter instrumental accompaniment. This allows a meaningful play on the change in vocal accompaniment.

Finally, the question of meaning seems central here. If it seems that the versions from the 1960s and 1970s have more or less the same meaning, the question can be asked about the 2016 version. Dylan says: 'Time allows me to find new meanings for each song, even the oldest ones, and it is important to always look for new ones' (Roe 2003: 90). Hence, what appears relevant in this song, but also in Dylan's artistic approach, is the distance taken from the hit that 'Blowin' in The Wind' had been. If he recreated it musically in its entirety, it's finally maybe because he can afford to do so. Dylan's accomplishment thus brings him to surpass his own creation.

References

Bjorner, O. (n.d.). '1962 Concerts and Recording Sessions', *I Happen to Be a Swede Myself* website. Available online: www.bjorner.com/DSN00150%201962.htm (accessed 7 April 2020).

'"Blowin' in the Wind" – Concert at Newport' (1963) [Video clip], *DailyMotion*. Available online: www.dailymotion.com/video/x1q9zea (accessed 7 April 2020).

'"Blowin' in the Wind" – Concert for Bangladesh' (1971) [Video clip], *DailyMotion*. Available online: www.dailymotion.com/video/x4ur2zc (accessed 7 April 2020).

'"Blowin' in the Wind" – Folk Songs and more folk songs' (1963) [TV programme], *YouTube*. Available online: www.youtube.com/watch?v=8XW0JsqFOZc (accessed 7 April 2020).

'"Blowin' in the Wind" – Live at Berkeley' (2016) [Video clip], *YouTube*. Available online: www.youtube.com/watch?v=sObIImr6zjk (accessed 7 April 2020).

Brauner, C. A. (1983), 'A Study of the Newport Folk Festival and the Newport Folk Foundation', MA diss., Department of Folklore, Memorial University of Newfoundland, St John's.

Broadside #6 (1962), '*Broadside* Magazine: The Issues (1–26), *Sing Out!* website. Available online: https://singout.org/broadside/issues-p1/ (accessed 7 April 2020).

Coase, R. H. (1979), 'Payola in Radio and Television Broadcasting', *The Journal of Law and Economics*, 22(2): 269–328.

Dylan, B. (1963), *The Freewheelin' Bob Dylan* [Album], USA: Columbia Records.

Ford, C. (2012), 'The Development of Bob Dylan's Rhythmic Sense: "The Times They Were a'Changing" (1958-1964)', in S. Hawking (ed.), *Critical Musicological Reflections. Essays in Honour of Derrick B. Scott*, 159–78, Farnham: Ashgate.

Gracyk, T. (1996), *Rhythm and Noise. An Aesthetics of Rock*, Durham, NC: Duke University Press.

Gray, M. (2006), *The Bob Dylan Encyclopedia*, New York and London: Continuum.

Heylin, C. (2009), *Revolution in the Air: The Songs of Bob Dylan 1957–1973*, Chicago: Chicago Review Press.

Irwin, C. (2007), *Legendary Sessions: Bob Dylan's Highway 61 Revisited*, New York: Billboard Books.

Lacasse, S. (2006), 'Composition, performance, phonographie: un malentendu ontologique en analyse musicale ?', in S. Lacasse and P. Roy (eds), *Groove: Enquête sur les phénomènes musicaux contemporains*, 65–78, Québec: Presses de l'Université Laval.

Lubet, A. (2012), 'Listening to Bob Dylan', *Cognitive Critique*, 5: 37–58.

Mansion-Vaquié, J. (2016), 'L'interprétation et la performance en question', in N. Bénard and C. Poulet (eds), *Chant pensé, chant vécu, temps chanté*, 221–40, Paris: Editions Delatour.

Negus, K. (2008), *Bob Dylan*, London: Equinox Publishing.

Negus, K. (2010), 'Bob Dylan's Phonographic Imagination', *Popular Music*, 29(2): 213–27. Available online: www.jstor.org/stable/40926919 (accessed 7 April 2020).

No Direction Home: Bob Dylan (2005) [Film], Dir. Martin Scorsese, USA: Paramount Pictures.

Rings, S. (2013), 'A Foreign Sound to Your Ear: Bob Dylan Performs "It's Alright, Ma (I'm Only Bleeding)", 1964–2009', *MOT (Music Theory Online)*, 19(4), December. Available online: https://mtosmt.org/issues/mto.13.19.4/mto.13.19.4.rings.php (accessed 7 April 2020).

Roe, N. (2003), 'Playing Time', in Neil Corcoran (ed.), *Do You Mr. Jones? Bob Dylan with the Poets and Professors*, 81–104, London: Pimlico.

8

'Behind Every Beautiful Thing There's Been Some Kind of Pain': Melancholia in Dylan's Songs and Paintings

Anne-Marie Mai

Bob Dylan's renewal of the American song tradition draws on a deep well of the 'blues', a word that embraces not only a genre of music but also a poetic form, a social condition, a mental ailment, even a way of life: a mood, and more than a mood. Historically and more broadly speaking, that mood is also known as melancholia. While Dylan's contributions to the blues throughout his career are easily recognized – 1991's 'Blind Willie McTell', for example – how his work can be related to the broader field of melancholy is less widely understood. This chapter aims to redress that imbalance by exploring the concept in an original way, bringing together Dylan's songs and some of his *Brazil Series* paintings, in order to assess the ways in which both forms, musical and pictural, probe this challenging condition (Elderfield and Monrad 2010: 31).

1. Melancholia – an oxymoronic condition

The concept of melancholia has a long history and it has been deployed by various disciplines – theology, philosophy, poetry and psychology. In premodern medicine and proto-psychology melancholia was defined as one of the four temperaments (or 'humours'), representing a state of mind characterized by a dark mood, caused by the black bile.

Plato had related a special kind of madness to divine inspiration – in his *Phaedrus*, Socrates discusses how madness can be a divine gift: 'The third kind is the madness of those who are possessed by the Muses; which, taking hold of a delicate and virgin soul, and there inspiring frenzy, awakens lyrical and all other numbers' (Plato 360 BCE).

These two notions come together in Renaissance philosopher Marsilio Ficino's development of the concept of melancholy. He combined the ideas of the so-called pseudo-Aristotelian *Problemata,* where the disease of the back bile is said to be characteristic of men eminent within the realms of poetry, philosophy and politics, with Plato's ideas of the 'divine frenzy'. Ficino thus re-evaluated melancholia and related it to Saturn (hence the expression 'a saturnine temperament'), considering the latter to be the mightiest and the noblest star (Klibansky, Panofsky and Saxl 2019: 259). Ficino's concept enabled later Romantic ideas of melancholia as the particular mood of artists – a creative condition where the artist experiences both inspiration and despondency. Melancholia was thus interpreted as an oxymoronic condition, where opposed feelings and moods were present at the same time.

Contemporary psychology does not often use the concept of melancholia – one of its main concepts now is rather 'depression', and if melancholia is mentioned it is in relation to a severe form of mental illness, melancholic depression. The German psychologist Thomas Fuchs describes melancholic depression as a pathological condition, in which a human being falls out of common environmental time: the temporal relation of the individual and society is uncoupled. In Fuchs's opinion, modern social reality implies a construction of time, where time appears as 'an autonomous godlike force that demands its sacrifices' (Fuchs 2001: 186). It is thus a construction of time that everyone is subject to, but it is very difficult for the melancholic to handle this condition: 'It is this alienated and reified time that in melancholia falls back on the subject from the outside. The depressive shows us vicariously that as individuals and as a society we are equally confronted with the task of reappropriating the time that we have made our enemy, and to make it our friend again' (Fuchs 2001: 186). The time experience becomes pathological when the individual is not able to synchronize personal, internal time with interpersonal, external time. But in Fuchs's opinion this raises the question of whether the pathology lies in the individual who is not able to follow the speed of societal life, or rather in a sort of 'collective mania', caused by the construction of time (Fuchs 2001: 180).

In his *Ecology of the Brain,* Fuchs develops a theory that understands the brain as a mediating organ of the living being. Fuchs sees the brain as 'an organ of interrelations' (Fuchs 2018: xx): it is not the brain, but the human being of body and mind, that feels, thinks, acts and interacts with the environment. Fuchs understands the mind as a product of an activity of the living being which integrates the brain within the functions of the human body. In contrast to a more everyday state of mind, where we tend to understand mental processes as taking place inside the brain, Fuchs describes these processes as an ecological networking activity. The brain is not an isolated sanctuary of the individual, but part of an extensive network.

While providing a contribution to the understanding of mental illness, Fuchs's ideas on melancholic depression and the ecology of the brain can also be seen to correspond with several artists' perceptions of the melancholic state of mind. Melancholia is often seen by artists – from the poet John Keats and philosopher Søren Kierkegaard to the poet and songwriter Bob Dylan or film director Lars von Trier – as a modern mental condition, characterized by a sense of being left out of time and of being entrapped by a place or a feeling of placelessness. But it is also seen as the experience of a borderland between feelings and the world around, as well as the potential experience of a special kind of creativity.[1] With all this in mind, the following paragraphs will discuss the melancholy within some of Bob Dylan's songs and paintings.

2. Not dark yet

The title of this chapter is a line from Bob Dylan's 'Not Dark Yet' (*Time Out of Mind*, 1997). The song depicts melancholy through the story of a man who has experienced a conflict with his beloved and perhaps even marks the end of their love story. But although he has received a kind letter from his former partner, the love affair has lost its meaning and importance. The beloved and her attraction have gone, but an angry and deep melancholy remains. The man has an experience of being left out of time, of being hurt and entrapped by his wounded and hardened soul and by the place he is in, as the song's first verse points to the shadows falling, the weary lengthy day or 'slow time' experienced by the singer,

---

[1] John Keats thematizes melancholia in his poem 'Ode on Melancholy' (1819); Søren Kierkegaard discusses melancholia in his *Journals* from the mid-nineteenth century. Lars von Trier's film *Melancholia* (2011), concerns two sisters, Justine and Claire, and their reaction to the end of the world caused by a collision between Earth and the planet Melancholia. Claire's small son, Leo, is very frightened, but he is reassured by the melancholic Justine, who says that they can be safe in a 'magic cave', something she promises him to build several times throughout the film. The melancholic young woman helps the child and her own despairing sister – she is able to build the magic cave for the three of them and to face destruction in a calm and stoic way.

and the latter's hardened soul (Dylan 2016: 566). The singer observes how night is falling and in the twilight he feels that his sense of humanity has disappeared. He also notes that his discovery and experience of beauty are inseparable from suffering. He describes how he has been travelling, taking in London and Paris, but he seems disillusioned by what he has found in the world. He seems emotionless and he can't perceive the murmur of a prayer – a reflection, perhaps, of the isolated individual in postmodern society who has forgotten how to pray. But some form of inner or spiritual light still seems possible since, as the chorus line suggests, it is only almost dark (Dylan 2016: 566).

The singer of 'Not Dark Yet' experiences the borderline between day and night as both an outer and inner condition, and this makes him sensitive and creative. Melancholia has entrapped the man's body and soul and reminds him of death, and yet melancholia also enables him to sing and rhyme, to express his existential and human situation and his sad relationship with himself and with his surroundings. Melancholy is portrayed as a vulnerable and sensitive state of mind, an oxymoron of creativity and passivity, darkness and light, love and anger, beauty and pain, remembrance and forgetfulness, movement and stillness, song and silence. The song shows us Dylan's poetical mastery of oxymora. He often uses this device in his songs, for example in 'Love Sick' (*Time Out of Mind*, 1997) where he shifts the words around. The song describes a condition of being sick of love, while managing to be lovesick at the same time (Dylan 2016: 559), longing for the one he loves to return to him, no matter what.

In 'Not Dark Yet', he simply uses oxymoron to its full range, mentioning both physical and mental circumstances, showing how the mental processes function as an ecological networking activity where the inner and outer worlds connect as daylight disappears and darkness takes over. The singer is about to lose his senses – his nerves are numb, but poetry stays with him and he sings as darkness comes. The understanding of melancholia one may derive from Dylan's song is the perception that melancholia does not necessarily lead to severe mental illness: it is a special human condition, and though painful, it is a part of human life, which might lead to creativity, and because of that the singer stays with it and examines it. The second line of 'Not Dark Yet' has a clear reference to linear time (Dylan 2016: 566) – but the singer experiences a situation where the past, present and future mingle and he has lost his usual sense of time. He crosses and re-crosses the borderline between inner and outer, where melancholia comes to rule.

When he started to take painting lessons from Russian artist Norman Raeben in New York in the 1970s, Dylan learned to work with a new concept of time fragments that became important to many of his songs. Raeben influenced both his paintings and his songwriting with an awareness of reality and of time. In a painting and a song, the artist can break out of the linear sense of time and let pieces of time emerge from several angles. Dylan's approach seems to indicate that the difference between a song and a painting lies in the mood and the experience of reality (Elderfield and Monrad 2010: 29). Songs may often be influenced by moods; paintings are much more tangible and point to pictural art's greater autonomy in relation to mood (see Cartwright 1991). Paintings, then, might be said to represent the presence of absence (Elderfield and Monrad 2010: 16 ff.), and in this way some of the paintings also point to an aesthetic of paradox.

'Not Dark Yet' gives the listener a strong sense of the melancholic mood, and it has striking resemblances to Keats's 'Ode on Melancholy' (1819). Keats, too, expresses the oxymoronic character of melancholia. The poem warns the reader against forgetfulness and death, but praises melancholia that brings beauty, as well as pain and death. The beauty stanza expresses the interweaving of contradictions when 'Joy's grape' bursts:

> She dwells with Beauty—Beauty that must die;
>   And Joy, whose hand is ever at his lips
> Bidding adieu; and aching Pleasure nigh,
>   Turning to poison while the bee-mouth sips:
> Ay, in the very temple of Delight
>   Veil'd Melancholy has her sovran shrine,
> Though seen of none save him whose strenuous tongue
>   Can burst Joy's grape against his palate fine;
> His soul shalt taste the sadness of her might,
>   And be among her cloudy trophies hung.
>   Keats 1819

The fact that joy will end and beauty will die makes the experience of joy and beauty inordinately more intense and gives the poet access to a holy and secret melancholy.

In many songs Dylan has approached this 'sovran shrine', and sometimes the encounter almost turns the singer into a ghost, as in the song 'Red River Shore' – an outtake from *Time Out of Mind* (Dylan 2008) – where the melancholy of a broken heart makes the singer a restless, ghost-like wanderer. But melancholia has not yet transformed him into a 'cloudy trophy'.

3. A melancholic stranger

'Red River Shore' is one of Dylan's most emotional songs, connecting his late-twentieth-century songs with his twenty-first-century artwork. It describes in a broken chronology the unhappy love story of an artist who in his youth fell in love with a woman, who would not get involved seriously with him; ever since, he has been longing for this lost love. He seems to be a touring artist and wherever he goes many women are interested in him, but he does not want any of them; he is only longing for 'the girl from the Red River shore' (Dylan 2016: 576). The impossible love has made him a melancholic stranger, rambling and gambling, living in the past in a world of his own, where his most important experience is his unhappy love story and longing for the girl from the Red River shore: though he is 'a stranger ... in a strange land' (an echo of Moses' words in the Book of Exodus [2.21–22] and one of several religious references in the song), he knows he belongs there (Dylan 2016: 576). The singer describes how he once went back to find out what happened and to straighten things out. But although the people had known him and his girlfriend back then, they didn't recognize who he was talking about when he returned. Their denial seems to make his longing for the girl from the Red River shore even stronger and he wishes that he could have spent his whole life with her.

Although the singer feels miserable, he is able to hear the songs of the hills and keep on travelling. Therefore, this almost deadly melancholia is still related to art and to the lifestyle of an artist. When the singer returns to the place where he once met his beloved, he looks like a ghost to the people who now live there. He remembers the story of a man who knew how to bring the dead back to life, an allusion to Christ, and the song ends with this religious vision involving a special 'kind of language' used by that man – but now, it seems, it is lost (Dylan 2016: 576). Perhaps we are to understand it was the language of poetry.

Although his song may not wake up the dead, it has the beauty of Keats's melancholic shrine – the uncanny atmosphere gives it, surprisingly enough, a strong and almost lively mood and the invisible man seems very much present.

4. A melancholic microcosmos

From September 2010 to April 2011, Dylan exhibited his *Brazil Series* of paintings in Copenhagen.[2] Some of the paintings shown there have the same melancholic mood as 'Not Dark Yet' and 'Red River Shore'. Dylan made the series for the National Gallery in Copenhagen in the two years prior to the exhibition. It is a series of approximately fifty works, of which forty paintings and eight drawings were shown in Copenhagen. Since then, *The Brazil Series* has been shown by the English Castle Galleries, and the Brazil paintings have also been the basis of a series of hand-signed limited-edition prints. When the board of the Danish National Gallery first contacted Bob Dylan about an exhibition, the curators had no idea that Dylan would embark on a whole new series. The board had seen a catalogue based on Dylan's *Drawn Blank* Series, which had been shown in Chemnitz in 2007. It was at this exhibition that Dylan first revealed on a large scale the results of many years of work in drawing and painting. In light of the Chemnitz exhibition, the Danish museum hoped that Dylan would exhibit some works from his almost lifelong production. However, the request prompted Dylan to embark on a whole new series of paintings related to Brazil. These were not painted on a journey; they were created in his studio on the basis of sketches from his previous visits to Brazil.

Some art critics have argued that the link between Dylan's paintings and his songs is the narrative character of his work: both his songs and pictures often tell stories. According to the Danish curator of the exhibition, Kasper Monrad, the paintings and the songs complement one another as genres, but where the songs might mix dream and different dimensions of reality, the paintings are kept within one illusion (Elderfield and Monrad 2010: 13). The leading American art critic John Elderfield, an expert in the work of Henri Matisse, emphasizes that Dylan's paintings work with the human imagination. Using the imagination, the artist focuses on reality, even though reality may be absent from the painting. To express this fact, the paintings are shattered via fragmented references to time and place. Paradoxically, this fragmentation creates a sense of presence, of reality and the passage of time. The *Brazil Series* paintings often show artistic creation: characters that perform ('Ventriloquist', 'Sideshow'), sing ('Songbird'), sculpt ('Sculptor'), play music ('Piano Player'), dance ('Politician') or write

---

[2] Bob Dylan, *The Brazil Series*, 4 September 2010–10 April 2011, Statens Museum for Kunst, Copenhagen.

('Chrysanthemums') (Elderfield and Monrad 2010). The paintings are often dark; and pain, joy and sadness mingle. A melancholic interaction between mind, world, body sometimes appears – for instance in the painting entitled 'Chrysanthemums'.

The painting shows a room, perhaps an artist's study. A large vase of beautiful chrysanthemums is placed on a table at the front of the scene, and behind them a man is sitting by an open window with a written paper in his hand. He wears a white shirt with a cravat at the neck and his hair is wavy and grey. He resembles a poet of the Romantic era, so perhaps he belongs to a bygone age. He has a sad expression and his eyes are almost shut. His mouth is shut too but he seems to be on the brink of smiling and he looks as if he is concentrating deeply on something. The title of the painting is 'Chrysanthemums', but does it picture these flowers? It does; but it also pictures the interaction between its components: the flowers, the window, the man and the written paper. The borderlines between mind, body and environment are blurred. Some of the colours of the flowers are also the colours of the man's skin and of his clothes; the green leaves of the flowers connect with the green growth that is mirrored in the window. The written paper and the shirt of the man are the same colour. Is it the flowers that colour the face of the man or is it the mind of the man colouring the flowers? There is no precise answer to this question, but the painting has growth (the flowers), mental productivity and creativity (the written paper) and melancholia (the sad expression of the man's face and the dark colours around his head). The painting shows how an artist's creative concentration can be pictured as a melancholic microcosmos of environment, body, mind and brain. The painting has no linear narrative, but the use of colours connects the elements and creates the melancholic oxymoron that is one of the signatures of Dylan's art. Where the song 'Not Dark Yet' pictures a melancholic mood, the painting 'Chrysanthemums' expresses a tangible microcosmos where melancholia rules. The two art forms share the mastery of the oxymoron. In 'Not Dark Yet' the rhymes and the sound of the words point to melancholia, while in 'Chrysanthemums' absence and solitude are signalled by the invisible words on the paper which the poet is holding.

Another example of a melancholic interaction between mind, world and body appears in the painting 'The Ventriloquist' (Elderfield and Monrad 2010). The painting shows a sad young man, performing with his dummy (an old man wearing a top hat and glasses). The whole scene is dark and scary: the big grey doll looks like a speaking corpse and the face of the ventriloquist's female assistant looks angry. It seems that both the anger and the deadly mood emanate from the young man: the red shades of the woman and the grey and black of the dummy connect them closely to the mind and body of the young man. His melancholia is eerie like that of the artist in 'Red River Shore', but he can definitely not bring his doll to life. This creative melancholia is linked to anger and death.

5. Still moving

In Dylan's art, melancholia is connected to the modern social reality that he has so often pictured – most famously, perhaps, in 'Like a Rolling Stone' (released in 1965). The song is a complex modern anthem, describing the conditions of modern Western life, where traditions, belongings, communities and values are going through an accelerated process of change or demolition and where alienation, from oneself and others, is a reality. As described by philosopher Marshall Berman, all that was solid is melting: the modern experience, he explained, is that of being 'alive to new possibilities for experience and adventure, frightened by the nihilistic depths to which so many modern adventures lead. Longing to create and to hold on to something real even as everything melts' (Berman 1982: 13–14). The modern human being is unknown, left on his or her own without a direction home. The existential meaning of the modern human condition has been pictured by both poets and philosophers, and one of the most influential is Søren Kierkegaard (1813–55). He is most famous for his analyses of the concept of 'anxiety', which is relevant to an understanding of the existential theme of some of Dylan's songs. But Søren Kierkegaard also referred to melancholia as a modern condition, and he underlined that his personal experience of it was closely related to his own sad love story: he probably thought that it would be impossible for him to combine his philosophical authorship with a life as husband, and he made his fiancée break off their engagement. Kierkegaard mentions melancholia in his *Journals*, and to him it is something different from anxiety. As an author Kierkegaard tended to adopt pseudonyms, as Dylan has done. In a note from 1847, he wrote:

> My melancholy has for many years prevented me from saying, in any deep sense, '*Du*' [you] to myself. There lay between my melancholy and my intimate *Du* a whole world of fantasy. It is this that I have partly emptied out in the pseudonyms. As with someone without a happy home who goes out as much as possible and would rather be rid of it, my melancholy has kept me outside myself while I

discovered and poetically experienced a whole world of the imagination. Like someone who inherits a big estate and never becomes fully acquainted with it – that's how in my melancholy I have related to possibility.

Kierkegaard 1996: 256

The modern melancholic is restless, being without a home; he is creative, but also lonely, alienated from himself, but still not mentally empty: he lets himself be absorbed in his own vast and surprising fantasy world, as when the singer finds himself trapped in a deceitful world, as well as seeming to be moving though motionless ('Not Dark Yet', Dylan 2016: 566). As a human being you are on your own and need to make your own choices, and although you move around searching for help, you won't find it until you start to address the (spiritual) unknown. What Dylan adds to Kierkegaard's concept is an elaboration of what *moving around* means. The melancholic poet is actually caught in an oxymoronic situation of moving and standing still. He might travel the world, but mentally he is 'standing still' (Dylan 2016: 566).

In one of Dylan's most beautiful blues songs, 'Highlands' (Dylan 1997), the creative melancholia is accompanied by humour and a self-conscious irony. The song describes an artist who, like Kierkegaard, mentally travels around. Kierkegaard says his melancholy keeps him from himself while he is discovering and poetically travelling through a whole fantasy world of other poets, and in this song Dylan longs to go to the poetical world of the Scottish poet Robert Burns, and enter his song, 'My Heart's in the Highlands' (1789). In the song, Robert Burns praises the Highlands and describes how his heart is always 'there', rather than 'here', in Burns' native Ayrshire in the Lowlands. Burns' song is a farewell to this land of 'valour and worth' (Burns 1789), and an avowal of his true belonging. Dylan's song does not describe a farewell, but the longing for an arrival, and a direction to the final 'home': the Highlands are indeed linked to death. The title of Burns' song serves as leitmotif to Dylan's own, the singer adding in the fourth verse that the Highlands are 'where [he]'ll be when [he gets] called home' (Dylan 2016: 571). The Highlands are pure poetry, a place where you can hear the wind whisper in the trees 'in rhyme' (Dylan 2016: 571); they are the world of poets and they are surrounded by deep feeling and by pathos, but in Dylan's song the road to the Highlands is paved with dark humour and self-irony. The song describes how people tell him to lower the volume when the singer listens to Neil Young: no one seems to understand him any longer. The song becomes an oxymoronic experience of how pathos and humour intertwine in melancholy. The singer feels that he has lost his anchoring in time and place.

He is drifting around, an annoyance to his surroundings; he's being mocked and he feels caught in a rat race of dull repetitions. But humour takes over when he expresses the seriousness of his crisis, as he points to his inability to distinguish 'between a real blonde and a fake' (Dylan 2016: 571). Worse things could be imagined as happening, but the song continues with an account of his meeting in a Boston bar with a young waitress who asks him to draw her picture. His lame attempt at flirtation falls flat, and she ends up mocking his lack of knowledge of women authors. The rhymes of the stanza combine self-irony and sadness. He shows the waitress his attempt to make a drawing of her, but she turns him down, saying that his drawing does not resemble her at all, and she starts cross-examining him on his knowledge of women authors (Dylan 2016: 572). He refutes her accusation saying that he has read Erica Jong, but mischievously makes the latter rhyme with 'wrong'. The potential truth of his drawing of the waitress is not appreciated, but the potential truth of her comment on his lack of interest in women authors is also abandoned. The singer ends up wondering if he should buy himself a full-length leather coat – the classic tough-guy outfit. He wanders around looking at young people who dance and enjoy life and once again he imagines the beauty of the Highlands, hoping he finds some way of getting there, though his mind is there already, which is of course a consolation (Dylan 2016: 573). Although he is disappointed with other human beings, his mind is still open and he has access to a landscape of poetry.

6. Conclusion

Many internet testimonies on Dylan's songs show how people have used them in the difficult situations of their lives, confronting illness, sorrow or loss (see Mai 2018: 111–25). The motif of mental or physical borders seems especially interesting for a deeper awareness of Dylan's contribution to our understanding of what it means to be human. The paradoxical or liminal experience in Dylan's songs and paintings, between night and day, darkness and light, between sound and silence, pathos and humour, absence and presence, and between an inner and an outer world, is often related to an interaction between mind, body and the environment, and to melancholy as a creative state of mind where human beings are vulnerable and sensitive to their surroundings. Dylan insists on melancholia as an important and open state of mind, not an illness; a state of mind that reveals the coexistence of mixed attitudes and feelings toward life:

sadness, humour, self-irony and a deep sense of reality. Dylan shows us both in his songs and his paintings that melancholia reminds us of life, love and creativity through an awareness of death, loss, absence and destruction. Even his most recent shows give the audience a sense of creative melancholia as his stage persona is enigmatic and oxymoronic: a figure belonging to times long gone and still completely present, examining his enormous backlist and new material in front of his audience. And perhaps 'that's good enough for now' (Dylan 2016: 573).

References

Berman, M. (1982). *All That Is Solid Melts into Air: The Experience of Modernity*, New York: Simon and Schuster.

Burns, R. (1789), 'My Heart's in the Highlands'. Available online: https://kalliope.org/da/text/burns2019090704 (accessed 26 December 2019).

Cartwright, B. (1991), 'The Mysterious Norman Raeben', in J. Bauldie (ed.), *Wanted Man: In Search of Bob Dylan, 85–90*, New York: Citadel Press.

Dylan, B. (1997), *Time Out of Mind* [Album], USA: Columbia Records.

Dylan, B. (2008), *The Bootleg Series Vol. 8: Tell Tale Signs: Rare and Unreleased 1989–2006* [Album], USA: Columbia Records.

Dylan, B. (2016), *The Lyrics: 1961–2012*, New York: Simon and Schuster.

Elderfield, J. and K. Monrad, eds (2010), *Bob Dylan. The Brazil Series*, London: Prestel.

Fuchs, T. (2001), 'Melancholia as a Desynchronization: Towards a Psychopathology of Interpersonal Time', *Psychopathology*, 34: 179–86.

Fuchs, T. (2018), *The Ecology of the Brain*, Oxford: Oxford University Press.

Keats, John (1819), 'Ode on Melancholy'. Available online: www.poetryfoundation.org/poems/44478/ode-on-melancholy (accessed 26 December 2019).

Kierkegaard, S. (1996), *Papers and Journals: A Selection*, trans. A. Hannay, London: Penguin Books.

Klibansky, R., E. Panofsky and F. Saxl ([1964] 2019), *Saturn and Melancholy: Studies in the History of Natural Philosophy, Religion and Arts*, Montreal: McGill-Queen's University Press.

Mai, A.-M. (2018), *Bob Dylan. The Poet*, Odense: UP of Southern Denmark.

Melancholia (2011) [Film], Dir. L. von Trier, Denmark: Nordisk Film.

Plato (360 BCE), *Phaedrus*, trans. B. Jowett. Available online: http://classics.mit.edu/Plato/phaedrus.html (accessed 26 December 2019).

Part Two

Roll on Bob: Late Dylan in Text and Tribute

9

'A-Journeying over the Shadows and the Rain': Dylan's Late Style(s)

Jean Du Verger

In memoriam John Dowling

'The time must come wherein thou shalt be taught / the value and the beauty of the Past', American poet Henry Timrod wrote in his poem 'The Past' (1965). An artist's late works acquire an aura caused by his impending death. Consequently, his late works are tainted with the way in which he is coming to terms with his own mortality. In due time, they will constitute his musical testament with its emotional, and intellectual, impact on the reader-listener. The main contention of this chapter is therefore to present Dylan's journey into old age, a period French philosopher Vladimir Jankélévitch describes as 'a mode of being like youth and adulthood ... it just has another pace, another rhythm, another tempo; a different tonality' (Jankélévitch 2008: 207).[1] In the present essay I shall explore Bob Dylan's canon of texts over a period of twenty years or so, ranging from *Time Out of Mind* (1997) to his latest standards album *Triplicate* (2017). In terms of lyrical content, Dylan muses on the themes of death and nostalgia that haunt his lyrics. As a result, his songs convey a strong sense of introspection and melancholy, leading to self-reflexivity which, as art historian Kenneth Clark argued, characterizes old-age creativity (Hutcheon 2012: 6). Moreover, the songsmith's lyrics bear an intimate tone, and ooze with autobiographical references that loom throughout the albums. Dylan admitted the autobiographical dimension of his work in *Chronicles* (Dylan 2004: 199).

Seymour Chatman defines style as a form that 'signifies the manner or way in which something, including a work of art, is done, and, more particularly, the

---

[1] My translation from French: 'un mode d'être comme la jeunesse et l'âge mûr ... il a seulement une autre allure, un autre rythme, un autre tempo ; une tonalité différente'.

trace that the artist's way of working leaves on his artefact' (1979: 169). The concept of late style is the combination of the German *Spätstil* ('late style') and *Altersstil* ('individual old-age style') (Hutcheon 2012: 1). Dylan's late style(s) will be assessed in light of his *oeuvre* as this chapter will combine an autobiographical with an hermeneutical approach – German philosopher Friedrich Schleiermacher ([1828] 1985) defines hermeneutics as an art of understanding, an *ars interpretandi*. This approach will highlight the manifold textual significance of Dylan's lyrics, while never losing sight of the way in which the music showcases the lyrics. In an interview he gave to Bill Flanagan in 2009, Bob Dylan referred to his 'texted music' (Hutcheon 2012: 10), and to songs as '[a] theater of the mind' (Flanagan 2009a, part 2). It is therefore the aim of this chapter to show how Dylan stages his late style(s), as well as to show how Dylan's twenty-first-century recordings both illustrate and challenge Theodor Adorno's concept of 'late style' and Edward Said's concept of 'lateness'. I shall first examine *Time Out of Mind* (1997) that Dylan recorded before the turn of the century and which bears, I believe, the roots of his late style(s), before paying close attention to the four albums he produced between 2001 and 2012. In these late works, Dylan walks the reader-listener through the vast American landscape, as he goes hunting the phantoms and shadows of the past. Finally, I will show how his three albums of American standards illustrate another facet of his late style(s).

1. *Time Out of Mind*: examining 'the lost forgotten years' ('Dignity', Dylan 1989)

Bob Dylan's thirtieth studio album, *Time Out of Mind*, released on 30 September 1997 and produced by Daniel Lanois, marked the singer-songwriter's artistic comeback. The thematic threads woven throughout the songs reveal an over-awareness of the past as they resonate with the themes of loss, death and nostalgia. Richard Leppert remarks Adorno's interest in the past rests on 'that which has been left along the way, that which has been forgotten or dismissed as outdated – what he elsewhere names as "scars"' (Adorno 2002: 80–1). In the late 1970s, Dylan used the scar metaphor to describe the effects of life on the lived body: 'Remind me to show you the scars ... the price of this sweet paradise' ('Where Are You Tonight?', Dylan 1978). What probably surprised the listeners with *Time Out of Mind* was that Dylan's vocal style had taken on a new tone as he sounded markedly different from what he had sounded like on *World Gone Wrong* (1993). Barb Jungr, who explores the ways in which voice may influence us, argues that it 'gives us access to the singer's deepest emotions' (Jungr 2002: 102). Dylan's rasping voice grates on the listener's ear giving shape to his inner feelings as it despondently addresses a former lover. The album's introspective nature came as a surprise even to Dylan's friends themselves (Sounes 2001: 491). The album's opening song 'Love Sick' evokes images of death, ruin, desolation and loneliness. The reader-listener follows the narrator as he moves down deserted dark streets while wandering through a desolate landscape (Dylan 1997). Dylan's spectral vocals are backed up by a pulsating beat and a reverberating guitar, which enhance the sense of angst and weariness that informs the song.

The effects of old age are described in an almost ætiological manner: 'the flesh falls off my face' ('Standing in the Doorway', Dylan 1997). The 'decay of the body' is, as Said avers, characteristic of 'the last or late period of life' (2017: 3). In 'Cold Irons Bound' the narrator is even beginning to feel the effects of what resembles senile dementia: 'I'm beginning to hear voices and there's no one around' (Dylan 1997). Certain descriptions are reminiscent of Ovidian shape-shifting scenes in which a fixed state of petrification brings to an end the animate existence of a character: this is somewhat reminiscent of Niobe's petrification in Ovid's *Metamorphoses*, Book VI, 277-312, (Ovid 2000: 142). The narrator's soul feels as though it has been transformed into 'steel' ('Not Dark Yet', Dylan 1997) and he has 'Got ice water in [his] veins' ('Standing in the Doorway', 1997). The repetition of words evoking walking ('Love Sick', 1997), which function as 'lexical anchors' (Bickford 2007: 449) to which the lyrics return, paradoxically creates a sense of motionlessness that reinforces the overall impression of stillness. The narrator's body and his lineaments are progressively torn asunder, thus mirroring the fragmentation that characterizes late style: 'Well, I'm torn and I'm tattered / But I'm holding all the parts of it together' (Dylan 2008). These lines are from the alternate version of 'Can't Wait' that appears on the album *Tell Tale Signs*. Dylan writes in his autobiography that broken things 'can't be pieced back together' (Dylan 2004: 172-3). Furthermore, the narrator is overwhelmed by an acute weariness with life as Dylan's recurrent use of the *tædium vitæ* mode attests to – 'Well, I'm tired of talking, I'm tired of trying to explain' ("Til I Fell in Love with You', 1997) – echoing the album's opening song ('Love Sick', 1997). Dylan goes on to explore the dark recesses of his memory – a memory that seems incapable of recollection, since the narrator of 'Not Dark Yet' has forgotten what he went there to escape from (1997). While the narrator of 'Can't Wait' is 'strollin'' through the lonely graveyard of [his] mind', his whole life seems to unfold before his eyes, as it does in the last song on the album, the nearly seventeen-minute-long 'Highlands' (1997). Dylan borrowed a riff from Charley Patton in 'Highlands': 'I had the guitar run off an old Charley Patton record for years and always wanted to do something with that' (Cott 2017: 423). As the song drifts onwards, the lyrics shed light on the way time flows regardless of everything. Dylan walks the reader-listener from one situation to another and, as we move from one scene to the next, we are made aware of life's transiency. Dylan's persona, while expressing the desire to escape into the past, senses the pointlessness of holding back time as his lyrics highlight the infinite flow of time and space. The blues is a perfect vehicle for achieving this effect. Musically, it is an unfixed structure, an infinite loop, which calls for a sense of openness that can begin or end anywhere, offering an almost endless set of resonances. Time is an explicit theme in 'Highlands', as it is throughout the entire album. But more essential is its fragmented character, consisting of episodes in which the singer's persona drifts from one scene to another, combining seemingly unconnected narratives interspersed with flashes of indefinite past and future as the narrator moves from an oneiric world to scenes of everyday life. Throughout the song, a sense of alienation emerges now and then ('Life in the same ol' cage', 1997), imparting a feeling of claustrophobia. A feeling countered by the vast open landscape of the highlands that creates an oscillatory effect between closed and open spaces.

While time constitutes the album's main theme, Dylan also dwells on themes of travel and space – for instance with the 'Dixie-bound' narrator from "Til I Fell in Love With You' (1997). The South, which occupies a specific place in Dylan's works, provides him with a map of marginal places that have been left behind, evoking a sense of nostalgia that reverberates through his lyrics. The spatial representation of the South mirrors Dylan's ontological concerns as he revisits his musical roots, suggesting that the South's *genius loci* reflects the experiences of the singer's persona. Moreover, the album's lyrics herald the musical journey Dylan's persona will be embarking on in his four subsequent albums of self-composed songs. The singer-songwriter's musical journey will enable the reader-listener to follow his perambulations down the Mississippi to New Orleans ('Tryin' To Get To Heaven', Dylan 1997), bearing in mind that the river stands as an old metaphor for the life of man.

2. Seeking the ghosts of the past: Dylan's musical journey through the South

The four albums of original material Dylan produced from 2001 to 2012 – *"Love and Theft"* (2001), *Modern Times* (2006), *Together Through Life* (2009) and *Tempest* (2012) – express 'the explosive force of subjectivity' that Adorno (2002: 566) defined as a feature of late works. Works which, as they become more introspective, more personal, touch the reader-listener with greater effectiveness, especially as the subject is also – in Adornian terms – the object of Dylan's lyrics. These albums were produced by the artist himself under one of his numerous pseudonyms – Jack Frost – the well-known figure in popular culture who personifies winter. The latter-day Dylan emerges through the themes and musical influences that permeate the lyrics and music of the albums, as the artist's 'phonographic imagination' (Negus 2010: 213) maps his own musical journey through the South. Consequently, the readers-listeners, while following the course of the meandering Mississippi river, also tread on the heels of Dylan's own ramblings. Robert Palmer notes that blues musicians 'traveled around Mississippi' (1982: 38), and Dylan described *Together Through Life* as 'a kind of journey … a journey of self discovery … [that] takes place in the American South' (Flanagan 2009a, part 1). All four albums conflate the influence of rockabilly, blues, folk and country music, providing the reader-listener with an encyclopaedia of twentieth-century American popular music, thus contradicting Adorno's remark that '[t]he juxtaposition of various forms of music and musical practice is the opposite of reconciled diversity' (1988: 120). It is precisely this 'reconciled diversity' that Dylan achieves in the aforementioned albums. The songs on *Modern Times* were 'written and performed in the widest range possible so they had a little bit of everything' (Flanagan 2009a, part 1). When he composed this album, Dylan argued that he had 'somebody in mind as an audience', and he then went on to explain that his audience is not really interested in the period to which his songs belong as the people 'feel style and substance in a more visceral way' (2009a, part 1). His audience sees music as a dialogue with the past, not just the present. They will therefore approach his works in terms of their own interpretative framework. In 2007, discussing the themes on *Modern Times*, Dylan told Jann S. Wenner: 'You would have to ask every individual person who hears it what it would mean. It would probably mean many things on many levels to many different kinds of people' (Cott 2017: 483). This contrasts with Adorno's approach which is more concerned with music's production than with its reception, exposing its theoretical limits in the understanding of contemporary popular music. Ros Jennings claims that popular music is aligned with the idea of a continuum linking past, present and future experiences. Dylan's '"greying" older audience' (Jennings 2015: 77) have aged and changed with him. Consequently, they can also muster out of their own experience the sense of ageing, on the understanding that in turn the readers-listeners themselves develop their own late taste.

For the present purpose, our focus will be limited to the blues influences that resonate throughout the albums. Jon Pareles notes that '[t]he blues has always been a Dylan touchstone, for both words and music' (Cott 2017: 418). In terms of lyrical and musical content there is clearly a thematic unity between the four albums. '*Modern Times*, like *"Love and Theft"* and *Time Out of Mind* before it', writes Jonathan Lethem, 'seems to survey a broken world through the prism of a heart that's worn and worldly' (Cott 2017: 470). Through the use of echo and reverberation effects, their recording process provides them with an aural spatiality reminiscent of the sound produced by independent studios such as Sun Records, Dylan's 'favourite sound for a record' (Dylan 2004: 216). Dylan mentioned his admiration for Sam Phillips's 'uplifting' work in his autobiography (Dylan 2004: 216). The vibrating, stuttering vocals, the single guitar texture, the drums' percussion effects and the accordion, which Dylan views both as an orchestrative and percussive instrument, 'render aural vistas' (Doyle 2004: 32) in the listener's mind. The intensity produced by these recordings is enhanced by the fact that '[t]he sound is uncluttered. There's power and suspense. The whole vibration feels like it could be coming from inside your mind. It's alive' (Flanagan 2009a, part 1).

Like many early blues singers, Dylan has undertaken a metaphorical and musical journey down South. The singer-songwriter explained his own personal vision of the South: 'It's filled with rambling ghosts and disturbed spirits. They're all screaming and forlorning. It's like they are caught in some weird web – some purgatory between heaven and hell and they can't rest. They can't live, and they can't die' (Flanagan 2009a, part 3). In his autobiography, Dylan depicts the South as a ghostly, deeply melancholic place (Dylan 2004: 181). He went on to explain to Flanagan the perambulatory aspect of his songs: 'The streams, the forests, the vast emptiness. The land created me. I'm wild and lonesome. Even as I travel cities, I'm more at home in the vacant lots' (2009a, part 3). As Dylan's persona sets out on his journey down South, he conveys the impression he is about to begin his final journey: 'I'm watching the roads, I'm studying the dust / I'm painting the town making my last go-round' ('Bye and Bye', Dylan 2001). The wandering theme resurfaces throughout the above-mentioned albums: the world the speaker walks through is 'mysterious and vague' ('Ain't Talkin'', Dylan 2006). Old age itself is described in terms of landscape: 'You think I'm over the hill / You think I'm past my prime' ('Spirit on the Water', 2006). As shown by the lyrics of 'Mississippi' (Dylan 2001) – a song initially recorded for the album *Time Out of Mind* that later surfaced on *"Love and Theft"* – we will follow the artist's course down the river. Interestingly, the source of the river is located in Minnesota, Dylan's own home state. Progressively, the river will come to embody life itself. The opening verse depicts a growing feeling of claustrophobia as the narrator feels the footfalls of impending death around him: 'Your days are numbered, so are mine / We're all boxed in, nowhere to escape' (Dylan 2001).

Throughout his lyrics, Dylan considers the numerous contrasting and destructive faces water takes on in nature. The river holds lethal and destructive powers engulfing the narrator, while the notion of time itself comes to a standstill, as his persona is trapped in what resembles an everlasting present. Memories themselves are erased by the water: 'My memories are drowning / In mortal bliss' ('Beyond The Horizon', Dylan 2006). The river's treacherous and destructive nature resurfaces in 'High Water' (Dylan 2001) dedicated to the father of the Delta blues, Charley Patton.[2] As we move further down South, Dylan's peregrinations progressively shape a map oscillating between known and unknown locations. The untamed tributaries of the Mississippi stand as symbols of the South – 'They went down the Ohio, the Cumberland, the Tennessee / All the rest of them rebel rivers' ('Floater', Dylan 2001) – while in 'If Ever You Go To Houston' (Dylan 2009), the narrator draws up his own personal map of Texas.[3]

The geographical space shapes the narrator's memories of the past while his meandering meditations lose themselves in time. In 'This Dream of You', the geographical locations are blurred: 'How long can I stay in this nowhere café' (Dylan 2009). Asked about the location of this 'nowhere café', Dylan replied cryptically: 'It sounds like it's south of the border or close to the border' (Flanagan 2009a, part 4). As Dylan's persona progresses southward toward the Mississippi's

---

[2] Dylan's lyrics are based on Patton's original song 'High Water Everywhere', recorded in 1929.
[3] Dylan had already drawn up a map of the South and the West in 'Wanted Man' (*Nashville Skyline*, 1969).

mouth, we finally reach his ultimate destination: the Gulf of Mexico and 'the deep blue sea' ('Tempest', Dylan 2012). The song, which stands as a metaphor of death, is based on 'Titanic', an old folk song likely to have originated around 1915 in Alabama. The destructive power of water comes to represent the ravaging effects of time itself – endless, faceless with crippling and deadly effects – as the ship sinks '[i]nto the underworld'. The bodies of the passengers are scattered or engulfed in the tempestuous waters, while 'Death [is] on the rampage' (Dylan 2012). As the end nears, the captain reminisces and cries.

The lyrics are suffused with a feeling of alienation and loneliness. In 'Lonesome Day Blues' for instance, the twofold incremental repetition, which echoes blues structure,[4] places emphasis on the narrator's feeling of solitude: 'Well, today has been a sad ol' lonesome day / Yeah, today has been a sad ol' lonesome day' (Dylan 2001). Consequently, his perception of the world grows bleaker as he reads it through a dark lens, as the chorus from 'Nettie Moore' suggests (Dylan 2006). The sense of loss and loneliness also pervades the lyrics of 'Life Is Hard': 'I've lost the way and will / I felt that emptiness so wide' (Dylan 2009). The song depicts Dylan's growing feeling of estrangement and change, which also appears in his interviews: 'It's more about ... how sometimes we know people and we are no longer what we used to be to them' (Flanagan 2009a, part 3). Time has an almost physical effect on the narrator's body: 'Time and love has branded me with its claws' ('Po' Boy', Dylan 2001), while memories themselves are endowed with physical properties: 'These memories I got, they can strangle a man' ('Honest With Me', 2001). Death hovers over the lyrics of the mournful song 'When the Deal Goes Down' (Dylan 2006), the sense of human finitude depicted through its lyrics being reminiscent of Robert Johnson's 'Last Fair Deal Gone Down'. In 'Pay in Blood', while Dylan's lyrics allude to the process of dislocation and fragmentation – with dogs that can tear a body apart – one perceives a tinge of anger in his voice (Dylan 2012). Life is therefore viewed as a harsh experience that does not leave one 'unscarred' ('Narrow Way', 2012).[5] Relying on the blues tradition, the musical and lyrical fragments of the four albums we have been looking at display a coherent thematic pattern that foregrounds the eschatological quality of his lyrics.

---

[4] Robert Palmer considers that *ostinatos* or repeating patterns characterize blues lyrics (1982: 29).

[5] 'Narrow Way''s chorus is taken from 'It's Done Gone Wet' by the Mississippi Sheiks (1934), while the rhythm of the song is based on a quick tempo version of 'The Swag' by Link Wray (1958). In *Chronicles*, Dylan mentions the hypnotic quality of Wray's music which rests on syncopations (Dylan 2004: 160).

3. Dylan's interpretations of the Great American Songbook

Bob Dylan's three American Songbook standards albums – four, if we consider his Christmas album released in 2009 – belong to what critics have termed 'Dylan's long goodbye'. The imagery and themes that run through these albums convey the artist's ruminations on life and the urgency of passing time, while emotion hovers near the surface of the lyrics. Dylan's self-titled debut album (1962) was an album of mainly non-original material, comprising only three songs that he wrote and composed himself. Yet, his first album of non-original songs *per se* as an established artist, *Self Portrait* (1970), which was defined as 'an elaborate joke' (Roos and O'Meara 1988: 40), revealed an unexpected facet of the singer-songwriter, an aspect that critics did not grasp at the time – one still has in mind the opening line of Greil Marcus's review in *Rolling Stone*: 'What is this shit?' (2010: 7) – and which seems, with hindsight, to make greater sense when one considers his late works. Contrary to Beethoven's late works which are, according to Adorno, characterized by discontinuities, Dylan's late works express a clear sense of continuity as the motifs keep toying with the issues of death, nostalgia and alienation (Said 2017: 16).

In the three Songbook standards albums – *Shadows in the Night* (2015), *Fallen Angels* (2016) and the three-disc *Triplicate* (2017), all produced by Jack Frost (aka Dylan) – the present is shadowed by the revived receding past. Dylan explains his lyrical silence in no ambiguous terms: 'There's enough of my personality written into the lyrics so that I could just focus on the melodies' (Flanagan 2017). For Dylan, not writing one's own songs is not a problem – 'If you can write your songs, that's ideal, but nobody will fault you if you don't' (Flanagan 2017) – as words of others can reflect the artist's own feelings and thoughts. Adorno argues that in Beethoven's late style the subject disappears without a trace (Rosengard Subotnik 1976: 256). Yet Dylan's musical and lyrical approach in his interpretations of Songbook standards, while indisputably posing the question of the artist's inspiration, are crucial in his artistic strategy to overcome the silence brought upon him by the drying up of his own well of creativity.[6] In Dylan's case, the subject is wrenched out of obscurity as he continues to express his inner feelings through the words of others, enabling his persona to resurface in a rather unexpected way, as he seems to reinvent himself

---

[6] On the question of inspiration, see the interview Dylan gave to Ed Bradley on *60 Minutes* in December 2004 (McCandless 2016).

by forging autobiographical links between music and memory. Consequently, these songs bring into being Dylan's own memoryscape. Talking about *Christmas in the Heart* (2009), he confessed: 'These songs are part of my life, just like folk songs' (Flanagan 2009b). Dylan is therefore creating the 'soundtrack of [his own] li[fe]' (Hyltén-Cavallius 2012: 279) – as he told Flanagan: 'Now that I have lived them and lived through them I understand them better' (2017). Thus, lateness brings knowledge and wisdom: 'When I was young there were a lot of signs along the way that I couldn't interpret, they were there and I saw them, but they were mystifying. Now when I look back I can see them for what they were, what they meant' (Flanagan 2017).

The songs on *Shadows in the Night*, *Fallen Angels* and *Triplicate* are replete with nostalgia and melancholy. Let us briefly glance at the record covers. On the back cover of *Shadows in the Night*, Dylan is portrayed holding a Sun record, a reference to that recording sound he likes. The inside cover of *Fallen Angels* pictures a hand holding cards, concealing the face of the person holding them, a visual allusion to 'When the Deal Goes Down' (Dylan 2006). These two examples illustrate the way Dylan's late works are carefully enmeshed and create a network of citations suggesting that they – whether albums or sleeves – must be regarded as a whole. If we now examine the songs' titles and lyrics from *Shadows in the Night*, 'Why Try to Change Me Now', 'Where Are You Now?' and 'What'll I Do?' (Dylan 2015), all dwell on the themes of disenchantment, loneliness and melancholia. As for *Fallen Angels*, the song entitled 'Melancholy Mood' is self-explanatory (Dylan 2016). In the *Triplicate* trilogy, the themes are subtly intertwined and reverberate with one another. On the first record, the themes and lyrics of 'September of My Years', 'Stormy Weather' and 'It Gets Lonely Early' resound in some songs found on the second record such as 'As Time Goes By' and 'Here's That Rainy Day', which in turn will find an echo on the third disc, in songs such as 'Somewhere Along the Way' or 'When the World Was Young' (Dylan 2017). All these songs have been picked from the Great American Songbook that stands as a legacy of American popular music. Dylan has given them a new lease of life. His phrasing hollows out the meaning of these lyrics and the musical arrangements create, as Tom Piazza notes in the *Triplicate* accompanying notebook, 'a beautifully balanced sonic world to surround the voice at its centre' (Dylan 2017). Like Sinatra, Dylan keeps his persona beneath the music. His 'art of transforming things' enables him to use art as 'an expression of life' (Flanagan 2017). As Dylan excavates these texts, he brings them back to life and displays them in a very personal way. His voice superimposes itself on the voices of Frank Sinatra, Ella Fitzgerald, Tony Bennett, Nat King Cole, Billie Holiday, Sarah Vaughan and others, creating a vocal and musical palimpsest of sorts as he lays down his own voice in the Great American Songbook, perpetuating the tradition of American popular music. *Shadows in the Night* is a tribute to Frank Sinatra, who, as critic Adam Gopnik put it (2015), did not merely interpret the American Songbook but invented it. Dylan has moved from being a songwriter to an interpreter. The scribe, who recollected in his songs the memories of the past, has now become the echo chamber of the voices contained in the Great American Songbook. The choice of Sinatra may also be explained by the fact that his voice was always that of someone confiding and capable of expressing self-reflecting melancholy without emoting. Asked whether he tried for different emotions on different takes, Dylan said: 'Not really. The emotions would pretty much be the same on any singular take. The inflections would maybe differ if we changed the key and sometimes that might affect the emotional resonance' (Flanagan 2009b). In the same way, Dylan's ageing vocals convey a sense of nostalgia to listeners as they listen to the songs from 'yesteryear'.

4. Conclusion

'The end of time has just begun' ('Can't Wait', Dylan 1997): *Time Out Of Mind* marks the dawn of Dylan's late style, illustrating Adorno's view that late works address 'catastrophes' (Adorno 2002: 567; the Greek word *katastrephein* means 'coming to an end'). I would tend therefore to side with critic Sean Egan, who described *Time Out of Mind* as rock's 'first heartfelt treatise on mortality' (Egan 2011: xxvi). The album's overall tone and the elements of despair in certain songs convey the idea that Dylan remains a tragically lonely figure whose late works stalk new sonic and thematic territories. The way he recorded his 1997–2012 self-penned albums, using echo and reverb to express a sense of twilight, gives the impression that things are progressively losing their solidity as they blend into the surrounding soundscape. The lyrics on these albums unite all the various stances and feelings expressed through his multiple personae. They are an entire reimagining of the artist's creative possibilities that rest on old patriarchal musical forms such as blues, country and folk. As for Dylan's interpretations of standards, while focusing on what happens to creative people in their twilight years – when they stop inventing themselves – they also express the return toward something precious and deeply felt: the music of his youth. Dylan's ageing identities are reflexive constructs that draw on music, images and texts of the past. Listening to these standards from long ago, one cannot help thinking of Johnny Cash's late recordings of covers. Cash's landmark records are permeated – not unlike Dylan's – with a touch of sadness and darkness. However, Dylan's interpretations of standards lack the dramatic tension of Cash's covers as they exude a feeling of serenity, as if the singer-poet had come to terms with the idea of death. Moreover, unlike Cash, Dylan is not a bruised legend. Cash's final years, which were plagued with health ailments, resembled, as Graeme Thomson aptly remarks, 'the unflinching late-period self-portraits of Rembrandt, another artist who suffered indignities and struggled to negotiate a path through middle age and yet returned in the end to a point of courageous, visionary strength' (Thomson 2011: 11). As Dylan reopens and revisits the Great American Standards, he is not only reinventing himself, he is also making a statement. Dylan's late works seem to have been addressing lateness ever since 1997. It is as if 'The Never Ending Tour' – as the hundreds of concerts performed by Dylan since the late 1980s have been dubbed by the media, though it is an expression Dylan despises – had morphed unobtrusively into a 'Never Ending Lateness'. While his late works inevitably deal with the past and the question of mortality, one must keep in mind what Dylan told Mikal Gilmore about *"Love and Theft"*: 'Well, it doesn't deal with my mortality. It maybe just deals with mortality in general. It's one thing that we all have in common, isn't it? But I didn't see any one critic say: "It deals with my mortality" – you know, his own' (Cott 2017: 441). Although Dylan clearly has a point here, it seems however questionable, on an album he describes himself as being 'autobiographical on every front' (Cott 2017: 454), that those themes had no relation whatsoever with his perception of his own mortality. But suffice it to say that with Dylan one is always left guessing.

References

Adorno, T. W. (1988), *Introduction to the Sociology of Music*, trans. E. B. Ashton, New York: Continuum.

Adorno, T. W. (2002), 'Late Style in Beethoven' [1937], in *Essays on Music*, ed. Richard Leppert, trans. S. H. Gillespie, 564–8, Berkeley and Los Angeles: University of California Press.

Bickford, T. (2007), 'Music of Poetry and Poetry of Song: Expressivity and Grammar in Vocal Performance', *Ethnomusicology*, 51(3): 439–76.

Chatman S. (1979), 'The Styles of Narrative Codes', in B. Lang (ed.), *The Concept of Style*, 169–81, Philadelphia: University of Pennsylvania Press.

Cott, J., ed. (2017), *Bob Dylan: The Essential Interviews*, New York: Simon and Schuster.

Doyle, P. (2004), 'From "My Blue Heaven" to "Race with the Devil": Echo, Reverb and (Dis)ordered Space in Early Popular Music Recording', *Popular Music*, 23(1): 31–49.

Dylan, B. (1978), *Street Legal* [Album], USA: Columbia Records.

Dylan, B. (1989), *Oh Mercy* [Album], USA: Columbia Records.

Dylan, B. (1997), *Time Out of Mind* [Album], USA: Columbia Records.

Dylan, B. (2001), *"Love and Theft"* [Album], USA: Columbia Records.

Dylan, B. (2004), *Chronicles, Volume One*, London: Simon and Schuster.

Dylan, B. (2006), *Modern Times* [Album], USA: Columbia Records.

Dylan, B. (2008), *Tell Tale Signs* [Album], USA: Columbia Records.

Dylan, B. (2009), *Together Through Life* [Album], USA: Columbia Records.

Dylan, B. (2012), *Tempest* [Album], USA: Columbia Records.

Dylan, B. (2015), *Shadows in the Night* [Album], USA: Columbia Records.

Dylan, B. (2016), *Fallen Angels* [Album], USA: Columbia Records.

Dylan, B. (2017), *Triplicate* [Album], USA: Columbia Records.

Egan, S., ed. (2011), *The Mammoth Book of Bob Dylan*, London: Robinson.

Flanagan, B. (2009a), 'Interview with Bob Dylan', *The Beat Patrol* blog, 6 parts, 17 March–26 April. Available online:

Part 1: https://beatpatrol.wordpress.com/2009/03/17/bill-flanagan-interview-with-bob-dylan-part-1-2009/ (accessed 11 March 2019).

Part 3: https://beatpatrol.wordpress.com/2009/04/16/bill-flanagan-interview-with-bob-dylan-part-3-2009/ (accessed 11 March 2019).

Part 4: https://beatpatrol.wordpress.com/2009/04/20/bill-flanagan-interview-with-bob-dylan-part-4-2009/ (accessed 11 March 2019).

Flanagan, B. (2009b), 'Dylan for the Holidays', *Street Roots*, 10 December. Available online: https://news.streetroots.org/2009/12/10/dylan-holidays (accessed 14 April 2020).

Flanagan, B. (2017), 'Q & A with Bill Flanagan', *The Official Bob Dylan Site*, 22 March. Available online: www.bobdylan.com/news/qa-with-bill-flanagan/ (accessed 12 March 2019).

Gopnik, A. (2015), 'The Pure Artistry of Frank Sinatra', *The New Yorker*, 8 April. Available online: www.newyorker.com/culture/cultural-comment/the-pure-artistry-of-frank-sinatra (accessed 12 March 2019).

Hutcheon, M. and L. (2012), 'Late Style(s): The Ageism of the Singular', *Occasion: Interdisciplinary Studies in the Humanities*, 4: 1–11.

Hyltén-Cavallius, S. (2012), 'Memoryscapes and Mediascapes: Musical Formations of "Pensioners" in Late 20th-Century Sweden', *Popular Music*, 31(2): 279–95.

Jankélévitch, V. (2008), *La Mort*, Paris: Flammarion.

Jennings, R. (2015), 'Popular Music and Ageing', in J. Twigg and W. Martin (eds), *Routledge Handbook of Cultural Gerontology*, 77–84, London & New York: Routledge.

Jungr, B. (2002), 'Vocal Expression in the Blues and Gospel', in A. Moore (ed.), *The Cambridge Companion to Blues and Gospel Music*, 102–15, Cambridge: Cambridge University Press.

Marcus, G. (2010), *Bob Dylan by Greil Marcus. Writings 1968–2010*, New York: PublicAffairs.

McCandless, B. (2016), 'Bob Dylan: Songs Were "Almost Magically Written"', *60 Minutes Overtime*, 13 October. Available online: www.cbsnews.com/news/60-minutes-bob-dylan-on-songwriting-2004/ (accessed 14 April 2020).

Negus, K. (2010), 'Bob Dylan's Phonographic Imagination', *Popular Music*, 29(2): 213–27.

Ovid ([AD 8] 2000), *Metamorphoses*, trans. M. M. Innes, London: Penguin Books.

Palmer, R. (1982), *Deep Blues*, New York and London: Penguin Books.

Roos, M. and D. O'Meara (1988), 'Is Your Love in Vain? – Dialectical Dilemmas in Bob Dylan's Recent Love Songs', *Popular Music*, 7(1): 35–50.

Rosengard Subotnik, R. (1976), 'Adorno's Diagnosis of Beethoven's Late Style: Early Symptom of a Fatal Condition', *Journal of the American Musicological Society*, 29(2): 242–75.

Said, E. (2017), *On Late Style. Music and Literature Against the Grain*, London and New York: Bloomsbury.

Schleiermacher, F. D. E. ([1828] 1985), 'Foundations: General Theory and Art of Interpretation', trans. J. Duke and J. Forstman, in K. Mueller-Vollmer (ed.), *The Hermeneutics Reader: Texts of the German Tradition from the Enlightenment to the Present*, 72–97, New York: Continuum.

Sounes, H. (2001), *Down the Highway: The Life of Bob Dylan*, London: Black Swan Books.

Thomson, G. (2011), *The Resurrection of Johnny Cash: Hurt, Redemption and American Recordings*, London: Jawbone Press.

Timrod, H. (1965), 'The Past', *The Collected Poems of Henry Timrod*. Available online: www.poetryfoundation.org/poems/48891/the-past-56d22a7d9aef6 (accessed 14 April 2020).

10

'The Last Outback at the World's End': Dylan's Sense of an Album's Ending

M. Cooper Harriss

The most important song on any Bob Dylan album is its last song. Dylan's albums end with a flourish, often with a grand gesture of songcraft noteworthy for its length ('Sad-Eyed Lady of the Lowlands'), vivid imagery ('Where Are You Tonight? [Journey through Dark Heat]'), summative encapsulation of an album's themes ('Wedding Song' or 'It's All Over Now, Baby Blue'), or an arresting performance that offers a kind of strategic encore ('When He Returns'; 'Dark Eyes' as a peace offering in atonement for the sonic excess of *Empire Burlesque* [1985]; or 'Buckets of Rain' as what Nina Goss describes in the first chapter of this volume as a 'coda', the striking of the set or a period of recovery that follows the intensity of *Blood on the Tracks* [1975]). Dylan has doubled-down on the album closer's significance in his twenty-first-century work. Consider the monumental 'Highlands', closing *Time Out of Mind* (Dylan 1997), 'Sugar Baby' at the end of *"Love and Theft"* (Dylan 2001) and *Modern Times* 'Ain't Talkin'' (Dylan 2006) – a song we shall examine in closer detail later in this chapter – and now 'Murder Most Foul' on *Rough and Rowdy Ways* (Dylan 2020). Whatever else these songs may or may not share, their placement at the end of their respective albums reflects a strategic and meaningful curatorial impulse.

In one sense these final songs represent death, foreclosing the possibility that the album might continue forever. This terminal sensibility also reframes the significance of an album's beginning and middle, marking 'the album' itself as a narrative genre. In this way – consisting of a specific beginning, middle and end – individual albums become discrete representations of a human life. Frank Kermode argues in *The Sense of an Ending* from 1966 that endings in cultural forms (he speaks of 'fiction', and here I refer to the album as, like fiction, a narrative genre) provide an imaginative rehearsal of the end of the world (Kermode 2000). Narratives must end because human beings are mortal.

Therefore, forms of human creativity that imagine and stand in for death situate the experience of a discrete and bounded story within the context of eternity. The meaning of this story – and especially of the individual events that comprise it – becomes changed by this ending. Kermode speaks of a 'unitary system' (2000: 5) that endings shore up in narratives. They enclose, codifying the seeming contingency of day-to-day experience by bringing it to completion. In this way the end casts the beginning and the middle in new light.

This chapter deploys Kermode's argument, focusing on categories of time, narrative and eschatology in the attempt to generate new conceptual approaches to a series of related questions: What is an album – especially a 'Dylan album'? How does the album function as a narrative genre? What are the aesthetic and metaphysical arcs of Dylan's eschatology as the album generates meaning from both its formal and technological dimensions? Finally, given Dylan's consistent use of the album form over the course of a career that spans parts of seven decades, what insights emerge from these eschatological dimensions of Dylan's twenty-first-century work and personae, especially as they differ from his better-known output of the 1960s and 1970s? What are the terms of Dylan's own sense of an ending as he seeks, late in his career and thus approaching his own end, to shore up and master the narrative dimensions of his own myth and its legacy?

1. What is an album?

Historically speaking the album emerged by accident, a by-product of post-war audio technology when 33⅓ rpm long-playing records (LPs) extended the running length for recorded music beyond the roughly three-minute sides of 78 rpm records to the vicinity of twenty-five minutes. This boon for classical recordings also enabled jazz musicians to recreate on record the deliberate and expanded flow of club performances or informal jams. Eight-track and cassette tapes extended this time frame and, in some cases, eliminated side A and side B (and the necessity of physically 'turning over' the record upon the completion of one side, since a ninety-minute cassette may hold an entire album on one of its forty-five-minute sides). Cassettes also introduced the mix tape, a democratized genre of 'do-it-yourself' album building. Compact discs followed suit in the 1980s, introducing the option to 'shuffle' songs, or even to reprogramme the playing order, essentially fracturing the album's canonical sequence either at random or by design. More recently, downloading and streaming technologies have returned emphasis to the 'single' – a solitary song consumed separate from any album. These technologies also allow for the curation of playlists or random samplings that harness one's entire digital collection of recorded music (Shuker 10–11).

In light of such developments, a number of sources have suggested that the album is dying – if not already dead (Oswinski 2018). In 1998, less than six months after the release of *Time Out of Mind*, an article in the *New York Times Magazine* called the album form 'played out', correctly forecasting nearly a quarter-century ago (at the outset of the digital era) that the genre 'cannot ... hold its own in cyberspace' (Marzorati 1998). The shift from a material artefact spinning on a turntable to data on a hard drive or in the Cloud not only altered the rites of listening but also abetted new habits that would prove suboptimal for the flourishing of a cultural form that 'demands to be listened to all the way through, to be engaged, interpreted, identified with, inhabited' (Marzorati 1998).[1] An album's materiality proves difficult to untether from its formal demands as a narrative genre.

What it means to think about 'the album' as a genre – narrative, musical, or otherwise – remains a lacuna in the study of popular music. One difficulty with doing so raises questions about what 'counts' more for discerning meaning in popular music – words or music. Peter Kaminsky's detailed musicological study of Paul Simon's 1975 album *Still Crazy after All These Years*, for instance, dives deeply into harmonic structure with in-text notations of selected musical motifs (Kaminsky 1992). While words do figure in his scheme, Kaminsky writes as a musicologist comparing Simon's formal creation with Schubert's song cycles. By contrast, other treatments of popular music tend to focus more fully on words than music, including (to take but one example) the theologian James Cone's book *The Spirituals and the Blues* (1972), which draws almost exclusively on lyrical content to build its case.[2] Consider, too, Christopher Ricks's reflections on Dylan's poetics, emphatically concerned with words and wordcraft: Ricks's *Dylan's Visions of Sin* (2005) and his editions of Dylan's lyrics (Dylan 2014) present the songs as words on the page without any notation or other musical referents.

---

[1] Central to Marzorati's premise is what he calls 'the Big Album' – nomenclature he deploys to distinguish an album that deliberately cultivates meaning and significance as opposed to a more matter-of-fact use of 'album' as a collection of songs or a long-playing recording that may or may not aspire to something 'greater' (Marzorati 1998).
[2] Along similar lines, the primary mode of discussing blues songs from the beginning of their academic study has skewed hard toward lyrical content, as in the case of Oliver (1969) and Charters (1975), among others.

These volumes do point out Dylan's own sense that it is in fact words and music working together that make the meaning. Musicality is never far away from either Ricks's or Cone's readings, yet inverse to Kaminsky's method, their most meaningful dimensions derive from *logos,* from linguistic and poetic modes. Whatever the music may otherwise contribute, the emphasis remains upon – indeed the 'song' becomes synonymous with – the words.

To call the album a narrative genre attempts to locate middle ground between words and music. Dylan insists on their union in his Nobel Lecture, referring to his work not as 'literature', which he argues must be read, but as 'songs' that 'are unlike literature. They're meant to be sung, not read' (Dylan 2017). Specifically, albums permit words and music to conspire, thus stylizing a trajectory of narrative meaning over time. My divergence from Kaminsky and Ricks, however, derives most fully from formal concerns. Musicology and poetics in and of themselves matter less in this schematic than the meaningfulness that they generate in concert with one another. A song's words must always be considered in context of sound and modulation in their performance. Likewise, musical concerns in songcraft cannot exist independent from the lyrics that they buoy. In this way 'the album' should be understood as a narrative genre fed by the significant interplay of words and music within a sequence of songs. Selected Bob Dylan albums permit us to consider formal aspects of the genre and, in this way, to examine the conventions that Dylan has deployed through performance and cultural influence in the late twentieth and especially the early twenty-first centuries.

2. What is a Dylan album?

The album form and its generic conventions clearly matter to Dylan as a recording artist. It remains one of the few working constants over his long and variable career, making it possible to periodize his trajectory by albums alone. The 'beginning' of his career often dates to the first album, for instance, even though he had been performing professionally in some capacity for more than two years by the time *Bob Dylan* was released in 1962. Certain 'trilogies' of albums (those released in 1965–6 and during the so-called Gospel years spanning 1979–81 among them) frame entire Dylan epochs. Also well documented is Dylan's particularity in maintaining a conscious sonic and thematic flow for his albums, which several volumes of the *Bootleg Series* highlight the development of, as well as his willingness to sacrifice individual songs of extraordinary quality or potential ('Blind Willie McTell', for instance) in deference to his perception of an overall feeling or mood for the album it might otherwise have populated (in this case 1983's *Infidels*) (Wilentz 2011: 205–6).

What is more, Dylan has continued to deploy the album format well into the twenty-first century, even as the technology surrounding its dissemination has changed and the album's own generic significance has been transformed from cultural touchstone into – much like Dylan's twenty-first-century output more broadly – a deliberate anachronism, a provocation of form. What, then, becomes the function of a Bob Dylan album in a digital age, when the form is no longer taken for granted, no longer technologically necessary? What was it ever? And what does this difference mean for understanding Dylan's renewed vitality in the albums of his long twenty-first century – a period that arguably began in 1997 with *Time Out of Mind*? What purpose does an album serve post-album, when the age of albums has effectively ended?

Most immediately, of course, a Dylan album presents a discrete set of song performances that are recorded, compiled, released and marketed as a singular unit. From this product we may derive associations with specific soundscapes, voices and backing musicians – as well as certain historical periods or artistic visions to which these aspects contribute. *Another Side of Bob Dylan* (1964), for instance, marks a stylistic shift toward imagistic lyrics and more personal subjects (Hentoff 1964). *Desire* (1975) remains unimaginable without sonic contributions from Emmylou Harris and Scarlet Rivera. *"Love and Theft"* (2001) all but confirms Greil Marcus's vision of Dylan's 'old, weird America' (Marcus 2011) even as it offered – accidentally, by virtue of its release date of 11 September 2001 – an organizing principle for coming to terms with twenty-first-century cataclysm (Marcus 2001). Furthermore, whatever their particular differences, these representative Dylan albums also point beyond themselves, exceeding the sum of their parts. To speak their titles – *Blonde on Blonde* or *Knocked Out Loaded* – deploys a shorthand for fans and critics, denominating broader legacies and disputes over quality, affect and historical context.

While Dylan did not invent 'the album', he contributed to its development as a popular-musical genre across the rock era as it transformed from an assemblage of individual musical tracks (reminiscent of the collection of photographs or the songbooks from which the name 'album' likely derives) into a more deliberate artistic statement. The *OED* dates to 1904 an instance of 'album' describing the containers holding multiple records that comprised a longer classical work (like an opera). The boxes opened like a book with sequential 'leaves' that held individual records which one could flip through like a photo album. Though still a novelty in early rock and pop, this curatorial impulse was not a new development. Jazz musicians conceptualized their albums early on: Frank Sinatra's *In the Wee Small Hours* (1955) and its intimacy of sound explores themes of loneliness and late-night desolation; the modal arrangements of Miles Davis's *Kind of Blue* (1959) exhibit sonic and thematic coherence typical of instrumental jazz albums; Ray Charles' *Modern Sounds in Country and Western Music* (1962) builds on the theme of crossing over, drawing unity from the source material it transforms and, indeed, from the process of transformation itself. Dylan's important contribution to this legacy combines the curatorial instinct of these earlier albums with his own generative role not just as performer, but as a songwriter working at the nexus of words and music. Whereas the album always bore narrative potential as a genre, Dylan's intervention brings new immediacy. His songs amplify the temporal matrix of word and music, composition and performance, textuality and phenomenology – even of passing time and immutability – that an album performs. In this way Bob Dylan albums create complex narratives that gesture well beyond their material (and now digital) limits, even as such limits contain and shape the stories that they generate. In doing so, they extend and innovate the album form as a limited and discrete artefact with a taste for the infinite.

One of Dylan's primary interventions in the album form is the significance he ascribes to the final song. Again, he did not create such a convention wholesale, yet his emphasis upon these 'closers' and on the sheer quality of the songs themselves perfects this tendency. The album closer draws on legacies of the encore, the swansong, even the recounting of a story's moral at the end of a telling that codifies what an auditor has heard, read, experienced and so forth, orienting it toward 'greater' purposes, for other times and places. Customs of the end include unmasking, revelation, peripeteia, apocalypse, suggestions of continuity (the cliffhanger, for instance) that gesture to the ongoing-ness of a narrative's themes beyond the bounded artefact that frames it. The end calls forth a new beginning.

3. The sense of an ending

Frank Kermode argues that human beings possess 'a need in the moment of existence to belong, to be related to a beginning and an end' (Kermode 2000: 4).

This is the case because people are born in the middle of things, *in medias res* – the world has already begun; likewise they die *in mediis rebus*, meaning the world proceeds in their absence, 'and to make sense of their span they need fictive concords with origins and ends, such as give meaning to lives and poems. The end they imagine will reflect their irreducibly intermediary preoccupations. They fear it, ... [because] the End is a figure for their own deaths' (Kermode 2000: 7). We do not remember being born into a world that we did not create, and we shall never know what it means to die, to be annihilated from a world that proceeds in our unknowing absence. Humans possess but a finite span of time that means the world to us. We long to ascribe significance that exceeds experience to this patch of eternity, to write ourselves into some grander temporal frame. Kermode ascribes this reality to a perspective of time that dates back through Augustine to Aristotle. In this way Kermode anticipates Ricœur (1984), which theorizes this conjunction of narrative and 'kairotic' time to good effect.

Kermode is concerned with the relationship between chronological time (also known as linear or narrative time) and kairotic time (irruptive time or the time of the 'stolen moment'). Albums function in narrative time. We place the needle on the record, hit play on the cassette, CD, or streaming platform and the text moves chronologically, as on a timeline, from beginning to end as the needle traces the groove, the tape unspools, or the digital counters reflect the elapsed time. Along the way, a trajectory unfolds in narrative time. It moves meaningfully from song to song, beginning to end, and in the process narrates a representative 'story'. Some of these stories may seem clear, as *Blood on the Tracks* traces the evolving stages in the erosion of a romantic relationship.[3] In other cases the narrative proves more impressionistic or oblique. What matters most is the passing of time, over time, that an album's narrative time generates. The deliberate procession from 'Like a Rolling Stone' to 'Desolation Row' that constitutes *Highway 61 Revisited* (1965), from 'Duquesne Whistle' to 'Roll on John' that generates *Tempest* (2012), in fact emplots these trajectories.

Still, narrative time is not the only way that human beings experience time. At moments we may recognize irruptions of meaning that disrupt the rote chronology of listening. A phrase, a word, a chord – the sedimentary deposit of all of these – offers fleeting, yet real opportunities for continual meaning-making through the excavation of cultural allusions and their sonic adjuncts. In this way,

---

[3] Among numerous readings of *Blood on the Tracks*, Ben Burrell's five-part podcast that traces the trajectory of this narrative across the album, in particular, and pays careful attention to the album form more generally, is especially commendable (Burrell 2018).

if narrative time offers a horizontal trajectory along an x-axis, a timeline of sorts, then kairotic time irrupts vertically as if along a y-axis while narrative time proceeds. Consider 'Ballad of a Thin Man' on *Highway 61 Revisited* (Dylan 1965). The song lasts nearly six minutes as part of the album's roughly fifty-two-minute (narrative) running time. Simultaneously, 'Ballad of a Thin Man' provides arresting kairotic juxtapositions: words invoking 'F. Scott Fitzgerald's books' or carnivalesque homoeroticism sung over-top a Ray Charles piano riff and ghostly organ. It stacks layers of verbal and musical signification that emerge for an instant and then dissipate, yet are cumulatively inflected by and through other sequential kairotic moments on *Highway 61*'s narrative timeline: Napoleon in Rags, Yahweh and Abraham on a highway that bisects the USA alongside the Mississippi River, Ma Rainey and Beethoven, this Graveyard Woman, Cinderella's Bette Davis style, and a slew of purloined blues licks. These momentary irruptions, vertically articulated along a horizontal trajectory, conflating musical and lyrical meaning and allusion, represent kairotic time. Such irruptions require listeners to draw on and juxtapose imaginary pasts in order to innovate meaning that speaks to a future they may never see – the far country, an eternity beyond human ken.

This significance of kairotic time for filling in this narrative timeline proves true of human lives as well, Kermode suggests. This is why stories, albums, and plays all remain so compelling: they model the experience of life, which is simultaneously fleeting and very long. No album runs forever, just as our lives prove finite. The album as a narrative genre, then, exemplifies the shape of a human life – a 'middle' carved out of the beginning and the end, a narrative timeline of kairotic irruption. It is through such forms that human beings experience the end of things – a rehearsal for death and an emblem of the desire for something so bounded and finite to bear both internal cohesion and eternal significance. An album's final song, then, addresses eternity. It imposes kairotic finitude, providing encapsulation, a moral, or internal coherence, while also pointing to the ongoing-ness of things, a sense of futurity.

4. A twenty-first-century case study: 'Ain't Talkin''

4.1 Dylan's late eschatology

We have noted that Bob Dylan's twenty-first century arguably begins with the release of *Time Out of Mind*. A latter-day invocation of things past, the album signals an important shift in Dylan's late style. It was heralded at the time as a return to form – indeed, Dylan's best album in a decade or more – because of its clear reliance on American vernacular musical forms and lexicons. An added benefit was Dylan's renewed commitment to recording 'live' in studio. *Time Out of Mind* represented a 'new' tack only for critics and fans unfamiliar with his work in the previous decade or so. Albums like *World Gone Wrong* (1993) and *Good as I Been to You* (1992) present examples of the source material that Dylan mines in *Time Out of Mind* and later twenty-first-century work. Similarly, we should recognize a sonic link between *Time Out of Mind* and *Oh Mercy* (1989) – both of which were produced by Daniel Lanois. The point of periodizing Dylan's long twenty-first century as beginning with *Time Out of Mind* is not to declare a clean break from the past, but rather a clear arrival at the general mode that would characterize and shape Dylan's output (and broader performative sensibility – consider the stage costumes, the moustache, the relative proliferation of interviews and media accessibility) in the new century. In this way *Time Out of Mind* gives the appearance of a return to form. All of the former elements seem to be in place.

At the same time, the power generated by the return to these former elements stems from a noticeably different disposition. Nearly a quarter-century since the release of *Time Out of Mind*, it has become clear that the album inaugurates a period in Dylan's career that is obsessed with the category of time. Early reviewers proved quick to note that the album seemed to dwell upon questions of mortality – an interpretation bolstered in the wake of Dylan's own serious illness in the months before the album's release (but after it was recorded). Past his mid-fifties, the *enfant terrible* of 1960s youth culture was growing aware of his age, the story went, newly cognizant that his own end loomed nearer than his beginning. Accordingly, this central paradox of the album's reception sees Dylan returning to his original source material yet reshaping it with a signal difference that hinges on the identity of time and Dylan's relationship to it. 1960s Dylan represents an agent of changing times – he invokes this change, calls it into being (a slant version of the 'voice of a generation' moniker). He deploys American vernacular music in order to trouble, displace, and effectively to protest post-war complacency through an appeal to a radical understanding of these forms. Citing 'traditional music', staking claim to a usable past, young Dylan emphasizes a strangeness in the older vernacular songs that belied attempts to regiment and enforce conformity on US culture in its global contexts. It is fascinating to recall Dylan's mid-sixties comments on 'traditional' music as the antidote to protest, to topicality:

> Traditional music is based on hexagrams. It is based on legends, Bibles, plagues, and it revolves around vegetables and death ... All those songs about roses growing out of people's brains and lovers who are really geese and swans that turn into angels – they're not going to die. Songs like "Which Side Are You On?" ... They're not folk music songs; they're political songs. They're *already* dead.
>
> quoted in Marcus 2011: 110

'Traditional' music fostered the resistance to such regulatory standardization.

The persona of *Time Out of Mind* no longer registers as the firebrand unleashing American vernacular forms and tropes to challenge post-war cultural atrophy while auguring changing times. Conversely, this twenty-first-century iteration deploys vernacular forms and tropes to discipline and contain the excesses of millennial dread, to invoke a need for holding it all together at this late hour 'when things disintegrate' ('Can't Wait', Dylan 1997). Questions of agency loom prominently in this transformation. Whereas 1960s Dylan enacts change, imposes uncertainty, challenges cultural formalities, the twenty-first-century material feels more eager to manage it. Musical and lyrical structures bring form to experience, as does the attempt to conflate past, present and future. There remains something conservative about drawing on past or 'traditional' sources to stave off uncertainty – at least in theory, but such a diagnosis only goes so far. Dylan's willingness to remain with this material bespeaks another possibility that comes to life especially in *"Love and Theft"* and *Modern Times*, the two albums that follow *Time Out of Mind*.

4.2 'The Last Outback at the World's End'

The joke of naming an album *Modern Times* in 2006 is that there is nothing 'modern' or new about doing so. The title effectively calls back to Charlie Chaplin's 1933 film of the same name. The terms of this joke also make sense of what Dylan achieves with *Modern Times*. Populated by eight-bar and twelve-bar blues songs, a torch ballad, a couple of ambitious Tin Pan Alley knock-offs and many other recognizable figures, forms and sounds, the album stakes a claim for the presence of the past. Whereas this process proves irruptively jarring with an album like *Highway 61*, it feels more reassuring by 2006. In an age of organized blues tours of the Mississippi Delta and the nostalgia of blues clubs on the (tourist-friendly) North Side of Chicago that offer the simulacrum of a mid-century juke joint, the fact that Dylan comes close to reproducing wholesale (attributed to his own name) three extant and recognizable blues songs – 'Someday Baby', 'Rollin' and Tumblin'' and 'The Levee's Gonna Break' (Dylan 2006) – should come as little surprise. They have become part of the furniture, an old man's recitations of things past.

On another reading we might argue that Dylan is after something more subtle. An eerie accident of twenty-first-century Dylan's output saw the album *"Love and Theft"* released on 11 September 2001, meaning that many listeners first heard the album with an eye (or ear) tuned to ongoing news reports of that day's terror attacks in New York, Washington and Pennsylvania. Songs like 'Lonesome Day Blues' and 'High Water (for Charley Patton)' (Dylan 2001) seemed oddly prescient, as if Dylan was not imposing an old, weird perspective on contemporary American reality but, rather, excavating the present from this 'old, weird' sensibility. In this way, the twenty-first-century material functions as an act of recovery, an anachronism that exposes the lie that there is anything new under the sun. Another song in which Dylan achieves this excavation of present or 'modern' reality from more traditional forms is 'Workingman's Blues #2' (Dylan 2006), which has been credited with predicting the global financial crisis of 2008 (Deacon 2012: 102). In some ways, of course, this all qualifies as a fortune-telling act: say enough things vaguely and one is bound to hit close to a mark. At the same time there remains a diagnostic sensibility in Dylan's late return to these vernacular sources. They have shifted in more than a half-century from corrective to diagnostic.

Tracking the narrative dimensions of *Modern Times*, the album begins on a mountain and ends in a garden. An arresting tension appears in the first song, 'Thunder on the Mountain' which, following a 'timeless' first verse mentioning 'fires on the moon' and God's trombone, telescopes in with a contemporary reference to Alicia Keys (Dylan 2006). The effect proves disorienting in the midst of Dylan's eight-bar blues and other lyrics that feel as though they were describing nineteenth-century America ('All the ladies in Washington are scrambling to get out of town'). This play on time and simultaneity reflects Dylan's ongoing obsession as well as a willingness to shift things around in the process.

Time remains a primary concern across the album's narrative trajectory. 'Rollin' and Tumblin'' points to the anxieties of an interminable night. 'When the Deal Goes Down' announces fealty until death. 'Someday Baby' looks to a conditional future while 'Beyond the Horizon' stretches the realms of possibility. 'Nettie Moore' demarcates the position of the singer's happiness as 'o'er' (Dylan 2006). Time undergoes a gamut of permutations on *Modern Times*. In this way our aim here has less to do with offering a stable or specific interpretation of the album's middle – in no small way because such an interpretation of the middle is likely to change upon reaching the end, and in the way that the end should then recast the beginning and middle for future encounters. For this reason, we now proceed directly to 'Ain't Talkin'' (Dylan 2006) and its eschatological orientation – in this case a representation, quite literally, of the end of the world drawn from older (indeed biblical) sources.

'Ain't Talkin'' begins in a garden redolent of mystical powers, conjuring (among other gardens) Eden and Gethsemane. These Biblical instances include the flying wheels of Ezekiel's vision of the four-faced angels and Jesus's mandates of neighbour love and the Golden Rule. The singer walks without talking through a landscape that appears vacant or abandoned. Yet it also groans with concealed malevolence – wealth, power, unseen enemies and agents who attack the singer from out of nowhere (Dylan 2006). A chorus follows every single quatrain verse in which lines one and three repeat with variations in lines two and four. The repetition both of and within these choruses keeps the singer and listener on the lookout for some kind of secret, constantly looking back over his shoulder.

The final verse circles back around to replicate the first, with a slight modification that moves the singer's walk in the same garden from night to day. After the singer goes into the garden, trenchantly we find an extended Biblical allusion to the end of the Gospel of Mark in this address: 'Excuse me, ma'am, I beg your pardon / There's no one here, the gardener is gone' (Dylan 2006). The whole quatrain reframes this episode from the end of Mark's Gospel, when the women are informed by a 'young man' that Jesus's body is gone (Mk 16.5). Here is the episode in full:

> And he saith unto them, Be not affrighted: Ye seek Jesus of Nazareth, which was crucified: he is risen; he is not here: behold the place where they laid him. But go your way, tell his disciples and Peter that he goeth before you into Galilee: there shall ye see him, as he said unto you. And they went out quickly, and fled from the sepulchre; for they trembled and were amazed: neither said they any thing to any *man*; for they were afraid.
>
> Mk 16.6–8 [KJV]

The KJV in fact has more following verse 8, but that section has long been understood as an addition to the original text that attempts to clarify or more stringently define a remarkably ambiguous conclusion, one characterized by fear and irresolution (Metzger 2005: 123). Dylan's refrain, sung after the verses (with variations in each iteration) brings the listener into the first-person perspective of one fleeing the sepulchre, with the burning and desire reflecting end-times anxiety (Dylan 2006). At the end of the world, one retreats into a final outback or wilderness. The words leave the action (and the listener) suspended, unsettled, in the midst of things.

While 'Ain't Talkin'' may appear, on the basis of the words alone, to leave things unresolved, a fascinating musical cue suggests otherwise (or at least muddies the waters). As the final refrain ends, the band resurrects a motif heard earlier in the song – alternating A minor and D minor chords. In this instance, however, and unlike the earlier deployments of this musical motif, the band arrives on the tonic A minor, feigning a concluding chord that sustains the mystery and anxiety of the song. This ending proves false when, several seconds later, they resolve the A minor to A major – a brighter, 'cheerier' chord that, if nothing else, seems to melt the anxiety away into a note of hope (Dylan 2006). Perhaps other listeners will hear this resolution differently. What fascinates me about this example, however, is the way that the false ending – blending as it does into the resolution – seems to mirror the later additions to the end of the Gospel of Mark. It provides a musical augmentation that, in a way words alone cannot do, shifts the tone of the song and the album's eschaton entirely into something else.

A second dimension of this sense of an ending comes when we consider that such an ending reflects (or affects) the experience of listening to the album again. If we take this closing motif of A minor → D minor → A minor → A major, we find something set up nicely for the resurrection of the first song, 'Thunder on the Mountain' (Dylan 2006). Namely, it also begins with a cadence motif of two chords that are, like A minor and D minor, one fourth apart. In this instance the opening chord of *Modern Times* is an E major. This registers as a false start itself, in a manner of speaking, because the song's key is B. So the opening motif goes E → B → E → B, from dominant to tonic, where the accompaniment begins to gallop and the singing begins (it should be noted that this is a descending fourth, whereas 'Ain't Talkin'' ends with an ascending fourth). Separately we might argue that nothing unusual is in play here. Chords are chords and they progress. Taken in tandem, however, this recurring cadence of fourths ties together beginning and end in a remarkable way, pointing to a recursiveness between end and beginning – an eternal return.

One last point about how the end of *Modern Times* then influences later moments of listening: if we consider the end to mirror the anxious moment when the women discover what becomes the resurrection (via the absence of

Jesus's body), then one reading would have us return to the mountain and consider various Gospel mountains. One possibility would be the Transfiguration, which takes place on an unnamed mountain in Mt. 17, Mk 9 and Lk. 9. Jesus and his disciples ascend the mountain, converse with Moses and Elijah, and the disciples notice that Jesus begins to shine. They want to stay but Jesus demands that they need to go down from the mountain, often understood as going into the world to do the work that was set out for him (rather than resting on his laurels in glory). If this correspondence works out, the 'middle' of *Modern Times* would correspond with Jesus's time in the world as healer, teacher and political provocateur. Another possibility for interpreting the mountain, especially given the clear correspondences between the end of 'Ain't Talkin'' and the Gospel of Mark, is that it is the Mount of Olives – the location of the Garden of Gethsemane. It is here where Jesus brings a number of disciples on the night he is betrayed and arrested. Like the singer, Jesus weeps. The invocation of the Golden Rule and neighbour love (mentioned earlier) points to Jesus's example. In this way, we might consider the return to the mountain implied by a later listening to *Modern Times* to establish a narrative and temporal boundary of the album that moves from the Transfiguration mountain or the Mount of Olives to that anxious moment when the resurrection hangs in the balance. And the body may well have simply been stolen, rather than resurrected – though the latter is implied by the resolution from A minor to A major as the album's true eschaton and 'last word'.

5. Older than that now

The point of these interpretations is not to denominate *Modern Times* as a Christian narrative, per se. This reading would bear that conclusion as one among several, but it need not register as an exclusive one. What fascinates me more fully is what this process of reading/listening, of paying close attention to the sense of an ending in Dylan's albums – his eschatology – reveals about notions of time, narrative and eschatology itself in his twenty-first-century work. The Biblical material, much like the 'traditional' musical forms and songs, provides a structural dimension through which certain disorienting realities of the present find grounding and structure. Unlike – indeed, obverse to – the way Dylan in the mid-1960s sought to upset, ambiguate, to introduce a sense of chaos to a world embodied by the likes of Mr Jones in 'Ballad of a Thin Man',

Dylan's late style invokes structure, excavating it from the indeterminacy of modern times. It uncovers recognizable narrative and cultural templates to make sense where once he might have sought to defy it. This is not necessarily better or worse, to my mind, than the earlier mode. But it is a distinction worth considering. In the twenty-first-century period of his career, beginning with or around the release of *Time Out of Mind* in 1997, Dylan's obsession with time leads him to attend less to insisting upon *kairos* and more to emphasize the steady progression of narrative time.

A number of questions remain, and surely new ones have emerged over the course of this chapter. What matters most is recognizing and pursuing further implications of this transition in the twenty-first-century corpus – a body of work that continues to grow (and impressively so). Furthermore, understanding the album as a narrative genre, while fruitful for a specific eschatological circumstance here, provides a viable template for other Dylan albums and their own textual problems. Attending to the album as generating narrative not solely through words (or solely through music either, for that matter) encourages a truer sense of the songs that contribute to the broader trajectory of their albums, to the ways that their integrity of words and music – one of Dylan's remarkable strengths – augment and subvert one another for greater effect than either could achieve alone.

References

Burrell, B. (2018), 'Episode 6: *Blood on the Tracks*' [Podcast], *Bob Dylan: Album by Album*. Available online: www.bobdylanpodcast.com (accessed 10 April 2020).
Charters, S. (1975), *The Country Blues: Roots of Jazz*, New York: DaCapo.
Cone, J. H. ([1972] 1992), *The Spirituals and the Blues*, Maryknoll, NY: Orbis.
Deacon, D. (2012), 'Hello to All That: "Credit Crunches", "Great Depressions" and Journalistic Retrojection', in E. Keightley (ed.), *Time, Media, Modernity*, 102–22, New York: Palgrave.
Dylan, B. (1965), *Highway 61 Revisited* [Album], USA: Columbia Records.
Dylan, B. (1997), *Time Out of Mind* [Album], USA: Columbia Records.
Dylan, B. (2001), *"Love and Theft"* [Album], USA: Columbia Records.
Dylan, B. (2006), *Modern Times* [Album], USA: Columbia Records.
Dylan, B. (2014), *The Lyrics: Since 1962*, L. Nemrow, J. Nemrow and C. Ricks (eds), New York: Simon and Schuster.
Dylan, B. (2017), 'Nobel Lecture', *The Nobel Prize* website. Available online: www.nobelprize.org/prizes/literature/2016/dylan/lecture/ (accessed 3 April 2020).
Dylan, B. (2020), *Rough and Rowdy Ways* [Album], USA: Columbia Records.

Hentoff, N. (1964), 'Bob Dylan, The Wanderer', *The New Yorker*, 16 October. Available online: www.newyorker.com/magazine/1964/10/24/the-crackin-shakin-breakin-sounds (accessed 10 April 2020).

Kaminsky, P. (1992), 'The Popular Album as Song Cycle: Paul Simon's *Still Crazy After All These Years*', *College Music Symposium*, 32: 38–54. Available online: https://symposium.music.org/index.php/32/item/2090-the-popular-album-as-song-cycle-paul-simons-still-crazy-after-all-these-years.

Kermode, F. ([1966] 2000), *The Sense of an Ending*, Oxford: Oxford University Press.

Marcus, G. (2001), 'Music; Sometimes He Talks Crazy, Crazy Like a Song', *New York Times*, 2 September. Available online: www.nytimes.com/2001/09/02/arts/music-sometimes-he-talks-crazy-crazy-like-a-song.html (accessed 10 April 2020).

Marcus, G. (2011), *The Old, Weird America: The World of Bob Dylan's Basement Tapes*, New York: Picador.

Marzorati, G. (1998), 'How the Big Album Got Played Out', *New York Times Magazine*, 22 February. Available online: www.nytimes.com/1998/02/22/magazine/how-the-album-got-played-out.html (accessed 10 April 2020).

Metzger, B. (2005), *A Textual Commentary on the Greek New Testament*, 2nd edn, Peabody, MA: Hendrickson.

Oliver, P. (1969), *The Story of the Blues*, Boston: Northeastern University Press.

Oswinski, B. (2018), 'The Music Album Is Dead, But Not Everyone's Accepted It Yet', *Forbes*, 10 March. Available online: www.forbes.com/sites/bobbyowsinski/2018/03/10/album-dead/#3df98cc16986 (accessed 10 April 2020).

Ricks, C. (2005), *Dylan's Visions of Sin*, New York: Ecco.

Ricœur, P (1984), *Time and Narrative, Volume 1*, trans. K. McLaughlin and D. Pellauer, Chicago: Chicago University Press.

Shuker, R. (2017), *Popular Music: The Key Concepts*, 4th edn, New York: Routledge.

Wilentz, S. (2011), *Bob Dylan in America*, New York: Anchor.

11

'No Success Like Failure'? Dylan's Awards, from Princeton to the Nobel

Denis Feignier

For Jack Lang and Elliott Mintz

The very idea of *honouring* Bob Dylan might appear to be a bold one, given that neither his vision of the world (as we might imagine it), nor his personal temperament would lead us to expect him to be much interested in receiving public honours. He has, however, accepted an honorary doctorate from Princeton University, the title of *Commandeur des Arts et des Lettres* in France, the Medal of Freedom from Barack Obama and the Nobel Prize in Literature, to name but four.

'They are planting stories in the press', Dylan sang in 'Idiot Wind' (Dylan 1975). On almost every occasion, the announcement of the honour elicited a deluge of differing reactions and commentaries: often negative towards, if not outraged at, the idea of officially honouring Bob Dylan. The implication was that he should not accept. Some argued that Bob Dylan did not deserve the award: why him? Why not someone else? Some argued that the award did not deserve Bob Dylan, suspecting the authorities of attempting to use him to boost their own reputations. Others simply argued that no award can be deserved – that it is merely a trick, and the very idea of it should be rejected.

In 1990, when I was working for French Minister of Culture Jack Lang, I had the privilege of being closely involved in the entire process of offering Bob Dylan an official award. My experience of this ongoing display of 'images and distorted facts' ('Idiot Wind', Dylan 1975) was what inspired me to write about this controversial topic now, and to try to put my personal experience in perspective with the comparable circumstances of others.

The topic I would therefore like to explore is not whether Bob Dylan deserves these official marks of recognition or not, but how they are offered, and how he responds to them.

When it comes to honours and awards, the usual recommendation given in France is: 'Don't ask for them; don't refuse them; don't show them off',[1] and we might wonder why Dylan appears to accede to this received wisdom so remarkably well. Perhaps the answer lies in the simple coherence between the sense of what is fair or unfair expressed in Dylan's works themselves, as well as in the usual attitude of the recipient.

1. Don't ask for honours: 'I let the songs fly, and people respond' (Gundersen 1997: 52)

The first point is that Dylan asked for nothing. As early as 1965, he said about his growing fame: 'I just haven't really struggled for that. It happened, you know? It happened like anything else happens. Just a happening' (Dylan 1965). In 1970, in Princeton, he added: 'Fine, I didn't ask for it in the first place' (David Crosby quoted in Heylin 2000: 321). Why, then, would we want to 'honour Bob Dylan'?

In 1970, Princeton University invited Dylan to receive an honorary doctorate of music, for having expressed, through his music, 'the disturbed and concerned conscience of young America' (Armstrong 2015). During the twenty years that followed, no further official awards were offered to him. France was the next country, in 1989, to bestow upon him the second of what was to become a long list of honours.

Let us examine the motivations behind some of these awards. Bill Clinton, speaking at the Kennedy Center in 1997, believed that Dylan 'probably had more impact on people of [his] generation than any other artist' (Lyman 1997). In 2000 Dylan was awarded the Polar Music Prize. The prize's press material described his influence in these terms:

> Bob Dylan's ability to combine poetry, harmony and melody in a meaningful, often provocative context, has captivated millions in all age groups, and in most cultures and societies. Through his modest, persuasive musical approach, he has

---

[1] People interested in matters of protocol in France will find useful answers in A. Damien's *L'art et la manière de porter les décorations* (Art Lys, 1994) and J. Gandouin's *Guide du protocole et des usages* (Stock, 1972).

demonstrated an impressive ability to question the most determined political forces, to fight all forms of prejudice, and to offer unflinching support for the less fortunate. Even those who might not have shared his views would find it impossible to argue against Bob Dylan's musical and poetic brilliance.

Polar Prize n.d.

In the same vein, the citation for the Prince of Asturias Award in 2007 described Dylan as 'a living legend in the history of popular music and a guiding light for a generation that dreamt to change the world. [W]ith an austere manner and profound messages, [he] combine[s] music and poetry in an oeuvre that has gathered a large following and which determines the sentimental education of many millions of people' (Príncipe de Asturias n.d.).[2]

A year later, Oxford Professor of Poetry Sir Christopher Ricks expressed his opinion about Dylan's Pulitzer Prize. As reported in *The New York Times*, Ricks explained:

> The Pulitzer might be an appropriate prize if it is meant to acknowledge Mr Dylan as a poet in the sense of a visionary or paradigmatic seer, ... but not if it is given in its traditional spirit as a recognition of writing or composition. It tugs back at the idea that his accomplishment can be measured purely on the page, ... which it can't even remotely be.

Itzkoff 2008

In fact, the Prize was justified by Dylan's 'profound impact on popular music and American culture, marked by lyrical compositions of extraordinary poetic power' (Pulitzer 2008).

The Presidential Medal of Freedom, the highest civilian award in the United States, 'is presented to individuals who have made significant contributions to the security or national interests of the United States, to world peace, or to cultural or other significant public or private endeavors'. It was presented to Bob Dylan in 2012, and his name appears – in distinguished company – alongside Madeleine Albright and Toni Morrison, amongst others. The citation said:

> Bob Dylan is one of the most influential American musicians of the 20th century. Releasing his first album in 1962, his work influenced the civil rights movement of the 1960s and has had significant impact on American culture over the past

---

[2] My translation from Spanish: 'Mito viviente en la historia de la música popular y faro de una generación que tuvo el sueño de cambiar el mundo; austero en las formas y profundo en los mensajes, Dylan conjuga la canción y la poesía en una obra que crea escuela y determina la educación sentimental de muchos millones de personas.'

five decades. He has won 11 Grammys, including a lifetime achievement award. He has written more than 600 songs, and his songs have been recorded more than 3,000 times by other artists.

Presidential Medal n.d.

In 2013, the American Academy of Arts and Letters explored more specifically the poetical area, stating that '[f]or more than 50 years, defying categorization in a culture beguiled by categories, Bob Dylan has probed and prodded our psyches, recording and then changing our world and our lives through poetry made manifest in song – creating relationships that we never imagined could exist between words, emotions and ideas' (Clarke 2013).

The pinnacle of Bob Dylan's awards must surely be his Nobel Prize in Literature in 2016 – not only recognizing his general artistic impact, but also focusing upon his literary and poetic talents. Horace Engdahl, a member of the Swedish Academy and the representative of the Nobel Committee for Literature, justified the decision as follows: 'In the most unlikely setting of all – the commercial gramophone record – he gave back to the language of poetry its elevated style, lost since the Romantics. Not to sing of eternities, but to speak of what was happening around us. As if the oracle of Delphi were reading the evening news' (Engdahl 2016).

Put briefly, from 1970 to today, Dylan has received awards for 'the influence and outstanding beauties of his works' (Engdahl 2016). As we can see, the awarding bodies do not have suspect intentions towards the recipient, and there seems to be no attempt at 'using' him: '"Did you think that Carter might have been using you by inviting you there?" "No, ... he just wanted to check me out"' (Cott 2017: 245). There is nothing as dubious as Ronnie Gilbert's statement, in Newport in 1965, telling the crowd attending the Festival to take Dylan because they knew him and he was theirs (Dylan 2004: 115). Nobody is supposed to *own* Bob Dylan; offering him an award is not an attempt to gain a political or other benefit. Although it may appear incredible to some commentators, it appears to be correct to say that the 'Dylan file' has not been treated so very differently from that of other laureates by the authorities giving awards. That being the case, I cannot help but think that the driving force behind many cases of official recognition has been the influence of a particular Dylan fan. For evidence of this, we need only to hear the way in which Horace Engdahl speaks of Bob Dylan: those who attended his Paris lecture about Dylan's Nobel Prize for the December 2016 event *La Saison des Nobels* can testify to this.

In real terms, how does this come about? Having experienced the process personally, I can offer the example of what happened in Paris in 1990, when Bob Dylan was made a *Commandeur des Arts et des Lettres*. This honour recognizes 'people who have distinguished themselves through their artistic or literary creations or for their contribution to arts or literature in France or overseas' (Arts et Lettres, n.d.).[3] For Jack Lang, the French Minister of Culture who proposed Bob Dylan, it was a wish to underline the link between France and a foreign artist of major importance, who was both influential *in* France and influenced *by* France. As it was the first official honour given to Dylan since Princeton twenty years previously, the minister took special precautions to avoid any potential snub from Dylan. Having established contact with the artist's representatives in June 1989, it was then actually fairly straightforward to obtain an agreement in principle, by evoking examples of other American artists who had received the honour, such as Elizabeth Taylor, Ella Fitzgerald, Dizzy Gillespie and Charles Schultz. This agreement, made orally, was confidential. There was no press release. A few months later, in January 1990, in a similarly informal fashion, the arrangements were made for an official award ceremony. Dylan's agent, Elliott Mintz, said quite simply, two days before the ceremony was due to take place: 'Mr Dylan said "Yeah"'[4] – and only then were we able to invite guests and inform the media.

2. Don't refuse them: 'Well, it's always been my nature to take chances' ('Angelina', Dylan 1991)

Bob Dylan does agree to honours, but in a straightforward way. Interviewed in 1997, he explained: 'Such honors are unexpected and unsolicited, and I'm not nonchalant about it, because it really does matter; I am very appreciative' (Gundersen 1997). Because he thinks it is a serious matter, rather than the polite indifference expected by some, he runs the risk and chooses to give a discreet acceptance (naturally, he may have refused some offers we do not know about).

---

[3] My translation from French: 'les personnes qui se sont distinguées par leurs créations dans le domaine artistique ou littéraire ou par la contribution au rayonnement qu'elles ont apportée au rayonnement des Arts et des Lettres en France et dans le monde.'
[4] Elliott Mintz, phone call to the author, Sunday 28 January 1990 at 1.15 am. The ceremony took place on Tuesday 30 January at 6 pm.

'Alright, I'll take a chance', Dylan sang in 'Is Your Love in Vain?' Yet the Tom Paine Award ceremony, held on 13 December 1963 – Dylan's first official award, offered by the Emergency Civil Liberties Union (ECLU) – turned into a fiasco, Dylan's acceptance speech being awkward and inappropriate (Heylin 2000: 137). This experience might have taught him early on to be more cautious in such circumstances – 'I've had good and bad accolades', Dylan said in an interview with *The Sun Sentinel* (Dolen 1995) – comparable to the hostility of certain members of the audience when he 'turned electric' or, later, when he became a born-again Christian. Several years later, the so-called 'China controversy' became an example of the way things can be twisted by inaccurate reporting. Dylan had to deny publicly that it was the Chinese government who had made the decision as to which songs were allowed to appear on the set-list of his concert in Beijing (Dylan 2011). In 2013, the French media took great interest in the decision of the French government to make Bob Dylan a *Chevalier de la Légion d'Honneur*, and it developed into a political issue because some politicians were extremely critical of the decision. Hence Dylan's circumspection: in order to avoid the risk of ridicule, the circumstances must be properly understood by the public – and this is not always the case. The deal appears to be: accept the honour and, if necessary, certain formalities that go along with it, but nothing more.

In any case, this reticence seems to be a well-established character trait of his. We might recall an exchange during the San Francisco KQED television press conference in December 1965: '"Mr Dylan, you seem very reluctant to talk about the fact that you're a popular entertainer – a most popular entertainer." "Well, what do you want me to say? ...You want me to jump up and say "Hallelujah!" – and crash the cameras or do something weird?"' (Cott 2017: 78). In 1970, he went to Princeton and agreed to wear the gown, but not the cap, and remained silent (Heylin 2000: 321). Later, in 'Day of the Locusts', an unusually autobiographical song referring to his Princeton degree, he sang: 'There was little to say, there was no conversation' (Dylan 1970), and in *Chronicles, Volume One* he merely writes that the ceremony 'had been a weird adventure' (Dylan 2004: 132). In 2000, for the Polar Music Prize awarded to him by the King of Sweden, he attended the ceremony but gave no speech. And in 2012, in Washington, from behind dark glasses, he accepted his award from President Obama with a simple 'Thanks, man', according to the account of a stunned Toni Morrison (Busnel 2016: 45).

Coming from such a public figure, this 'no comment' attitude has often been misunderstood and criticized. The Nobel controversy is the most recent and significant example. On 13 October 2016, the world was informed by the Nobel Committee that Bob Dylan was being offered the Nobel Prize in Literature. The ensuing (apparent) silence of the recipient was to start a new controversy. In fact, Dylan neither gave a press conference nor published any statement to his audience about his acceptance of the Nobel Prize in Literature. What was even more badly received was that he snubbed the official Nobel Banquet on 10 December. The Banquet speech written by Dylan and delivered for the occasion by the US Ambassador to Sweden, Azita Raji, is a carefully crafted piece of work, in which Dylan says how proud he is to be distinguished in this way (Dylan 2016). A few days later, on 14 December, Horace Engdahl, a member of the Nobel Committee and the person who reported the Dylan candidacy, informed the audience at a lecture he gave in Paris that a meeting with Bob Dylan might happen in Stockholm in early April 2017.[5] Despite this, during Spring 2017 the newspapers continued to comment on Dylan's supposed lack of education and manners. On 2 April 2017, *The Guardian* wrote: 'After months of uncertainty and controversy, Bob Dylan finally accepted the 2016 Nobel Prize in Literature' (Agence France Press 2016). In fact he had done so several months earlier. Maybe part of this uncertainty can be explained by the expectation that Dylan would give an official Nobel Lecture, as requested by the Nobel rules, but the official Nobel Lecture by Dylan was to be submitted, on time, to the Nobel Academy on 5 June.

Of course, Bob Dylan may not appear to be very talkative, but some of his behaviour can be read as a sign of being appropriately proud – or at least appreciative – of these honours: such might be the case with the Oscar he won for 'Things Have Changed' featured in the film *Wonder Boys* (2000) – the golden statuette now appearing on stage during his concerts.

Even more clearly, Dylan has referred to his appreciation for honours that have been awarded him on at least three occasions. In Paris, on 30 January 1990, he simply said, in French: 'Merci beaucoup, de tout mon coeur, pour l'honneur que vous me faites, qui me touche énormément' (Dobbels 1990: 41).[6] Several months later, he completed his acceptance speech in Brisbane, Australia: '[t]hat was a heavy thing, being given an award by a French Government, especially in the area of creativity, you know, because of the French influence on my own stuff' (Coupe

---

[5] Horace Engdahl, 'Le Printemps des Nobels', Paris, 14 December 2016.
[6] 'Thank you so much, with all my heart, for this honour, for which I am enormously grateful'. See also Roques 1990.

1992: 33). He knew very well why he had accepted the honour, and what he was thankful for. Likewise, when he was named MusiCares Person of Year on 6 February 2015, he made, to the audience's delighted surprise, a more effusive acceptance speech, paying a lengthy homage to the greats who had preceded him (Dylan 2015). Finally, in 2016, he addressed the Nobel Academy briefly, but with feeling: 'Not once have I ever had the time to ask myself, "Are my songs literature?" So, I do thank the Swedish Academy, both for taking the time to consider that very question, and, ultimately, for providing such a wonderful answer' (Dylan 2016). He later expanded on this theme during his 2017 official Nobel Lecture (Dylan 2017), and I will say more about this later.

In my opinion, Dylan put it in the clearest possible way in November 2013, in his acceptance speech to the French Minister of Culture, Aurélie Filipetti, who had just given him the *Croix de Chevalier de la Légion d'Honneur*: 'I feel humble and proud. That's all.'[7]

3. Don't show off your medals: 'Humble and proud. That's all.'

What can Dylan's motives be for accepting honours, and also for not making a big show of it? Should we be surprised by this slightly self-contradictory position?

Could one of his motives be curiosity? As Liam Clancy, an old acquaintance from Dylan's first years in New York, said: 'He had this immense curiosity. He was ready to suck everything that came his way' (quoted in Heylin 2000: 73). Or does he, perhaps, have a business motive? Could accepting an award be considered as a simple business decision? He felt it was something that was respectable and that, as it were, he might be able to use (Dylan 2004: 132–3). But is that enough?

I would therefore now like to suggest that this may in fact be a matter of justice. Justice is a common theme in Dylan's work, as noted by Sir Christopher Ricks: 'Many of Dylan's songs hinge upon the cardinal virtue of justice ("cardinal" means pertaining to a hinge)' (Ricks 2011: 221). Ricks draws on the example of 'The Lonesome Death of Hattie Carroll', a song showing an instance of double injustice: not only is Hattie senselessly killed by William Zanzinger, but the killer

---

[7] Palais Royal, Paris, 13 November 2013. My own personal memories, as a guest. See also 'Nous étions à la remise de la Légion d'Honneur à Bob Dylan', *Le Parisien*, 13 November 2013, available online: www.leparisien.fr/culture-loisirs/nous-etions-a-la-remise-de-la-legion-d-honneur-a-bob-dylan-13-11-2013-3311851.php (accessed 6 April 2020).

himself does not get the punishment he deserves, receiving a sentence of only six months. I suggest we should balance the sharp end of punitive justice with the idea of recompense: it is not unjust to expect a reward for hard work. Bob Dylan is not as cryptic as he is often said to be, and my opinion is that one can rely (albeit carefully) on the words he chooses to employ. In 'Where Are You Tonight (Journey Through Dark Heat)', he tells us: 'If you don't believe there's a price for this sweet paradise, remind me to show you the scars' (Dylan 1978). 'I'm glad for my songs to be honored like this. But you know, they didn't get here by themselves. It's been a long road and it's taken a lot of doing', he insists (Dylan 2015). It is evidently the just reward for hard work and not the celebration of a hero that counts – as 'If Dogs Run Free' has it: 'Just do your thing, you'll be king' (Dylan 1970). As Law Professor Xavier Magnon wrote: 'Over and above justice, it is perhaps the defence of that which is just that dominates in Dylan's vision' (Magnon 2011: 78).[8] Bob Dylan will not let himself be manipulated, but he also will not deprive himself of the recognition he deserves: 'Everything's been returned which was owed' ('Visions of Johanna', Dylan 1966). He accepts honours in the same way that others before him have done.

Dylan himself does not hesitate to praise the success of other people. 'I used to worship Woody Guthrie, Robert Johnson. I know what hero-worship is. I also know that it's an enlightening thing ... It's nothing that holds you back' (quoted in Gray & Bauldie 1988: 15). The very public nature of this recognition makes him part of a club to which he can legitimately be proud to belong: 'That I now join the names on such a list is truly beyond words' (Dylan 2016). And we know it matters to him to be able to join that list. As early as 1962, he gave his girlfriend Suze Rotolo a book of the poems of Byron, which he signed for her 'Lord Byron Dylan' (Rotolo 2008: 172). We can see multiple references to Homer, Shakespeare, Byron,[9] Balzac and Tolstoy (Dylan once even rode Tolstoy's bicycle in Yasnaya Polyana [Dylan 2004: 38]) liberally scattered throughout his work, both old and new. He never hesitates to pay homage: not only to the 'Old Greats' but also to all of those he admires. The nature of such recognition can be summed up by his special tribute to the great Robert Johnson, to whom he returned the idea of creating surprising lyrical reversals: 'There's no success like failure, and failure's no success at all ...

---

[8] My translation from French: 'Plus que la justice, c'est peut-être la défense de ce qui est juste qui domine dans la vision de Dylan.'
[9] Lord Byron is mentioned no fewer than five times in the first ninety pages of *Chronicles, Volume One*. See Feignier 2008.

I didn't invent this . . . Robert Johnson would sing some songs and out of nowhere there would be some kind of Confucius saying that would make you go, "Wow, where did that come from?"' (Hilburn 2004). 'Dylan has a genius for gratitude', Christopher Ricks noted (Lesinska 2008).

As for Dylan himself, he can simply appreciate receiving the recognition that he and his work deserve, whether it comes from his audience, from the approval of his peers, or from official awards. His songs are played all over the world. 'When I started writing songs as a teenager, . . . [i]f I was really dreaming big, maybe I could imagine getting to make a record and then hearing my songs on the radio. That was really the big prize in my mind' (Dylan 2016). 'I'm lucky to have an audience . . . a lot of my contemporaries really don't have any' (Wilmot 1992). Dylan can appreciate the breadth of the fan base he has won, kept, expanded and renewed, as an indication of the quality of his work. Of course a limited audience should not be identified as a weakness, but quality deserves to be recognized, and it is appropriate to fight for recognition.

Dylan may never have agreed to be labelled as 'the voice of his generation', but that has not stopped him from being a part of the lives of others: 'My songs seem to have found a place in the lives of many people throughout many different cultures and I'm grateful for that' (Dylan 2016). On the one hand, Dylan may think that fame is a trick: the song 'Stack a Lee' says that 'no man gains immortality thru public acclaim. Truth is shadowy . . . No Rights Without Duty is the name of the game & fame is a trick' (Dylan 1993). But, on the other hand, he hopes for a lasting legacy, as he told Allen Ginsberg:

> You want to live forever, right Allen? Huh? In order to live forever you have to stop time. In order to stop time you have to exist in the moment, so strong as to stop time and prove your point. So that you have stopped time. And if you succeed in doing that, everyone who comes into contact with what you've done – whatever it might be, whether you've carved a statue or painted a painting – will catch some of that; they'll recognize that you have stopped time – they won't realize it, but that's what they'll recognize, that you have stopped time. That's a heroic feat! I'd like my work to survive, yeah. . . . It's not enough to be an observer all the time. You have to know that you've stopped time.
>
> Dylan quoted in Williams 2005: 253

Beyond the public approval he has enjoyed, Dylan has received recognition from his peers: John Lennon, Paul McCartney, Leonard Cohen, Bruce Springsteen, Mick Jagger, Lou Reed and others have all spoken about him with praise, and none of them have appeared to begrudge him the awards he has received.

Perhaps, like Byron in his own time, he has become the central figure on the stage, and everybody else has had to position themselves with regard to him.

Also, even if he is personally more attuned to the recognition of the quality of his work and not to his social impact (a concept he has always mistrusted), I suggest there is no major contradiction between the motives which have led to Dylan being offered public awards and the motives which have led to his acceptance of them. The awards appear to be his achievement as a cultural and artistic presence.

4. 'I have dined with kings... And I've never been too impressed' ('Is Your Love in Vain?', Dylan 1978)

This does not mean Dylan's awards are easy for him. Things may have changed but, as he said, he's only 'passing through' (Dylan 2000). And an uncomfortable last step has to be taken: the recipient has to participate in (or endure) a ceremony. It is unlikely that the ceremonies themselves have been particularly enjoyable to Dylan, as those who have witnessed them tend to agree. He shows awkwardness and uneasiness, without a doubt. Not because he is overwhelmed but probably, as his agent Elliott Mintz warned me when we were organizing the Paris ceremony in 1990, because 'Mr Dylan is painfully shy'.[10] Actually, the ceremony lasted only two and a half minutes, including the acceptance speech. In Stockholm, thirty-seven years later, when meeting the Nobel Committee, Dylan looked like 'an old Indian chief coming reluctantly to negotiate with the white men'.[11]

Although he may not be in control of this kind of situation, nevertheless, despite his uneasiness, Dylan can defend himself well. Even if he is anxious during the ceremony, he can be good-humoured afterwards – perhaps remembering that, as Christopher Ricks wrote, 'humour is the penetrating disinfectant' (Ricks 2011: 193). On 30 January 1990, the newly made *Commandeur des Arts et des Lettres* gave a fabulous concert at the Grand Rex Theatre, and played the song 'Tight Connection to my Heart' (Dylan 1985). I cannot help but think that this particular choice of song was relevant – and humorous – as he, as

---

[10] Elliott Mintz in conversation with the author, 29 January 1990.
[11] Email from Horace Engdahl to Anny Romand, April 2017, quoted here with the recipient's kind permission.

it were, alluded to it at several points during the ceremony. The ribbon of the medal had to be tied around the *Commandeur*'s neck – 'I gotta move, but I can't with your arms around my neck', he would later sing. He had to look for his coat just after the ceremony – 'I'm gonna get my coat', he told us. And, last but not least, there was an allusion which provides a precious memory for me. Just after the ceremony came to an end, and we were preparing to leave the Ministry, the door seemed to be locked and the gatekeeper was nowhere to be seen. Just then, I heard a clinking sound behind me: Dylan was offering us his own keys! Later he would be singing: 'You're the one I'm looking for, you're the one that's got the keys'. I came to the conclusion that, even if Dylan did suffer during the ceremony, he was certainly not resentful!

His way of accepting honours seems like another way of illustrating the classic Dylan-ness with which he resists both melodrama and sentimentality, and I can only suggest that he accepts these distinctions because he believes that he deserves them, and that they are worth it. In any case, Dylan-esque acceptance is a style to emulate. In France, in the months following his visit to the Palais Royal, it was to be the turn of Mick Jagger, Lou Reed, Peter Gabriel, and many others. There, too, Dylan had opened a door.

References

Agence France Presse (2016), 'Bob Dylan finally accepts Nobel prize in literature at private ceremony in Stockholm', *The Guardian*, 2 April. Available online: www.theguardian.com/music/2017/apr/02/bob-dylan-finally-accepts-nobel-prize-in-literature-at-private-ceremony-in-stockholm (accessed 3 April 2020).

Armstrong, A. C. (2015), 'This Week in Princeton History for June 8–14', *Mudd Manuscript Library Blog*, 8 June. Available online: https://blogs.princeton.edu/mudd/2015/06/this-week-in-princeton-history-for-june-8-14/ (accessed 1 April 2020).

Busnel, F. (2016), 'Grand Entretien avec Toni Morrison', *America*, 1: 45.

Clarke, J. (2013), 'Bob Dylan Inducted into American Academy of Arts and Letters', *Rolling Stone*, 16 May. Available online: www.rollingstone.com/music/music-news/bob-dylan-inducted-into-american-academy-of-arts-and-letters-243564/ (accessed 3 April 2020).

'Conseil de l'Ordre des Arts et des Lettres' (n.d.), *Ministère de la Culture*. Available online: www.culture.gouv.fr/Nous-connaitre/Organisation/Conseil-de-l-Ordre-des-Arts-et-des-Lettres (accessed 3 April 2020).

Cott, J., ed. [(2006) 2017), *Bob Dylan: The Essential Interviews*, New York: Simon and Schuster.

Coupe S. (1992), 'Interview', *ISIS* [Fanzine], 42 (April-May): 33–35.
Dobbels, D. (1990), 'Les mémoires Dylan', *Libération*, 31 January: 40–41.
Dolen, J. (1995), 'A Midnight Chat with Dylan', *The Sun Sentinel*, 28 November. Available online: www.sun-sentinel.com/news/fl-xpm-1995-09-28-9509270260-story.html (accessed 3 April 2020).
Dylan, B. (1965), KQED Television Press Conference, San Francisco, 3 December, *YouTube*. Available online: www.youtube.com/watch?v=m68JY-7LfpQ (accessed 3 April 2020).
Dylan, B. (1966), *Blonde on Blonde* [Album], USA: Columbia Records.
Dylan, B. (1970), *New Morning* [Album], USA: Columbia Records.
Dylan, B. (1975), *Blood on the Tracks* [Album], USA: Columbia Records.
Dylan, B. (1978), *Street-Legal* [Album], USA: Columbia Records.
Dylan, B. (1985), *Empire Burlesque* [Album], USA: Columbia Records.
Dylan, B. (1991), *The Bootleg Series, Vols 1–3: Rare & Unreleased, 1961–1991* [Album], USA: Columbia Records.
Dylan, B. (1993), 'About the Songs (what they're all about)' [Album liner notes], *World Gone Wrong*, USA: Columbia Records.
Dylan, B. (2000), 'Things Have Changed' [Single], USA: Columbia Records.
Dylan, B. (2004), *Chronicles, Volume One*, New York: Simon and Schuster.
Dylan, B. (2011), 'To my fans and followers', *The Official Bob Dylan Site*, 13 May. Available online: www.bobdylan.com/news/my-fans-and-followers/ (accessed 3 April 2020).
Dylan, B. (2015), 'Read Bob Dylan's Complete, Riveting MusiCares Speech', *Rolling Stone*, 9 February. Available online: www.rollingstone.com/music/music-news/read-bob-dylans-complete-riveting-musicares-speech-240728/ (accessed 3 April 2020).
Dylan, B. (2016), 'Banquet Speech', *The Nobel Prize* website. Available online: www.nobelprize.org/prizes/literature/2016/dylan/25424-bob-dylan-banquet-speech-2016/ (accessed 3 April 2020).
Dylan, B. (2017), 'Nobel Lecture', *The Nobel Prize* website. Available online: www.nobelprize.org/prizes/literature/2016/dylan/lecture/ (accessed 3 April 2020).
Engdahl, H. (2016), 'Award Ceremony Speech'. *The Nobel Prize* website. Available online: www.nobelprize.org/prizes/literature/2016/ceremony-speech/ (accessed 3 April 2020).
Feignier, D. (2008), 'Lord Byron Goes Electric: Lord Byron and Bob Dylan, Reluctant Voices of their Generations', in C. Vigouroux (ed.), *Lord Byron's Correspondence(s)*, 373–87, Paris: F.-X. de Guibert.
Gray, M. and Bauldie, J., eds (1988), *All Across the Telegraph: A Bob Dylan Handbook*, London: Futura.
Gundersen, E. (1997), 'At the Heart of Dylan', *USA Today*, 28 September. Available online: www.interferenza.net/bcs/interw/97-set28.htm (accessed 1 April 2020).
Hentoff, N. (1990), 'Preface', in C. McGregor (ed.), *Bob Dylan: A Retrospective*, 2nd edn, ix–xii, Cambridge, Massachusetts: Da Capo Press.

Heylin, C. (2000), *Dylan: Behind the Shades (Take Two)*, New York: Viking.
Hilburn, R. (2004), 'Rock's Enigmatic Poet Opens a Long-Private Door', *Los Angeles Times*, 4 April. Available online: www.latimes.com/archives/la-xpm-2004-apr-04-ca-dylan04-story.html (accessed 3 April 2020).
Itzkoff, D. (2008), 'Bob Dylan Finally Gets His Pulitzer. His What?', *The New York Times*, 13 April. Available online: www.nytimes.com/2008/04/13/weekinreview/13Itzkoff.html (accessed 3 April 2020).
Lesinska, I. (2008), 'A Lesson in Dylan Appreciation', *Eurozine*, 11 April. Available online: www.eurozine.com/a-lesson-in-dylan-appreciation/ (accessed 3 April 2020).
Lyman, R. (1997), 'A Wind of Gratitude Blows Through the Performing Arts', *The New York Times*, 8 December. Available online: www.nytimes.com/1997/12/08/arts/a--wind-of-gratitude-blows-through-the-performing-arts.html (accessed 3 April 2020).
Magnon, X. (2011), 'La Vision de la Justice dans les chansons de Bob Dylan', in J.-P. Marguénaud, W. Mastor, F. Marchadier (eds), *Droit et rock*, 65–78, Paris: Dalloz.
'The Polar Music Prize: Bob Dylan', The Polar Music Prize Official Site. Available online: www.polarmusicprize.org/laureates/bob-dylan/press-material/ (accessed 3 April 2020).
'Premio Príncipe de Asturias de las Artes 2007: Bob Dylan' (n.d.), *Fundación Princesa de Asturias*. Available online: www.fpa.es/es/premios-princesa-de-asturias/premiados/2007-bob-dylan.html?texto=acta&especifica=0 (accessed 3 April 2020).
'The Presidential Medal of Freedom' (n.d.), *The Obama White House Archives*. Available online: https://obamawhitehouse.archives.gov/campaign/medal-of-freedom (accessed 3 April 2020).
'The Pulitzer Prize Winners' (n.d.), *The Pulitzer Prize Official Site*. Available online: www.pulitzer.org/winners/bob-dylan (accessed 3 April 2020).
Ricks, C. ([2003] 2011), *Dylan's Visions of Sin*, Edinburgh: Canongate.
Roques, D. (1990), 'They Call Him The Commander', *The Telegraph* [Fanzine], 36: 44–54.
Rotolo, S. (2008), *A Freewheelin' Time*, New York: Broadway Books.
Williams, P. (2005), *Bob Dylan, Performing Artist, 1986–1990 & Beyond*, London: Omnibus Press.
Wilmot, P. (1992), 'Dylan interview: Jokes, Laughter and a Series of Dreams', *The Age*, 3 April. Available online: www.interferenza.net/bcs/interw/92-apr03.htm (accessed 3 April 2020).

12

'How Could It Be Any Other Way?' Dylan's Editorial Decisions in *The Lyrics: 1961–2012*

Simon McAslan

In a delectable scene in the Marx Brothers' film *Duck Soup*, Mrs Teasdale sees Groucho leave her room, but behind her back Chico, disguised as Groucho, emerges from under the bed. She is surprised to see him and says, 'I thought you left'. When Chico denies ever leaving, she says, 'But I saw you with my own eyes'. Chico replies, 'Who you gonna believe – me or your own eyes?' (*Duck Soup* 1933). Bob Dylan might very well be asking us a similar question as we gaze with baffled ears on the pages of his latest lyrics book. Who are we going to believe, Dylan or our own ears? The printed lyrics are not always faithful to what Dylan actually sings; editorial changes create new texts of some songs, and of Dylan too as he re-reads self and subject, revisiting his highway of inspiration from '61–2012.

As editor as well as artist, Dylan decides how to present who and what 'Bob Dylan' is. His public silent editing creates in *The Lyrics: 1961–2012* not a reference book, but a separate artistic venture, characteristic of the re-visioning of self in much late Dylan. As with his other recent subversive written gestures (*Chronicles, The Nobel Lecture*), it partly undermines what it purports to preserve. This lyrics book chronicles Dylan's words while simultaneously subverting some of that very documentation, erasing previous Bob Dylans even as it creates and recreates them. The conundrum of transcriptive accuracy in this new lyrics edition is worth exploring, as is the question of the book's ultimate purpose.

A related text with two faces, oral and written, is Dylan's *The Nobel Lecture*, delivered as a speech on 5 June 2017 and published as a book in October of the same year. The tinkling piano in the background of the spoken version reinforces the notion that this text is something to be listened to; on the other hand, the printed text allows for a detailed contemplation in a way that the ephemeral oral recording does not. However, the spoken delivery underscores sound, especially in the final paragraph that foregrounds alliteration, assonance, consonance, rhyme and rhythm that in the printed prose might remain hidden. Thus, Dylan says – or writes:

> Our songs are alive in the land of the living. But songs are unlike literature. They're meant to be sung, not read. The words in Shakespeare's *plays* were meant to be acted on the *stage*. Just as lyrics in *songs* are meant to be *sung*, not read on a *page*. And I hope some of you get the chance to listen to these lyrics the way they were intended to be heard: in concert or on record or however people are listening to songs these days.
>
> Dylan 2017: 23; my emphases

Despite stressing the orality of song, Dylan has in fact published several editions of collected lyrics, presumably to be read on a page. *The Lyrics: 1961–2012* was published in 2016 between the announcement of Dylan's Nobel Prize and his eventual lecture.

1. 'What our Dutch ears thought they heard': unauthorized diligence

This most recent edition is the latest in a long line of books chronicling Dylan's lyrics, all with varying degrees of accuracy. Before Dylan published his first official book of lyrics, *Writings and Drawings* (Dylan 1973), several unauthorized attempts were printed, notably the first unofficial collected edition of Dylan's lyrics titled *(Approximately) Complete Works*, published by De Bezige Bij and Thomas Rap in Amsterdam (Dylan [c.1969] n.d.). The cover bears the title *complete works*, while in significantly smaller font size the title page adds the word *approximately*, very likely a nod to Dylan's song title 'Queen Jane Approximately', the syntax echoing the title 'Absolutely Sweet Marie'. Both the title and Bob Dylan's name are rendered in lower case. No year or editor is mentioned, but Tom Willems dates it as 'late October 1969' and identifies Jacob Groot as compiler (Willems 2014: 84). The songs are presented alphabetically rather than chronologically, and the book is indexed. Though seemingly meticulous, this handsome volume is approximate, in both completeness and accuracy. For example, 'It's Alright Ma (I'm Only Bleeding)' is rendered as 'It's allright Ma, I'm only bleeding', and the line 'Outsiders they can freely criticize' is misheard as 'Outsiders aching freely criticize' (Dylan [c.1969] n.d.: 83). Furthermore, in 'Gates of Eden', the possessive pronoun 'its' is misspelled as 'it's', and 'wishing' becomes 'whishing' (Dylan [c.1969] n.d.: 54). More egregious is the question of not securing rights. Although the book lists American and European copyrights, with accompanying copyright symbols, this edition is apparently compromised: 'Shortly after publication, the publishers hear from New York [that the] official copyright holders of Dylan's music within the Netherlands ... should never have granted permission for the publication' (Willems 2014: 85). Despite this error, *(Approximately) Complete Works* stands as the first publication of Dylan's collected lyrics, albeit pirated and sometimes inaccurate.

That an interest in Dylan as primarily a wordsmith existed early in his career is also evident in *Dylan: Words to His Songs,* printed anonymously in 1972. Without editors, transcribers or publishers named, the only identification is the title on the cover, and the first page bearing only the date in lowercase, 'may 1972', followed by a short introduction and the words 'illustrated by the HOLY CAT' (Dylan 1972). Like Dylan, this artist had changed his name. Born Petrus Josef Gerardus Pollmann in The Netherlands, he decided 'in the name of the battle against the evil ego' to go by 'Holy Cat' (Willems 2014: 139). He later adopted the name Peter Pontiac and became 'generally considered the "godfather" of Dutch underground comix' (Schuddeboom and Knudde n.d.). Clinton Heylin calls Pontiac's artwork for the 1972 pressing of Dylan's bootleg album *Little White Wonder* 'perhaps the most inspired bootleg cover of them all' (Heylin 1994: 152). A member of an online discussion group claims to have contacted the artist 'for any stories he had around the creation of the Little White Wonder [c]over' and posts what is apparently Pontiac's response:

> In 1969 I lived in a hippie-commune in a squat in the town of Leiden. Selling acid (LSD) and hashish was our source of income ... but to keep a straight front for the Law we made bootleg-lyrics-books, by playing records over & over again and writing down what our Dutch ears thought they heard. The resulting collection of lyrics then was mimeographed.
>
> Cube 2014

While their 'Dutch ears' may not have been able to catch all of Dylan's words, any errors are to be expected, considering that even the ears of native English speakers also face difficulties. Although this lyrics book is very much a product of the counterculture – as Pontiac's recollections of the 'hippie-commune', the 'squat' and the selling of drugs attest – the transcribers' dedication is evident in their repeated playing of the records to catch the right words. Appraising the cover art for *Little White Wonder*, Heylin says that Pontiac 'display[s] an obvious love for, and understanding of Dylan's work' (Heylin 1994: 152–3). This appreciation for Dylan is also witnessed in *Dylan: Words to His Songs,* both in Pontiac's artwork as Holy Cat and in the painstaking transcription by the team of Dutch ears.

Stating that 'this book has no pretensions but to offer you the words to dylan's songs' (Dylan 1972), these editors seem more concerned about accurate transcription of the oral words than about conventional written mechanics. The entire text is set in lower case, with the exception of the first-person *I* capitalized throughout. The brief introduction is punctuated by commas and periods, which appear nowhere else in the book. Sometimes spaces are used to indicate commas. Since punctuation is silent, this transcription emphasizes the orality of Dylan's lyrics, reminding us that the songs were composed to be heard, not read. On the other hand, official editions of Dylan's lyrics use punctuation and capitalization, but inconsistently. If the purpose of the lyrics book is to highlight the words as they are heard, Dylan's own presentation of the words seems to undermine their oral aspect.

2. 'Fooled-around-with lyrics': authorized inaccuracy

Dylan published his own authorized book *Writings and Drawings* possibly as a riposte to these unauthorized editions circulating from late 1969 through 1972. That it was originally conceived as a collection of only the lyrics is suggested by the emendation of the title on a sticker on the proof's front wrapper. The typed title 'Words' is crossed out and 'Writings and Drawings' added in handwritten block capitals. The publisher's description below the title emphasizes the completeness of the volume:

> This is the first time that all the lyrics of the legendary songwriter and folksinger have been collected in one volume. Besides the songs on his fourteen record albums, the book contains many which have not been recorded and still others which were recorded by Columbia and not released. It also includes a number of poems and prose writings, fragments of which have passed from hand to hand for many years, but which have never appeared in print.
>
> Dylan 1973b: front wrapper

While not acknowledging the previous unauthorized *(Approximately) Complete Works,* this blurb situates this edition as somehow connected to the counterculture. Phrases such as 'which have not been recorded' and 'not released' suggest that the book provides a revelatory access to forbidden texts; the phrase 'passed from hand to hand' implies a clandestine elite exchanging secrets that we will now be privy to. The description of this official authorized book evokes the underground culture, a stance that Columbia / Sony will later echo with the release of the *Bootleg Series*.

In 1973, the purpose of that early edition might have seemed to be a way of correcting errors in Dylan's printed lyrics, but in fact *Writings and Drawings* and the subsequent authorized lyrics books, including the 2016 edition, have all been approximate and incomplete, perhaps deliberately so. In his discussion of *Writings and Drawings,* Paul Williams is confident that 'there can be no question that the decision to issue the book, and the basic choices as to content and form of presentation, were Dylan's' and that the drawings accompanying the lyrics 'were probably done in 1972' (Williams 1990: 270–1). His otherwise glowing admiration for the book is tempered by what he sees as 'inappropriate' rewrites to the lyrics, changes that he considers detrimental to the songs' integrity and made because Dylan 'just thought they'd read better this way or that it would be fun to make this change' (Williams 1990: 273). It would seem, though, that Dylan's altering of his lyrics goes far beyond what Williams calls '"fooled-around-with" lyrics' (1990: 273). There seems to be something else afoot.

Since Dylan is known for his frequent changes to lyrics and arrangements in both studio takes and live performances, the presentation of his lyrics in book format implies something frozen; rather than reflecting the flux of Dylan's art, the bound book instead suggests stasis. However, playing with these associations of permanence evoked by the book as object, Dylan instead creates new and variant texts that – despite being printed and bound – resist being fixed, thereby disrupting and subverting the notions not only of a definitive *text* but also of a definitive *book*.

Whereas the unauthorized editions had produced inadvertent transcription errors, Dylan in his own lyrics books, especially *The Lyrics: 1961–2012,* presents himself as being almost wilfully inaccurate. While the blurb on the Simon and Schuster website avoids the word 'complete', it does position *Lyrics* as a 'comprehensive volume'. By referring to 'the songwriter's edits to dozens of songs, appearing here for the first time', the description emphasizes Dylan's hand at work and amplifies this by saying, 'Well known for changing the lyrics to even his best-loved songs, Dylan has edited dozens of songs for this volume, making *The Lyrics* a must-read for everyone from fanatics to casual fans' ('Lyrics:

1961–2012'). But 'fanatics' will of course notice lyric changes as well as the omission of several songs, 'Tell Ol' Bill' and 'All the Tired Horses' among them. Since the physical book contains no editorial information, though, 'casual fans' – whatever that means – might miss the problematic transcription and take the book at face value.

3. 'The sound of the words and sounds': writing the oral

Apart from the lyric changes here, transcription itself is already suspect since the printed text cannot convey vocal phrasing. Transcription is but a shadow of the full self of a song. The written text, then, offers the most conundrums. In what way can we capture how Dylan's voice expresses the language, how it stretches or compresses syllables, how it emphasizes words that might not seem stressed when we read them? Analyzing 'It's Alright Ma (I'm Only Bleeding)', musicologist Steven Rings discusses Dylan's 'performative inflections' and the ways in which Dylan's vocal performances of that song have changed over time. Rings says, 'For Dylan, it seems, the recorded "track" ... is subordinate to the continually morphing "song"' (Rings 2013: 113). This idea echoes Dylan's statement, 'Many of my records are more or less blueprints for the songs' (Parales 1997). The studio version is not a definitive one. However, as Rings notes, even staunch fans who enjoy how Dylan transforms his songs in performance also frequently extol the studio performance. If so, the final studio takes play the role of both blueprint and definitive version simultaneously, each function negating the other. The reworked live renditions rely on the audience's previous knowledge of the 'fixed' studio version, so the echo of the 'original' is always in the re-imagined and re-visioned text of the concert performance. Similarly, the written text trapped in a book is seen as definitive even though the 'original' oral performance haunts it. If the familiar studio performance is both the flexible blueprint as well as the static definitive version, then the one is always written upon the other, each negating and recreating the other. The difficulty is compounded when Dylan's own authorized words on the page are clearly not those heard on the studio recording.

Dylan's official written texts pay little attention to capturing the oral experience in print, yet some Dylan scholars have struggled to rectify this. In *Song and Dance Man*, Michael Gray provides an interpretation of 'Fourth Time Around' (Dylan 1966) that relies on Dylan's pauses in the song; Gray's argument rests on the 'sexual innuendo' these pauses create. He explains what the performance sounds like and then offers an example:

> Dylan's technique for delivering sexual innuendo ... is almost like a parody of a schoolboy reading Shakespeare aloud in class; instead of the frequently required line overflow, there is a pause – encouraged, but not exaggeratedly, by the tune – at the end of odd lines in the lyric. Into each pause comes all the innuendo and ambiguity that Dylan can muster.
>
> Gray 2000: 148

Gray then breaks up the lines to represent what he hears, making Dylan's fifteen lines into twenty-one lines. For example, he turns two lines of verse into four, thus:

> Her
> Jamaican rum
> And when she did come
> I asked her for some.
>
> Gray 2000: 148

This is all, of course, particular to Gray's ear, but the point is salient: how does one convey the pauses, the hesitations and the verbal play that in many cases inform the theme and sense of the song? This song in particular is an exercise in breathing and phrasing. Unlike some other songs from the *Blonde on Blonde* sessions, the lyrics to 'Fourth Time Around' seem to have been completed before recording began. Only some minor changes have been made to the words themselves; however, the several takes show Dylan trying to find the right cadence and stress (Dylan 2015). In order to give an approximation of this oral acrobatics, Gray breaks up the lines where he thinks the pauses appear. Similarly, playing with layout, Gray also represents how Dylan pushes the line length in 'Leopard-Skin Pillbox-Hat' (Dylan 1966):

> In the second verse ... he marries the long, downward trail of the standard blues third line to this:
>> You know it balances on your head just like a mattress balances on a bottle of
>> w
i
n
e
.
>
> Gray 2000: 150

In the two previous editions of *Song and Dance Man* (1972 and 1981), Gray had quite a different way of presenting those lines, using what seems to be a typewriter, the first line cascading across the page, with the word 'balances' directly underneath 'mattress'. The decision to change that whimsical representation to the more staid even line suggests that Gray is not sure how best to demonstrate what the line sounds like. Gray's varying representations of Dylan's words are symptomatic of the subjectivity of rendering sounds in print. In his attempt to discuss the phrasing and timing, Gray seems almost to have changed his mind about where those pauses actually appear.

In his discussion of *Lyrics: 1962–1985*, the first collection of Dylan's lyrics in book form since 1973's *Writings and Drawings*, Stephen Scobie also questions how Dylan's lyrics appear on the page, arguing that in performance 'Dylan's phrasing cuts across the regular printed lines to such an extent that he produces an aural equivalent of free verse' (Scobie 1991: 34). Presenting an example from a live performance of 'I Dreamed I Saw St. Augustine' from a 1987 London concert, Scobie lineates the lyrics as he hears them:

> No martyr is
> among you now
> that you can
> call your own,
> so go on your way a-
> ccording-
> ly
> but know
> you're not a-
> lone.
>
> Scobie 1991: 35

And that's just one performance of one song.

Scobie's example could be set against the poetry of, for instance, Charles Olson. Thinking back to Olson's idea of Projective Verse, in which breath is central to what he calls the 'THE LAW OF THE LINE' (Olson 1997a: 244), we can see a parallel to the problems of transcribing Dylan. Olson says lineation is 'how [the poet] would want any reader, silently or otherwise, to voice [the poet's] work' (Olson 1997a: 245). In his poem 'Love' (1954), Olson places words carefully on the page to signal the breath and pace. The last lines of the poem demonstrate the effect of such a strategy:

                                               This can also be
Love.
                                               Olson 1997b: 300

Here Olson's lineation indicates the breath, the space and the rhythm of the poem. The final word 'Love', for instance, is different from the same word appearing three lines previous. The combination of enjambment and a pause created by the spacing allows the final word its extra resonance; that the first letter is upper case adds to the distinction between these words. The problematics of authorial intention aside, Olson's notions of 'Projective Verse' indicate quite clearly the direct relationship between the placement of the words on the page and the sound – the *voice* – of the poem.

Dylan, though, is a writer primarily of songs for performance, not printed words for reading. However, for the purpose of the *Lyrics* to be clear, to be the approximation of what we hear when he sings, they must let us hear Dylan too. And if we are to hear Dylan, it seems we need to organize the words on the page to reflect the performance. Of course, since each Dylan performance is perforce different, such an undertaking could simply not be achieved in print form at all; even a comprehensive web-based approach would prove insurmountable. All this demonstrates how much Dylan's words rely on their performance. During his London concert on 27 May 1966, after playing 'Tell Me Momma', Dylan says, 'What you're just hearing here now is the sound of the songs. You're not hearing anything else except the songs, the sound … of the words … and sounds…' (Dylan 2016b). Despite him being under the influence and having just previously said, 'Forgive me … Anything I say now, please don't hold against me', his statement articulates the essence of what Dylan may be attempting to do with sound.

This capturing of the oral experience in print poses a considerable challenge for anyone attempting the task, Dylan himself included. In *The Lyrics: Since 1962*, Christopher Ricks and his co-editors tackle this problem head-on, presenting Dylan's work 'to the eye in such a way as to help the eye see what the ear hears' (Dylan 2014: viii). Large pages let lines breathe and play unrestricted; variant versions of the lyrics show each song's evolution. However, Ricks concedes that the limits of transcription mean that any such project must necessarily fall short of a full reckoning of what Dylan *does* with his words. Ricks asks, 'since the lyrics by themselves are clearly not "the whole thing" (as Dylan put it), why present them by themselves?' (Dylan 2014: ix). Hence an editor's overwhelming challenge of, on the one hand, recognizing the written text as only a ghost of the whole song and, on the other hand, portraying in print Dylan's elusive oral gymnastics to emphasize the importance of the words separate from music and voice.

4. 'Which one is correct?': the 'problem' of variant lyrics

Haunting this endeavour is the ever-present matter of Dylan's frequent redrafting. All the printed alterations Dylan makes to his songs create new texts altogether. In his editorial comments on the official lyrics to the outtake from *Shot of Love*, 'Let's Keep It Between Us', published in the Bob Dylan fanzine *The Telegraph*, John Bauldie voices concerns about the fidelity of Dylan's published lyrics. Commenting on these lyrics 'officially supplied' by Dylan's music publisher Special Rider, he cautions that 'these "official" lyrics beg a few questions themselves, and don't correspond to the performed lyrics – which themselves changed and developed a little as the year wore on and the tour ... wore out' (Bauldie 1983: 32). In the next issue, Patrick Webster's response underscores the problems of presenting Dylan's work in print:

> [I]s it possible to achieve a definitive version of the lyrics of each Dylan song? I mean, how loyal to the words Dylan is singing are the published songbooks? ... A good example of this ambiguity is the line from 'Gates of Eden': 'Leaving men wholly, totally free'. *Writings and Drawings* [1973] prints this, whilst in the songbook it's 'Leaving me holy, totally free'. So which one is correct?
>
> Webster 1983: 7

Bauldie and Webster position Dylan's songs as essentially unstable texts impossible to represent satisfactorily on the page, yet both seek something in print that is definitive and 'correct'. However, any seemingly 'official' or 'authorized' version will always butt against both the aural reality of its several studio takes as well as the various transformations as the song evolves in concert. 'Which one is correct?' is a question that folds in on itself since the notion of 'correct' is always a problematic proposition in relation to the fluidity of Dylan's work. Bauldie draws attention to the complexity of hearing and reading Dylan when he says that he favours the words of 'Let's Keep It Between Us' in the performed version to those in the published lyrics, adding, with his typical ironic humour, 'But then again, who am I to voice such preferences?' (Bauldie 1983: 32). Here, Bauldie seems to accept that the 'official' lyrics take precedence over his own inclinations, but with mock humility he simultaneously rejects this dominance of the printed text and calls attention to the subjectivity of listening to Dylan's words. The 'correct' version of a song's lyrics for Bauldie might not be the same for Webster, or for you or me, but lying at the heart of the problematic of deferring to the primacy of Dylan's lyrics as written text is this very tension between the desire for the 'correct' and the acknowledgement of our subjective 'preference'. Further complicating matters is the fact that two years after Bauldie's comments on 'Let's Keep It Between Us', Bob Dylan published the song in *Lyrics: 1962-1985* with significantly different lyrics from the ones Special Rider had earlier provided to *The Telegraph*.

Clinton Heylin has explored the transcription of another *Shot of Love* outtake, 'Caribbean Wind', which has changed through several versions both live and in print. In his 1986 *Telegraph* review of *Lyrics: 1962-1985*, Heylin notes that 'unhappily, the errors in the first edition which ought to have been put right with careful revision still remain' (Heylin 1986: 56). This 'carelessness in the revising', as Heylin puts it, detracts from what he sees as the book's role as a 'volume which offers [Dylan's] words to posterity' (Heylin 1986: 63). Years later, in *Still on the Road*, Heylin again touches on the transcription of this particular song, stating bluntly, 'The published lyrics to "Caribbean Wind" stand as a mess of titanic proportions' (Heylin 2010: 195). According to Heylin, the main problem behind all the wildly variant lyrics is that apparently a single source was not used, but rather,

> it was the April 7, 1981 version – sullied by a series of horrendous mistranscriptions – that was used in the 1985 *Lyrics*. This was 'corrected' when the official website published the lyrics online in 1997. Unfortunately, the version used then was apparently one given to Dylan's then-lawyer Naomi Saltzman in 1981, being a composite of the versions recorded on March 31 and April 7, making it neither one thing nor the other. Nonetheless, it is this version that appears in the 2004 *Lyrics*.
>
> Heylin 2010:195

Lyrics: 1962-1985 also proves problematic for Neil Corcoran, who characterizes the changes as 'evidence... of how frequently Dylan misreads himself' (Corcoran 1987: 93). Corcoran seems to place Dylan as both victim and culprit. Since Corcoran's 1987 review, Dylan has continued to revisit, reread, rewrite, and 'misread' himself over and over, as we too do the same thing. But if the writer indeed misreads himself, what chance have *we* got when we consult the *Lyrics* book to aid in exegesis, especially when Dylan's 'misreading' might be a deliberate act?

In his song about the *Titanic*, 'Tempest' (2012), Dylan sings, 'Jim Dandy smiled, he never learned to swim'. At least that's what the most recent lyrics book tells me (Dylan 2016a: 664). But I am not alone in hearing Dylan bark the name as 'Jim Backus', the actor who played the millionaire Thurston Howell III in the 1960s sitcom *Gilligan's Island*, an entirely appropriate allusion that links the shipwrecks of the real – and fictional – *Titanic* and the entirely fictional *Minnow*. However, the 1956 LaVern Baker song 'Jim Dandy' has a Jim Dandy in a nautical context, on a submarine rescuing a 'mermaid queen' (Baker 1956). Dylan's Jim Dandy, though, 'never learned to swim'. *The Lyrics: 1961–2012* tries to convince me that I hear 'Jim Dandy', and I do, sometimes, but mostly I still hear 'Jim Backus' – on LP, CD, or MP3 or however I'm listening to songs these days. With Dylan's delivery, it is often possible to hear both names sung simultaneously. Am I mishearing, or is Dylan misreading, or is something altogether different going on?

Dylan's printed lyrics are not so much transcription as *translation* of one experience into another. Dylan's notions of translation, transcription, origin, authorship, language, and indeed self are at play in his comments about Hugues Aufray's translations of his songs: Dylan says, 'sometimes it makes me think they were written in French to begin with and it was me who translated them back' (Dylan 2009). This rupture between self and creation echoes his recent statement about his earlier songs: 'there are a lot that I don't remember writing. I mean I know I wrote them, but I can't say where or when' (Dylan 2018: 9).

5. 'Tweedle Dee & Tweedle Dum' revisited: recreating the self

The revisited lyrics in the hands of this artist dissociated from their very genesis are entirely new creatures, dizygotic twins, neither page-poetry nor song, yet both and more and then some. For example, the reworked lyrics of 2001's 'Tweedle Dee & Tweedle Dum' in *The Lyrics: 1961–2012* (Dylan 2016a: 581) differ in form, content and tone from those on the album recording (Dylan 2001) and in the previous *Lyrics: 1962–2001* (Dylan 2004: 579–80).

The latest text (Dylan 2016b) exemplifies Dylan's awareness of creating a *written* document 'on a page', separate from lyrics being sung. In this meditation of self versus self, Dylan privileges the written by adding commas and periods, voiceless visual marks that 'pass by so silently', living only on the page. Although he peppered his 1971 book *Tarantula* with ampersands, only two Dylan-penned song titles feature this sign that straddles the line between punctuation and sounded word: 'Rainy Day Women #12 & 35' and 'Tweedle Dee & Tweedle Dum'. The latter is the only one that uses the ampersand to join names.

In *The Lyrics: 1961–2012*, Dylan's concern for the page is evident too in his restructuring of the song. He changes twelve verses of four lines each into five verses of eight lines. Although the first twenty-four lines remain intact, a full verse is omitted, including a line in which the first-person speaker addresses a second-person love interest ('I got love for you and it's all in vain'; Dylan 2004: 579). Dylan also rearranges lines and deletes two separate couplets, one talking of the speaker's lover in third-person, the other mentioning that Tweedle Dee and Tweedle Dum 'run a brick-and-tile company' (Dylan 2004: 580).

Excising the first-person speaker removes romantic love from the narrative that focuses now on the divided selves of the Tweedles. Defined self gives way to ambiguity. In the new final verse from *The Lyrics: 1961–2012*, they are temporarily shorn of identity as their individual traits, in turn pathetic and brutal, are not attributed to each by name. This song that opens with images of violence and death ends with Tweedle-dee Dum's final brooding threat to Tweedle-dee Dee, 'I've had too much of your company' (Dylan 2016b: 581); however, this line loses the playful pun of the now deleted phrase 'brick-and-tile company'. Overall, the new lyrics focus on the destructive fellowship of the Tweedles, with no counterbalance of love, and the song is much darker for that. Despite these lost lines, the tightened song gains much.

The editorial changes to this song and others in this book make *The Lyrics: 1961–2012* a text that is both faithful and unreliable. It chronicles a collision of texts as it represents the likewise changing self of the artist and reveals how the mutability of art and multiplicity of selves resist the construct of the definitive. The book is a living document of an ever-shifting artist, but on the front and rear covers of the dust jacket, Jerry Schatzberg's 1965 portraits seem to freeze Dylan in the 1960s, an era he has consciously moved far beyond. In this context, these pictures contradict rather than celebrate the protean multiplicity that is Dylan, and instead reinforce the popular conception of Dylan – and his words – as being fixed in time, the totality of his work able to be summed up in these iconic photographs of the 1960s rebel. Such wholeness can be a comforting conceit despite its impossibility.

6. Indefinitively Dylan

The reverence shown by scholars to authoritative editions of authors' works shows how seductive the idea of completeness can be. In his survey of the several editions of James Joyce's *Ulysses* over the years, Edward L. Bishop quotes the claim of the 1932 Odyssey Press publication: 'The present edition may be regarded as the definitive standard edition' (quoted in Bishop 1994: 31). He adds that it is in fact not definitive and says, 'What is interesting is the assurance, once again, that though the text has been faulty in the past, now it is fixed' (Bishop 1994: 31). The Odyssey Press *Ulysses* has since been superseded by the Gabler edition, named for its editor Hans Walter Gabler. In the preface to its second impression, Gabler notes the impossibility of perfection: 'the literary text itself never wholly achieves a definitive state. Neither do scholarly and critical procedures of editing in their turn bring forth definitive texts, but at the most approximations to the best possible text' (Joyce [1922] 1986: vii). Another ambitious editorial undertaking is John Butt's multi-volume Twickenham Edition of *The Poems of Alexander Pope*, referred to as 'definitive', although it now exists also more popularly as a one-volume 'reduced' edition, first published in 1963 and 'Reprinted with corrections' in 1968 (Pope [1963] 1996: vi). That the offspring of an authoritative text was itself not error free says much about the challenges of ever creating a definitive text.

Anyone attempting an authoritative text of Bob Dylan's lyrics will be met with certain disappointment. As Christopher Ricks writes in his introduction to *The Lyrics: Since 1962*, 'Definitive is the reviewer's word of praise these days for anything at all (a biography, a reference book, a performance). It is always an untruth, fortunately. There is no such thing as a definitive setting-down, or version, interpretation, or performance, of any work of art' (Dylan 2014: xi). Seeming to contradict this directly, though, Simon and Schuster's online press release states, 'The Lyrics is the first comprehensive, rigorously annotated, and *definitive* collection of Bob Dylan's lyrics to be published' ('Simon & Schuster' 2014; my emphasis). However, as with critical editions of Joyce and Pope and others, a *book* of Dylan's words seems attractive because it is some kind of 'assurance' (as Bishop would have it) of a reliable text, even if in fact Dylan's songs are constantly fluctuating oral texts, their written versions always necessarily incomplete.

In contrast to the description of Ricks's edition, Simon and Schuster's blurb for *The Lyrics: 1961–2012* draws not on the cachet of an academic authorized text being 'rigorously annotated' by an external scholar, but rather positions the book as being connected with Dylan himself, making the author the authority. Saying that 'Dylan has edited dozens of songs for this volume' ('Lyrics: 1961–2012') suggests also that this editing is an exceptional personal offering for the book the reader now holds. In contrast, though, the blurb evokes the language of literary study and critical texts by characterizing this edition as 'a comprehensive and definitive collection of Dylan's most recent writing as well as the early works that are such an essential part of the canon' ('Lyrics: 1961–2012'). The phrase 'the canon' is ambiguous. It speaks of a closed group of approved texts, but whether it refers to only Dylan's oeuvre or all of established literature is unclear. Either way, combined with the words 'comprehensive', 'definitive' and 'essential', it frames the book – as well as Dylan himself – as frozen and preserved.

But this is also the alluring language found in the proliferation of lucrative 'essential' or 'definitive' versions for sale in popular culture: films repackaged on DVD and reissued in their 'original' format, with additional deleted scenes and alternate endings; collectors' limited edition CD box sets of music artists' back catalogues, re-released with outtakes. All of these come with the promise of completeness. However, the notion of the 'definitive' version is at odds in many ways with the endless variations of folk art, free collective creations, and the open-ended traditional music that Dylan cut his teeth on.

The Lyrics: 1961–2012 might then have the outward appearance of being definitive, but the gesture of the contents resists this limitation and instead embraces never-ending fluidity and change, reflecting the mutability of the artist himself. Therefore, it does not function like a volume of poetry or a reference book. It seems to suppose that the reader is either listening to or has listened to the songs whose words are on the page, but so-called 'casual fans' expecting verbatim texts might be dismayed, much as some despairing concert-goers are when Dylan doesn't talk to the audience or provide a nostalgia act. However, those who have sailed with Dylan do not see these as objectionable points. Quite the contrary. Likewise, this perfectly imperfect book of echoes and ghosts of performances and selves must always remain approximately incomplete as a reflection of that larger text of the entity known as 'Bob Dylan'. As Dylan says at the end of 'Tell Ol' Bill' (Dylan 2005), whose lyrics are mysteriously absent from *The Lyrics: 1961–2012,* 'How could it be any other way?'

References

Baker, L. (1956), 'Jim Dandy' [Song], USA: Atlantic.

Bauldie, J. (1983), 'Let's Keep It Between Us', *The Telegraph*, 10: 32.

Bishop, E. L. (1994), 'Re: Covering "Ulysses"', *Joyce Studies Annual*, 5 (Summer): 22–55. Available online: www.jstor.org/stable/26283621 (accessed 4 February 2020).

Corcoran, N. (1987), 'Going Barefoot: Thinking About Bob Dylan's Lyrics', *The Telegraph*, 27: 93–8.

Cube, T. (2014), 'Bob Dylan's Basement Tapes – Where We're Currently At (Part 3)' [Forum discussion], *Steve Hoffman Music Forums*. Available online: http://forums.stevehoffman.tv/threads/bob-dylans-basement-tapes-where-were-currently-at-part-3.381361/page-21 (accessed 11 April 2020).

Duck Soup (1933) [Film], Dir. L. McCarey, USA: Paramount Pictures.

Dylan, B. ([c.1969] n.d.), *(Approximately) Complete Works*, Amsterdam: De Bezige Bij / Thomas Rap.

Dylan, B. (1966), *Blonde on Blonde* [Album], USA: Columbia Records.

Dylan, B. (1972), *Dylan: Words to His Songs*, Amsterdam: n.p.

Dylan, B. (1973a), *Writings and Drawings*, London: Jonathan Cape.

Dylan, B. (1973b), *Writings and Drawings*, uncorrected proof, London: Jonathan Cape.

Dylan, B. (1985), *Lyrics: 1962–1985*, New York: Knopf.

Dylan, B. (2001), 'Tweedle Dee & Tweedle Dum' [Song], *"Love and Theft"*, USA: Columbia Records.

Dylan, B. (2004), *Lyrics: 1962–2001*, New York: Simon and Schuster.

Dylan, B. (2005), 'Tell Ol' Bill' [Song], *North Country: Music from the Motion Picture*, USA: Columbia / Sony Music.

Dylan, B. (2009), Sleeve Notes, in Hugues Aufray, *New Yorker* [Album], France: Mercury.

Dylan, B. (2014), *The Lyrics: Since 1962*, eds J. Nemrow, L. Nemrow and C. Ricks, London: Simon and Schuster.

Dylan, B. (2015), *The Bootleg Series Vol.12: The Cutting Edge 1965–1966 (Collector's Edition)* [Album], USA: Columbia Records.

Dylan, B. (2016a), *The Lyrics: 1961–2012*, New York: Simon and Schuster.

Dylan, B. (2016b), 'Tell Me Momma' [Song], *The 1966 Live Recordings*, USA: Columbia.

Dylan, B. (2017), *The Nobel Lecture*, New York: Simon and Schuster.

Dylan, B. (2018), *Mondo Scripto*, London: Halcyon Gallery.

Gray, M. (2000), *Song and Dance Man III: The Art of Bob Dylan*. London: Cassell.

Heylin, C. (1986), '*The Lyrics 1962–1985*: A Version Short of the Definitive', *The Telegraph*, 23: 55–67.

Heylin, C. (1994), *The Great White Wonders: A History of Rock Bootlegs*, London: Penguin.

Heylin, C. (2010), *Still on the Road*, Chicago: Chicago Review Press.

Joyce, J. ([1922] 1986), *Ulysses: A Critical and Synoptic Edition,* ed. H. W. Gabler, New York: Garland.
'The Lyrics: 1961–2012' (n.d.) [Book description], *Simon and Schuster* website. Available online: www.simonandschuster.com/books/The-Lyrics/Bob-Dylan/9781451648768 (accessed 5 February 2020).
Olson, C. (1997a), *Collected Prose,* ed. D. Allen and B. Friedlander, Oakland: University of California Press.
Olson, C. (1997b), *The Collected Poems of Charles Olson, Excluding the* Maximus *Poems,* ed. G. F. Butterick, Oakland: University of California Press.
Parales, J. (1997), 'A Wiser Voice Blowin' In the Autumn Wind', *New York Times,* 27 September. Available online: www.nytimes.com/1997/09/28/arts/pop-jazz-a-wiser-voice-blowin-in-the-autumn-wind.html (accessed 15 November 2019).
Pope, A. ([1963] 1996), *The Poems of Alexander Pope: A One-Volume Edition of the Twickenham Text with Selected Annotations,* ed. J. Butt, London: Routledge.
Rings, S. (2013), 'A Foreign Sound to Your Ear: Bob Dylan Performs "It's Alright, Ma (I'm Only Bleeding)", 1964–2009', *Music Theory Online,* 19.4. Available online: www.mtosmt.org/issues/mto.13.19.4/mto.13.19.4.rings.pdf (accessed 15 November 2019).
Schuddeboom, B. and K. Knudde (n.d.), 'Peter Pontiac', *Lambiek Comiclopedia* website. Available online: www.lambiek.net/artists/p/pontiac1.htm (accessed 15 November 2019).
Scobie, S. (1991), *Alias Bob Dylan,* Markham, Ontario: Red Deer College Press.
'Simon & Schuster Announces Limited Edition of Bob Dylan's Lyrics' (2014), *Simon and Schuster* website. Available online: http://about.simonandschuster.biz/news/simon-schuster-announces-limited-edition-of-bob-dylans-lyrics/ (accessed 6 February 2020).
Webster, P. (1983), 'What Publishers Do to Dylan's Lyrics', *The Telegraph* [Fanzine], 11: 7.
Willems, T. (2014), *Bob Dylan in the Netherlands 1965–1978,* Frederick, MD: America Star Books.
Williams, P. (1990), *Performing Artist: The Music of Bob Dylan. Volume One, 1960–1973,* Novato, CA: Underwood-Miller.

13

Dylan's Resources

Christopher Ricks

Among the things that everybody knows is that the art of Bob Dylan owes (and is happy to acknowledge and repay) a great deal to the art of T. S. Eliot, even as Eliot's art owes and no less gratefully repays so much to the art of John Donne, say, or of Tennyson.

Dylan 'Through hostile cities and unfriendly towns' (Dylan 2016: 509)
Eliot 'And the cities hostile and the towns unfriendly' (Eliot 1963: 109)

Not exactly the same (the sequence, the syntax, the cadence), indeed exactly *not* the same, and yet – as Eliot once put it – 'original with the minimum of alteration' (Eliot 2015: 169). Nothing hostile or unfriendly about the relation between these two poets, even if once upon a time Ezra Pound and T. S. Eliot, for their parts, were fighting in the captain's tower, there on the *Titanic* that was Modernism.

So for the delighting conference at the University of Artois on Bob Dylan and his twenty-first century, I tried to give salience to – or rather, to show the salience of – some Eliot-features of Dylan's resourcefulness. Dylan's resources brought to mind Eliot's words when in 1948 he was awarded the Nobel Prize in Literature: 'the expression of one's feelings calls for resources which language cannot supply' (Eliot 1948). Eliot's thought has the amplitude to accommodate the ways in which voice and music, for instance, are evidently resources which language cannot supply – but with which language is then happy co-operatively to achieve compound interest in the art of song.

A short report, here, on a few of the intersections that I sought to identify.

The starting point needed to be the applicability and adaptability of Eliot's thinking in his grateful Address of 1948:

> When I began to think of what I should say to you this evening, I wished only to express very simply my appreciation of the high honour which the Swedish

Academy has thought fit to confer upon me. But to do this adequately proved no simple task: my business is with words, yet the words were beyond my command.

Eliot 1948

No less than your sons and your daughters, not just *the* words but *your* words are beyond your command. Dylan once lovingly insisted that his songs lead their own lives; this can go, too, for the thought that his words, too, lead their own lives, as the best words have a way of doing. This would include 'words of appreciation', as Eliot granted:

> Were the Nobel Award similar in kind to any other award, and merely higher in degree, I might still try to find words of appreciation: but since it is different in kind from any other, the expression of one's feelings calls for resources which language cannot supply.
>
> Eliot 1948

The occasion of the Bob Dylan in the Twenty-First Century 2018 conference did not call for any defence of the Swedish Academy's decision, for good sense understands that any notion of Literature that would exclude, for instance, *Shakespeare* (whose medium as a dramatist was not words, but people moving about on a stage using words – people and words plus music plus sets and costumes and and and) would be simply vacuous. If Literature had to mean *made of words alone*, then the Prize should never have been given to Dario Fo, Samuel Beckett, or George Bernard Shaw. Moreover, the words of songs need to be as deeply right as any words anywhere – and as the other constituents of song. And in a *compound*, no constituent is any less important, essential even, than anything else, whatever the proportion of it.

Much of what I hoped to illuminate consisted of instances attended to: say, the geranium that flourishes in Eliot (thanks to Jules Laforgue) as well as in Dylan (thanks to Eliot). Or the surface that is intimate with depths:

Eliot 'The surface glittered out of heart of light' (Eliot 1963: 190)

Dylan 'resign from mind the heart of light' (Dylan 2005: 45)

– this from an evocation in *Tarantula* (1966), which knows (as Eliot did) about Conrad's 'heart of darkness', and which has its affinities with the world of Eliot and with a world behind Eliot, that of Shakespearean tragedy and comedy: 'tragedy, the broken pride, shallow & no deeper than comedy – . . . his path, his noise, his shadow . . . resign from mind the heart of light' (Dylan 2005: 45). Eliot: 'Resign resign resign' (Eliot 1963: 143). There, for Dylan, 'where a nosebleed would disturb the universe' (*where* from *dare*: 'Do I dare / Disturb the universe?', wonders J. Alfred Prufrock) (Eliot 1963: 14).

The case that I wished more sustainedly to explore was that of Hamlet and of *Hamlet*, surfacing again and again in Dylan's – as in Eliot's – imagining and re-imagining ('then you wonder why you flunked the hamlet exams' [Dylan 2005: 61]). But perhaps the thing to select here would be the crucial concurrences of principle. Eliot in 1948 makes a necessary concession:

> Poetry is usually considered the most local of all the arts. Painting, sculpture, architecture, music, can be enjoyed by all who see or hear. But language, especially the language of poetry, is a different matter. Poetry, it might seem, separates peoples instead of uniting them.
>
> Eliot 1948

But what Eliot then adds about poetry proves to be richly applicable to song and to its international traditions and heritages: 'To enjoy poetry belonging to another language, is to enjoy an understanding of the people to whom that language belongs, an understanding we can get in no other way' (Eliot 1948). But then song is itself another language:

> We must remember the immense debt of every considerable poet to poets of other languages than his own; we may reflect that the poetry of every country and every language would decline and perish, were it not nourished by poetry in foreign tongues. When a poet speaks to his own people, the voices of all the poets of other languages who have influenced him are speaking also ... partly through translation, which must be also a kind of recreation of his poems by other poets.
>
> Eliot 1948

This to include the re-creation that may be song, itself then – as a performed art – gleefully or poignantly or thrillingly open to a multiplicity of re-creations.

Eliot knew that 'the poet does many things on instinct, for which he can give no better account than anybody else' (Eliot 1948). Dylan, likewise a creator and re-creator, turned his train of thought to those trains that always mean so much to his art:

> Creativity is not like a freight train going down the tracks. It's something that has to be caressed and treated with a great deal of respect. If your mind is intellectually in the way it will stop you. You've got to program your brain not to think too much.
>
> Gundersen 1995

That said, it should be said, too, that it was a very happy thing that the programme of the Conference had us all helping one another to think, and this with a great deal of respect.

*

STOP PRESS
Let's face it. Or,
NOBEL LITERARY LAUREATE ROUNDS SQUARELY ON NOBEL LITERARY? LAUREATE

21 March 2019
Wole Soyinka (interviewed by Henry Louis Gates Jr. in the *New York Review of Books*)

> **Gates** Were you surprised when the Swedish Academy named Bob Dylan a laureate?
>
> **Soyinka** Yes, I was surprised, and at the beginning I had a sort of mixed reaction toward it. Afterward I came down heavily on the side of the negative. One, compared to the music industry, I believe that literature is very shortchanged in terms of accessibility to funds, to popular recognition. Let's face it: the literary worker has to work twice as hard as a music worker, especially pop music. I'm not talking about classical music, the heavy stuff. I considered it one of those gestures: 'Let's break the mold for the sake of breaking the mold.' I wasn't impressed at all. Even if you're going to do that, you should proceed as you do normally for literature. You want to take the lyrics out of the music and say this is literature also, in spite of its being in the musical mode? Then you must apply the same stringent standards, and I do not believe that those standards were applied. I look at the list of poets who've been nominated in the past. I compare their work with the lyrics of Bob Dylan, and it is ridiculous.

Half-wracked prejudice leaped forth?

References

Dylan, B. ([1966] 2005, *Tarantula*, London: Harper Perennial.
Dylan, B. (2016), *The Lyrics: 1961–2012*, New York: Simon and Schuster.
Eliot, T. S. (1948), 'Nobel Prize in Literature Banquet Speech', *The Nobel Prize* website.
  Available online: https://www.nobelprize.org/prizes/literature/1948/eliot/speech/ (accessed 29 April 2020).

Eliot, T. S. (1963), *Collected Poems 1909–1962*, London: Faber and Faber.
Eliot, T. S. (2015), 'Introductory Essay to *London: A Poem* and *The Vanity of Human Wishes* by Samuel Johnson', *The Complete Prose of T. S. Eliot: The Critical Edition: English Lion, 1930–1933*, 168–75, eds J. Harding and R. Schuchard, Baltimore: Johns Hopkins University Press.
Gundersen, Edna (1995), 'Dylan on Dylan: "Unplugged" and the Birth of a Song'. Available online: www.bjorner.com/Interviews_90s.pdf (accessed 29 April 2020).
Soyinka, W. and H. L. Gates Jr. (2019), '"There's One Humanity or There Isn't": A Conversation', *The New York Review of Books*, 21 March. Available online: www.nybooks.com/articles/2019/03/21/one-humanity-conversation-henry-louis-gates-wole-soyinka/ (accessed 29 April 2020).

14

Dylan Nobelized? Dylan Ricksified?

Adrian Grafe

1. Strategically placed?

Some readers may be familiar with what began in 1963, 'Between the end of the *Chatterley* ban / And [Dylan's] second LP' ('Annus Mirabilis', Larkin 1981: 34).

Not quite: it was 'the Beatles' first LP'. In September 2017, a certain Nobel Prize-winner for literature, a novelist and lyricist, published a novella entitled *Souvenirs dormants*, in which he wrote: 'I feel that, during the years 1963 and 1964, the old world was holding its breath for the last time before collapsing' (Modiano 2017: 22).[1] One can reckon Dylan responsible for contributing to the collapse of that old world and the ushering in of a new one, with his second LP in particular, *The Freewheelin' Bob Dylan*, somehow managing both to retain and to revolutionize both the art and entertainment value of the American song, if not the art of song full stop. Interviewed just after the announcement of the Nobel Prize-winner for Literature 2016, Margaret Atwood, perhaps in a fit of sour grapes, said the choice of Dylan was 'a strategically placed win', a response to the American presidential election, Dylan being a 'countercultural figure from the sixties' (Atwood 2016). Some members of the public were even surprised to learn that Dylan is still alive (and even more surprised that he's still recording and performing on stage). What about the seventies, 'Knocking on Heaven's Door', 'Idiot Wind', 'You're a Big Girl Now', 'Tangled up in Blue', 'Shelter from the Storm', *Desire* and 'Hurricane'? What about the eighties, *Oh Mercy*, 'Political World', *Slow Train*, 'Precious Angel', *Infidels*, *Empire Burlesque*, 'Dark Eyes', 'Jokerman', 'Every Grain of Sand'? The nineties? *Time Out of Mind*, 'Not

---

[1] My translation from French: 'Il me semble … qu'au cours de ces années 1963, 1964, le vieux monde retenait une dernière fois son souffle avant de s'écrouler'. Many thanks to Marc Porée at whose POEM workshop an early version of this chapter was delivered.

Dark Yet'? 'Cold Irons Bound', which won the Grammy for best male vocal performance of the year 1996 (so much for those who say Dylan can't sing)? What about the 2000s? 'Things Have Changed', Dylan's song for the film *Wonder Boys*, Oscar for best original song in 2001? *"Love and Theft"*? 'Moonlight'? 'Mississippi'? *Together Through Life*? 'Beyond Here Lies Nothin''? *Tempest* in 2012? The song 'Tempest' is nearly fourteen minutes long, a waltz with forty-five quatrains on the sinking of the Titanic, worthy to be set alongside other epic sea sagas like 'The Rime of the Ancient Mariner'. Not forgetting: five albums' worth of standards, sung with a maximum amount of feeling, taken from the golden age of American songwriting and Tin Pan Alley, between the 1920s and the 1950s. Is Dylan, after all, merely a mediocre popular entertainer who seems to make a good living out of it? How can one forget Eliot's so-called 'Critic with Gusto' in *To Criticise the Critic*, an instance of whom he describes as 'an erudite and genial man with an insatiable appetite for the second-rate' (Eliot 1991: 12)? Is Dylan then a 'second-rate' artist who attracts Eliot's 'critics with gusto'?

2. Category and quality – too much confusion?

It is straightforward enough to summarize the controversy over Dylan's Nobel Prize in Literature: is his work literature (or poetry)? The Swedish Academy was hardly revolutionary in this respect: Christopher Ricks had been discussing Dylan's work in public partly from this viewpoint since the mid-seventies; scholar Betsy Bowden brought out her *Performed Literature: Words and Music by Bob Dylan* in 1982. If it is literature, is it good enough to win the Nobel Prize in Literature? Category is the overriding issue; and then it would seem to be quality. Add to this the cries of outrage: why Dylan? Protestors crawled out of the woodwork: what about Leonard Cohen, a greater and more legitimate poet? What about Joni Mitchell, whose lyrics are more literate than Dylan's? Richard Williams wrote a piece in *The Guardian* just after the Nobel Prize announcement entitled 'Why Bob Dylan Deserves his Nobel Literature Win'. The last sentence of his piece reads: 'In songs such as Tangled Up in Blue (1975), Blind Willie McTell (1983) and Cross the Green Mountain (2002) he explored ways of playing games with time, voice and perspective, continuing to expand the possibilities of song in ways that disarm all possible criticism of this new and perhaps greatest honour' (Williams 2016). All the same, it is notable that Williams, the most articulate rock critic writing in English, does not affirm that song is a literary form. Salman Rushdie did not bother arguing about what was literature and what was not, writing: 'Dylan towers over everyone . . . and I am delighted by his Nobel win' (Rushdie 2016).

Anyone who followed the events after the announcement of the prize in autumn 2016 will know that there is a further controversial dimension: the prize-winner's own response or non-response to the announcement. And when he did finally respond, it was by proxy: by sending Patti Smith to the prize-giving ceremony in his stead, by having his banquet speech read out by the US Ambassador (two women, each voicing Dylan: shades of Cate Blanchett in *I'm Not There*); and finally by his taped Nobel Lecture, broadcast in mid-2017. Marc Porée's intuition, according to which Dylan's remarks on *Moby-Dick* sounded rather banal and schoolwork-like ('un brin scolaire', Porée 2017), turned out to be only too correct, when it was discovered that several of Dylan's remarks bore a strange word-for-word resemblance to online *Sparknotes* material on Melville's novel. It is true that right from the start, as soon as it was possible to get any reaction at all out of him, and that was after two weeks, Dylan sounded rather underwhelmed by the whole business. 'Isn't that something?' (Gunderson 2016).

This chapter will take stock both of the possible significations of Dylan's prize and of the critical work that Christopher Ricks devoted to the singer, *Dylan's Visions of Sin*, without which Dylan might well not have won the Nobel.

First, however, a brief word about the Nobel Prize in Literature and its relevance to Dylan is in order. Arguably, the contemporary Nobel Prize in Literature is two-thirds hype, one-third criticism. It is probably good for the authors, their reputations and their pockets. Whether it is critically serious is another matter. It is a financial prize, not only critical recognition. W. B. Yeats wrote to John Quinn a fortnight before the announcement was made: 'I see I have a chance of the Nobel prize. If I get there I shall be well off once more and can pay off my debts'; he also told W. F. Stead: 'I am glad of the prize and glad of the money' (Foster 2003: 247). There is nothing shameful about Dylan's sending in his lecture a few hours before the deadline by which he could receive his prize money. Some previous winners of the literature prize have been two philosophers and one historian and statesman: Bergson won the literature prize in 1923, Bertrand Russell in 1950 and Winston Churchill in 1953. The 1995 Nobel Prize in Literature went to Wislawa Szymborska: although just over twenty years on, one wonders whether she is much read nowadays outside her native Poland. With Dylan's Nobel, the prize did not make an artist global, as it did, albeit briefly, in the case of Szymborska. It simply went global: it went to a global artist.

Dylan was certainly not a conventional Nobel winner, if there is such a thing. He did not attend the award ceremony. His banquet speech, gracious enough, was delivered by the American ambassador to Sweden. His taped Nobel Lecture is notable both for Dylan's highly rhythmic, Beat-poetry-style spoken delivery and for the cocktail-lounge piano playing in the background. Many of the sentences or phrases in them are dimeter ones, and it is easy to imagine Dylan singing them. After saying he will discuss the link between his songs and literature in a 'roundabout' way, he begins with the non-literary figure of his first hero, Buddy Holly (Dylan 2017). However, soon on in the lecture, he tackles the question of 'the vernacular', which he mentions twice: 'you pick up all the vernacular' and 'I had all the vernacular down. I knew the rhetoric' (Dylan 2017). The art of song is, for Dylan, a matter of language. And in his Nobel Lecture, when he insisted on songs being 'unlike literature' because they were 'meant to be sung, not read' (Dylan 2017), he was – perhaps – shifting his position slightly, in comparison with his Nobel 'Banquet Speech'. The latter concluded with an expression of gratitude to the Nobel Committee for providing 'such a wonderful answer' to the question as to whether his songs were '*literature*' (Dylan's emphasis) or not (Dylan 2016a). Their answer but possibly not his own? (One might speculate that between December 2016 and June 2017 Dylan had grown fed up with the whole circus around his Nobel Prize and the talk of 'literature'.)

Inspired by his early hero, first heard on the radio, through intense listening and a talent he discovered he had for learning different types of folk songs fast, he was able to reproduce their language, in the broadest sense of the term, the mode of expression specific to them. Dylan's use of language itself in the speech is intriguing: the way in which he switches between the autobiographical 'I' and the generic 'you'. He seems to do this as though he were saying that anybody could do what he did, although Patrick Modiano in *his* (2014) Nobel Lecture does the same thing, so perhaps it is simply a question of modesty. Modiano quotes from two lyric poets, Yeats and Mandelstam (Modiano 2014). Dylan alludes to the lyrics of various songs in quick succession, but quotes them not as lyrics but as facts: 'You learn the details … You know that Washington is a bourgeois town' (Dylan 2017) – a quotation from 'The Bourgeois Blues', a song about racial prejudice by Lead Belly (1889–1949), whom Dylan names second in his influences after Buddy Holly. By presenting these allusions to songs and song lyrics as actualities, he somehow gives listeners a clue as to how he perceives his own songs and lyrics. It is from this that he moves on to name some novels and then discuss three literary texts in particular that he read 'way back in grammar school' (Dylan 2017), 'way back' meaning before he came into contact with folk songs. From reading literature he picked up, to add to the 'lingo' of folksong, 'principles and sensibilities and an informed view of the world' (the plural 'sensibilities' is striking, suggesting different ways of responding to the world, not just one sensibility). He presents himself as a musical autodidact, and does not state explicitly whether he was introduced to the three works he comments on – *Moby-Dick*, *All Quiet on the Western Front* and the *Odyssey* – in class or simply while he was at school. Dylan ends his account of *All Quiet on the Western Front* with several lines from an anti-war song by Charlie Poole entitled 'You Ain't Talkin' To Me': Dylan gravitating naturally back to the art of song (though the song itself is by Charlie Poole, the lines quoted by Dylan are much later additions by Jim Krause). His Nobel Lecture probably does not have the smooth, immaculately thought-out approach and structure of Modiano's. But it has its own qualities and extreme suggestiveness. He begins by referring to 'my songs', but ends with 'our songs': his songs along with those of all songwriters including an epic poet like Homer, since Dylan ends his lecture by quoting Homer's invocation to the Muse: 'Sing in me, oh Muse, and through me tell the story' (Dylan 2017). Dylan presents himself here in the role he so often adopts: a storyteller in song, a bard.

Simon Armitage argued that Dylan's work was not up to the standard expected of Nobel Prize-winners: there were 'howlers' in Dylan's work which in Armitage's opinion disqualified him from the prize (Malvern 2016). Armitage seems to get tangled up in his own objections when he claims on the one hand that 'Songwriters are not poets. Or songs are not poems' (Armitage 2008), and on the other that Dylan commits 'howlers' in his lyrics which are unworthy of a Nobel Prize in Literature winner. If song lyrics are not literature, whether Dylan's lyrics are unworthy of the Nobel is beside the point, since as a lyricist he is anyway ineligible for the Nobel.

How can such arguments be countered? First, Dylan likes and speaks the vernacular, the common tongue. Ain'ts and don'ts ('ain't no use', 'it don't matter') pepper his songs and speech. Second, the vernacular has always been part of literature. Third, we recall N. F. Blake's comment in *The Language of Shakespeare*: 'wordplay puts sound before sense. Surface grammaticality may be sacrificed' (Blake 1983: 27). Fourth, if Armitage wants to balk at Dylan's howlers, one might reply that howling lies at the heart of Dylan's poetics, like Ginsberg's: 'Sweet Melinda … / She takes your voice / And leaves you howling at the moon.' ('Just Like Tom

Thumb's Blues', Dylan 2016b: 179); 'Outside in the distance a wildcat did growl / Two riders were approaching and the wind began to howl' ('All Along the Watchtower', 2016b: 224). Has ever a song if not a poem ended in such an ominous way? The soundscape combined with the two cinematic riders approaching feels like the true beginning of the song, or the real action of the song (hence, on stage, the lengthy improvisations that often follow the final words).

3. Ricks's regrettable decision?

Given Christopher Ricks's pre-eminence in the world of English-language literary criticism and editing, and the fact that he was previously known for critical and editorial work on Milton, Keats and Tennyson, among others, his fondness for Dylan's work has confounded some critics. Along with *Geoffrey Hill and the Tongue's Atrocities* (1978), *Dylan's Visions of Sin* seems to be the only critical work, and the only full-length one (*Geoffrey Hill and the Tongue's Atrocities* is the text of a lecture, thirty-six pages long), Ricks has devoted to a living author (living, that is, at the time of publication). In the *Visions of Sin* book, Ricks discusses Dylan in the company of, if not in the same breath as ... Milton, Keats and Tennyson. Ricks uses the seven deadly sins, the four cardinal virtues and what he calls the three heavenly graces, as the matrix for his discussion of Dylan's songs. He takes two or three Dylan songs for each of his fourteen categories and discusses the lyrics in terms of those categories (Ricks 2005).

The phrase 'Ricks's regrettable decision' alludes to Geoffrey Hill's inaugural lecture as Oxford Poetry Professor (Hill 2010). Towards the end of his lecture, Hill states that it is customary to pay tribute to one's predecessor in the post, though admits he has a 'little local difficulty' in this respect:

> I regret his decision to publish the book on Bob Dylan. Not – not that I think Dylan is execrable – some of the melodies stay long in the mind – but because as a verse writer he is merely not good enough to merit even the protracted suspended animation of a great mind that in addition to the major works on Milton, Keats, Tennyson and Eliot, has also conceived and presented such formidable and formative essays as those on Gower, Donne, Wordsworth, Beddoes and Lowell. When Ricks is at his best – and he is so, more often than the rest of us – he can move the axis of the earth with his little finger. But Dylan is

not an axis. He is a marvellously accomplished skimmer and has been since he first skimmed his effective stage name from the name of a famous Welsh poet.

Hill 2010

First of all, Hill does not say Ricks's book is bad. Hill counterweights his critique of Dylan with flattery of Ricks. Hill praises Dylan's melodies, as opposed to his lyrics, precisely to provoke the audience's mirth on the one hand – and he is successful in this – and on the other, to get at Ricks. He is using Dylan as a stick with which to beat Ricks for a lapse in critical discernment; for example he calls Dylan a verse writer instead of a poet. Why did Hill use the word 'axis' here? Is it because Ricks had applied the word to Dylan, and Hill wanted to get back at him? Ricks says of Dylan's songs: 'The words constitute an *axis*. They do not point in one direction' (Ricks quoted in Ross 1999). Hill would perhaps have preferred Ricks to apply the splendid word 'axis' to his own, Hill's, poetry.

Hill sometimes complained of being sick of being told he was the greatest English-language poet in the world when his book sales were so few: 'It would be very nice to sell tens of thousands of copies and get the royalties, but if that's not to be, that's not to be' (Hand and Crespi 2015). When the late René Gallet was preparing his French translations of Hill's poems, he wrote to Penguin Books to request copyright permissions. They wrote back saying: 'We have never heard of this author' (personal communication). On the other hand, there's no doubt that Dylan's publisher, Simon and Schuster, and his record company, Columbia, have heard of *him*.

As for Geoffrey Hill himself and the Nobel Prize, in his long poem *The Triumph of Love*, the speaker prays to the Mother of God to bless two people, presumably the Nobel father and son, the founders of the Nobel Prize, which could be interpreted as his preempting his own failure to win it – or was Hill shooting himself in the foot? 'Bless, / of your charity, for your orator's sake, / worthless *N*. and *N*. now Swedish millionaires' (Hill 1998: 45).

4. Not 'Is Dylan a poet?' but 'What kind of poet is Dylan?'

Bob Dylan's repeated publication of collections of his lyrics over the years shows their value to him on the page, as Simon McAslan argues in this volume. To take Dylan's work in the 2000s: five albums of original songs and six of other songwriters' material, the commercials for cars, the hundred and fifty-odd editions of Bob Dylan's *Theme Time Radio Hour*, beyond the exhibitions of his paintings, beyond the metal sculptures, beyond *Chronicles, Volume One*, the texts written for his exhibition catalogues, the sleeve notes written for his own and other artists' albums, films, and rockumentaries like Martin Scorsese's *No Direction Home*, Dylan is also a poet, a poet to whom you can listen as he performs his work, or read on the page. Setting aside the question as to whether he's a poet or not, or whether his work is of literary prizewinning standard or not, or worthy of Hill's or Ricks's attention, let us take as read that Dylan is a writer of lyric poetry if lyric poetry is, as Seamus Heaney (1995) said in his Nobel Lecture, a matter of 'tone and cadence, rhyme and stanza'; and song and lyric poetry indeed share a metrical matrix, and simply ask: what kind of poet is Dylan?

First, he's an empathizer-with-the-condition-of-women poet: 'Sister, lemme tell you about a vision that I saw, / You were drawing water for your husband, you were suffering under the law' ('Precious Angel', Dylan 2016b: 403).

Second, he can be a sexist poet: 'You know, a woman like you should be at home / That's where you belong' ('Sweetheart Like You', 2016b: 465).

Third, he's a nature poet: see 'Huck's Tune', in which nature makes the singer's 'heart rejoice'; 'Play me the wild song of the wind' (2016b: 624).

Fourth, he writes narrative poetry with dialogue: 'Oh God said to Abraham, "Kill me a son" / Abe says, "Man, you must be puttin' me on"' ('Highway 61 Revisited', 2016b: 178).

Fifth, he is a poets'-name-dropping poet: 'Situations have ended sad, relationships have all been bad / Mine have been like Verlaine's and Rimbaud' ('You're Gonna Make Me Lonesome When You Go', 2016b: 338).

Sixth, he's an end-rhymer: 'Sailing round the world in a dirty gondola / Oh to be back in the land of Coca-Cola!' ('When I Paint My Masterpiece', 2016b: 271).

Seventh, he's an internal rhymer – the whole of the lyric of 'When the Deal Goes Down' is based on this technique: 'The midnight rain follows the train ... / The moon gives light and shines by night' (2016b: 610).

Eighth, he's an intertextual poet: the whole song 'Roll on John' (2016b: 668–9) is a take on the folk song of the same name which Dylan recorded in 1962. It carries echoes of Paul Simon's 'Fifty-Ninth Street Bridge Song' ('Slow down, you're moving way too fast'); the second and fourth lines of Lennon and McCartney's 'Come Together' ('Lord, you know how hard that can be'); Blake's 'Tyger' appears directly, while 'I pray the Lord my soul to keep' is the first line of a child's bedtime prayer.

Ninth, he's a punning poet: 'I'm going off into the woods, I'm huntin' bare' ('Honest with Me', 2016b: 594).

Tenth, he's a Tin Pan Alley love poet (witness the rhyme 'crimson / limbs an''): 'The clouds are turnin' crimson / The leaves fall from the limbs an' / The branches' ('Moonlight', 2016b: 593).

Eleventh, he's a love poet, a hate poet and an anti-love poet all in one: 'I'm sick of love but I'm in the thick of it / This kind of love I'm so sick of it' ('Love Sick', 2016b: 559).

Twelfth, assuming it has now been shown that Dylan is a lyric poet, he is also an epic poet, recent examples being songs such as 'Tin Angel' (2016b: 658–60) and 'Tempest' (2016: 661–5).

Thirteenth, he's a Biblical poet with at times an old-testamentality: in 'Spirit on the Water', the first two lines (2016b: 607) allude to Genesis 1.2: 'And the earth was without form, and void; and darkness was upon the face of the deep. And the Spirit of God moved upon the face of the waters'.

Fourteenth, he's a religious poet: 'I know God is my shield and he won't lead me astray' ("Til I Fell in Love with You', 2016b: 565).

5. Conclusion: No Ricksification, no Nobelization

Ricks does a lot, does a huge amount with Dylan; which means he does a huge amount for listeners – and readers – of Dylan. This is partly due to one of his methodological principles, what we – although perhaps not he – would call intertextuality: and it is true that as Eric Ormsby (2011) says, the slightest phrase of Dylan's can produce reams of intertextual reminiscences from Ricks's unbelievably well-stocked mind. Contrary to Hill's opinion, Ricks was right to do the book on Dylan and therefore did not make a mistake in doing so. Apart from anything else, at least in America it brought him (Ricks) a readership the size of which most literary critics can only ever dream of, if that. His work is, in part, based on a general principle, either intertextuality or, more accurately, intertextual analogy, or intertextual comparison. This consists in taking a quotation from a Dylan song and aligning it with (generally) English-literature texts on the same subject. For example, Ricks quotes the whole of Philip Larkin's poem 'Love Songs in Age' in order to discuss Dylan's love song 'Love Minus Zero/No Limit' (Ricks 2005: 20–5). He quotes Pope's *Dunciad* with its apocalyptic ending in order to compare Dylan's 'A Hard Rain's A-Gonna Fall' to it: 'Lo! thy dread Empire, CHAOS! Is restor'd' (2005: 329). Ricks quotes some lines from Dylan's 'High Water (for Charley Patton)' in the context of a discussion of blindness and animals; he here mentions Homer, Milton and nursery rhymes (2005: 78). The title 'High Water' is an allusion to Charley Patton's song 'High Water Everywhere' (1929), itself drawing, perhaps, on the saying 'to go through hell or high water'. Incidentally, Ricks could have gained some support from Dylan himself (not that he needed it) if his book had not predated *Theme Time Radio Hour*, weekly radio programmes in which he deejayed, talked and recited dozens of poems – his most-oft recited author was Shakespeare: 'the kid is good' (Bals 2008).

Ricks's study of Dylan is so full of insight that if we didn't know the kid was good when we started the book, we do when we put it down. Ricks situates Dylan, through his use of intertextual analogy and comparison, in the literary tradition. Marc Porée in his article adduces a quotation from Sartre's *Situation de l'écrivain en 1947*: 'The American writer thinks less of glory than he dreams of fraternity, and it's not against tradition, but because of not having a tradition, that he devises his own way of being' (Porée 2017).[2] Sartre claims that the American writer invents his way of being not against tradition but because he does not have a tradition. That was certainly true in 1947; but tradition builds up through a process of slow accretion (and sometimes through revolutions like the Modernist revolution). But what if the *écrivain* in question were an *American* songwriter? The Nobel Committee for Literature place Dylan 'within the great American song tradition' (Nobel 2016). And so the Committee members suggest a possible expansion of Ricks's approach.

Nobel motivations very rarely mention the country of origin of the winner, and even more rarely the name of any country. Let's again set aside category: literature, verse-writing, poetry, counter-culture, popular culture, pop culture, high culture, low culture, and examine the phrase 'the great American song tradition'. This phrase is close to 'the great American Songbook', by which an ill-defined canon of American songs of roughly the twenties to the fifties are known. Standards, classic songs, Tin Pan Alley songs, sentimental journeys, (these) foolish things, stardust. Dylan's albums *Shadows in the Night* (2015), *Fallen Angels* (2016) and *Triplicate* (2017) are composed entirely of songs from 'the great American Songbook' and show Dylan as wanting to be included within

---

[2] My translation from French: 'L'écrivain américain songe moins à la gloire qu'il ne rêve de fraternité, ce n'est pas contre la tradition mais faute d'en avoir une qu'il invente sa manière d'être'.

that tradition. Therefore the Swedish academy has reminded us of a crucial path to follow in relation to Dylan: one would need to take separately all the strands and varieties of American song – folk songs, cowboy songs, mountain ballads like those beloved of Aaron Copland and his *Appalachian Spring*, Woody Guthrie's dust-bowl ballads, work-songs, Afro-American blues and jazz, the different kinds of blues including Chicago blues and country blues, the spirituals which Dylan has so often sung, country and western, Buddy Holly, Jerry Lee, rock 'n' roll and Elvis Presley's Sun Studio recordings, the American girl groups of the late fifties and early sixties like the Poni-Tails, whose song 'Born Too Late' Dylan name-checks in 'Simple Twist of Fate' ('I was born too late'; [Dylan 2016b: 334] or, in recent live versions, 'I must have been born too late'), the American tradition of the musical from, for instance, Cole Porter and Rodgers and Hammerstein, through to Stephen Sondheim and the contemporary historical hip-hop musical *Hamilton*,[3] the NY Hit Factory with singer-songwriters like Carole King – all that Dylan himself calls 'that pedigree stuff' (Lethem 2017: 480), not forgetting the great American poetic song tradition, the songs and ballads of Edgar Allan Poe, Walt Whitman, the Beats, Allen Ginsberg.

Ricks is too modest a critic, too gifted a thinker, to want to Ricksify Dylan (or anyone else), even if he could, just as the Nobel Committee can award Dylan the Nobel but cannot Nobelize him: as Dylan says himself, he's '*way* gone from the corner' (Lethem 2017: 480).

References

Armitage, S. (2008), 'Propelled Towards Legend', *The Guardian*, 27 June. Available online: www.theguardian.com/music/2008/jun/27/arcticmonkeys.popandrock (accessed 13 April 2020).

Atwood, M. (2016), 'On Bob Dylan Winning Nobel Prize for Literature' [Interview], *BBC Newsnight*, *YouTube*. Available online: www.youtube.com/watch?v=XIUjcijy-3g (accessed 13 April 2020).

Bals, F. (2008), 'Episode 52 – Poetry Readings with Your Host, Bob Dylan' [Podcast], *Dreamtime – Commentary Inspired By Bob Dylan's* Theme Time Radio Hour, 19 March. Available online: www.dreamtimepodcast.com/2008/03/episode-52-poetry-readings-with-your.html (accessed 13 April 2020).

Blake, N. F. (1983), *The Language of Shakespeare*, Basingstoke: Palgrave Macmillan.

---

[3] The genre of the musical is a perfect setting for Dylan's songs, as shown by *Girl from the North Country* (2017), based on Dylan's songs, written by Irish playwright Conor McPherson.

Bowden, B. (1982), *Performed Literature: Words and Music by Bob Dylan*, Bloomington: Indiana University Press.
Dylan, B. (2016a), 'Banquet Speech', *The Nobel Prize* website. Available online: www.nobelprize.org/prizes/literature/2016/dylan/25424-bob-dylan-banquet-speech-2016/ (accessed 3 April 2020).
Dylan, B. (2016b), *The Lyrics: 1961–2012*, New York: Simon and Schuster.
Dylan, B. (2017), 'Nobel Lecture', *The Nobel Prize* website. Available online: www.nobelprize.org/prizes/literature/2016/dylan/lecture/ (accessed 3 April 2020).
Eliot, T. S. (1991; 1965), *To Criticise the Critic and Other Writings*, Lincoln and London: University of Nebraska Press.
Foster, R. F. (2003), *W. B. Yeats: A Life. Vol. 2: The Arch-Poet*, Oxford: Oxford University Press.
Gunderson, E. (2016), 'World Exclusive: Bob Dylan – I'll be at the Nobel Prize Ceremony . . . If I can', *The Telegraph*, 29 October. Available online: www.telegraph.co.uk/men/the-filter/world-exclusive-bob-dylan---ill-be-at-the-nobel-prize-ceremony-i/ (accessed 13 April 2020).
Hand, D. and S. Crespi de Valldaura (2015), '"If I Write about Destruction It's Because I'm Terrified of It": An Interview with Geoffrey Hill', *Isis*, 27 April. Available online: https://isismagazine.org.uk/2015/04/if-i-write-about-destruction-its-because-im-terrified-of-it-an-interview-with-geoffrey-hill/ (accessed 13 April 2020).
Heaney, S. (1995), '"Crediting Poetry": Nobel Lecture', *The Nobel Prize* website. Available online: www.nobelprize.org/prizes/literature/1995/heaney/lecture/ (accessed 13 April 2020).
Hill, G. (2010), 'How Ill White Hairs Become a Fool and Jester' [Lecture], University of Oxford, 30 November. Available online: www.english.ox.ac.uk/professor-sir-geoffrey-hill-lectures (accessed 13 April 2020).
Hill, G. (1998), *The Triumph of Love*, Boston, New York: Houghton Mifflin.
Larkin, P. ([1974] 1981), *High Windows*, London: Faber and Faber.
Lethem, J. ([2006] 2017), 'The Genius of Bob Dylan', in Jonathan Cott (ed.), *Bob Dylan: The Essential Interviews*, 469–81, New York: Simon and Schuster.
Malvern, J. (2016), 'Dylan Lyrics are Childish, Says Poet', *The Times*, 17 October. Available online: www.thetimes.co.uk/article/dylan-lyrics-are-childish-says-poet-6g6cmtsdw (accessed 13 April 2020).
Modiano, P. (2014), 'Nobel Lecture', *The Nobel Prize* website. Available online: www.nobelprize.org/prizes/literature/2014/modiano/25238-nobel-lecture-2014/ (accessed 13 April 2020).
Modiano, P. (2017), *Souvenirs dormants*, Paris: Gallimard.
'The Nobel Prize in Literature Press Release' (2016), *The Nobel Prize* website. Available online: www.nobelprize.org/prizes/literature/2016/press-release/ (accessed 13 April 2020).

Ormsby, E. (2011), *Fine Incisions: Essays on Poetry and Place*, Erin, Ontario: Porcupine's Quill.

Porée, M. (2017), 'Avec son discours du Nobel, Dylan livre une performance aussi rusée qu'inédite', *The Conversation*, 12 June. Available online: http://theconversation.com/avec-son-discours-du-nobel-dylan-livre-une-performance-aussi-inedite-que-rusee-79277 (accessed 13 April 2020).

Ricks, C. ([2003] 2005), *Dylan's Visions of Sin*, New York: Ecco.

Ricks, C. (1978), *Geoffrey Hill and the Tongue's Atrocities*, Swansea: University College of Swansea.

Ross, A. (1999), 'The Wanderer', *The New Yorker*, 10 May. Available online: www.newyorker.com/magazine/1999/05/10/the-wanderer (accessed 13 April 2020).

Rushdie, S. (2016), 'Dylan Towers Over Everyone', *The Guardian*, 13 October. Available online: www.theguardian.com/music/2016/oct/13/dylan-towers-over-everyone-salman-rushdie-kate-tempest-and-more-pay-tribute-to-bob-dylan (accessed 13 April 2020).

Williams, R. (2016), 'Why Bob Dylan Deserves His Nobel Literature Win', *The Guardian*, 13 October. Available online: www.theguardian.com/music/2016/oct/13/bob-dylan-deserves-to-win-nobel-prize-literature (accessed 13 April 2020).

Coda: Late and Timely, Rough and Ready: A Review of *Rough and Rowdy Ways*

Adrian Grafe and Andrew McKeown

The more Dylan publishes of his work, the more it all seems to offer thematic and aesthetic cohesion. The more Dylan extends the boundaries of his musical expression, the more he wants to be different to his previous avatars and to experiment, as he clearly does here, and the more all the different components of the canvas that he has been painting for over sixty years fall into place. The more time goes on, the less contemporary Dylan seems, and the more he crafts a sound – or, perhaps, soundscape – that, if not timeless, lies out of time. Such is the case of the album *Rough and Rowdy Ways*, which was released on 19 June 2020.[1] In actual fact, he has invented a sound world that recreates that of many American popular singers and musicians, especially blues, rockabilly and early rock 'n' roll artists, from any time between the 1940s and early 1960s. This is especially apparent on 'False Prophet', which tips its hat to Sam Phillips's Sun Records and their proto-lo-fi sound.

In short, there is something crude and rugged about the sound of the record. The sound reflects the album title, and vice versa, and in itself functions as a tribute to the artists and producers of the mid-twentieth century. It is not paradoxical to say that the album sounds carefully put together and varied, and is high on entertainment value without being meretricious ('Goodbye Jimmy Reed' sounds like a natural crowd-pleaser). The faster songs are powerfully rhythmical and all the instruments, not just the bass and drums, play the actual beat of the songs. *Rough and Rowdy Ways* is a double album with the first disc containing

---

[1] This Coda was written when all other chapters were in proof stage (early June 2020), explaining some possible overlaps with the Introduction.

multitudes (nine tracks), and the second devoted entirely to 'Murder Most Foul' (containing multitudes of lyrics and names). The individual songs gain strength from being heard in context, resonating as they do with one another: put simply, these songs work as stand-alones, and may be heard as such whenever Dylan gets back on the road, but the cumulative effect is an intriguing and powerful listening experience. The overall impact of the album is further heightened by the consistency of approach: all the tracks feature Dylan's current touring band, while the stable quality of the singer's voice throughout the record argues for the recordings being done within a relatively short time span. The voice recites the words of 'Murder Most Foul' as an epic Beat poem: there are two keyboard players on the album, Benmont Tench of the Heartbreakers, and Alan Pasqua, the pianist whose playing can be heard on the recording of the Nobel Lecture the artist sent the Nobel Committee (see Sisario 2017). The tender love song 'I've Made Up My Mind to Give Myself to You' comes across, at moments, like a *parlando* Sinatra. Otherwise the voice has its own mellifluity, and this song in waltz time has a true melody, despite the artist's one-time disclaimer: 'I'm not a melodist' (Cott 2017: 466). In fact this track borrows from Offenbach's 'Barcarolle', whose lilting refrain is first reproduced, then reinvented, then developed in a minor progression in the chorus – waltzing whorls of melody entirely befitting the sentimental mood of the piece. If Dylan borrows from an older European tradition, as he does here, he is also in constant conversation with American song.

Keeping company with the Great American Songbook has revealed as never before the versatility, even the elasticity, of Dylan's voice, and rubs off on the delivery here. The voice performs 'False Prophet' with swagger, in a style reminiscent of *Tempest*'s 'Pay in Blood', and the violent attitude and obscenity (one word, but telling enough) of 'Black Rider' – shades of Weber, Burroughs and Waits – verge on braggadocio even as the voice remains restrained, almost gentle. Some of the more hurtful, vengeful lines on the album, and there are a fair number, seem designed to be voluntarily repellent (from 'Black Rider': 'I'll take a sword and hack off your arm' or 'I'll cut you up with a crooked knife', from 'Crossing the Rubicon' [Dylan 2020]). Likewise, a statement like 'I'm the last of the best / You can bury the rest' in 'False Prophet' (Dylan 2020) cannot be expected to be taken at face value, but rather as an ironic reflection on the mortal narcissism (according to the myth of Narcissus, narcissism is by definition mortal) of the persona.

Song, story and memory lie at the heart of *Rough and Rowdy Ways*. The song 'Mother of Muses', and its chorus, 'Mother of Muses, sing to me' (Dylan 2020), may remind the listener of the last words of Dylan's Nobel Lecture, quoting the first line of the *Odyssey*: '"Sing in me, oh Muse, and through me tell the story"' (Dylan 2017). Mnemosyne, the Mother of the Muses, was, as her name suggests, the Muse of memory – not memory for the sake of remembrance, but rather as the source of artistic creation, *poesis*. This alone gives listeners a hint as to how, in one respect, the artist perceives his album, or how he would like it to be perceived: as an evocation, or reawakening, of memory, be it musical, cultural or historical. In the same song, the singer claims to have fallen in love with Calliope, one of the nine Muse daughters of Mnemosyne. Calliope was the Muse of epic poetry. Setting apart the length of songs like 'Key West (Pirate Philosopher)' (just over nine minutes) or 'Murder Most Foul' (nearly seventeen minutes) – '"It's too much and not enough," he said in reference to the extended nature of many of his songs' (Cott 2017: 391) – the lyrical vision that the album offers is literally both multitudinous and universal. As the gothic, hubristic speaker – there are some nasty personae especially on this album, but this Frankenstein-like persona is one of Dylan's nastiest – of 'My Version of You' claims: 'I can see the history of the whole human race' (Dylan 2020). The atmosphere here is distinctly Edgar Allan Poe (and Dylan in 'I Contain Multitudes' mentions Poe and the title of his short story 'The Tell-Tale Heart'), of dark places and dark intentions and, at the heart of the song, the body, dismembered then rebuilt so as to fit someone else's 'version of you'. And so the track leaps from Southern Gothic to Universal Contemporary, and seems to pivot especially on religion (of all stripes) and patriarchs (Godfather/Caesar/Marx), inviting the listener to connect Dylan's fear and loathing – widespread here and elsewhere on the album – to real (if unnamed) men of violence of our own times.

Which brings us naturally to the centrepiece of *Rough and Rowdy Ways*: 'Murder Most Foul'. Dylan's longest recording to date, this one-whole-side-of-the-album track is in fact a feat of concision. In just shy of seventeen minutes, Dylan packs in his vision of post-war America, his own 'American Pie': the putting to death of one instance of a mythical America, come to life in JFK's 'Camelot' (see Grafe 2020), and the inexhaustibility of the components of that dream (i.e. you and me), recorded in the songs and sounds of post-war American popular music, as played by Dylan's alter ego, Wolfman Jack, radio DJ from *American Graffiti*, who admits to the kid – in the film played by Richard Dreyfuss – that sure, it's all just a dream (a vacuum, a scheme, babe etc.), but hell, it's a damn good dream. Oh, play that thing!

'Goodbye Jimmy Reed' confirms the musician's fidelity to his beginnings (incidentally, the album takes its title from a Jimmie *Rodgers* song, 'My Rough and Rowdy Ways', not a Jimmy *Reed* one). A Hibbing girlfriend of the teenage

Dylan is quoted as asking him whether he knew 'Maybellene': '"'Maybellene' by Chuck Berry? You bet I've heard it!"... And on and on about Chuck Berry, Fats Domino, Little Richard, Jimmy Reed – Bob thought he was fabulous, the best!' (Heylin 2001: 20). In a 1989 interview, the musician was granted the all too rare opportunity to discuss musical technique, in this case the mouth organ: 'Jimmy Reed blew out instead of sucking in on [the harmonica]. He had his own style of playing – he'd play like three notes, sometimes the whole solo would be like three notes' (Heylin 2001: 64). 'Goodbye Jimmy Reed' does not bring the harmonica to the fore, but it does have several stabbing harmonica ejaculations in the instrumental passages between the verses. In the same way, in interviews almost twenty years apart, the artist cites Reed as being among those musicians who aroused his early enthusiasm (Cott 2017: 41 and 312).

Although quotation is part of the lyricist's stock-in-trade on *Rough and Rowdy Ways*, as it was to a lesser degree on *Tempest*, there is pleasure to be derived from recognizing – or discovering – that different phrases and lines (and even tunes and arrangements) have been loved and thieved. These borrowings can add layers of meaning and intention to the songs. 'I Contain Multitudes' rhymes 'all the young dudes' with the title line, evoking the Bowie glam-rock anthem 'All the Young Dudes' of 1972, the lyrics of which themselves mention the Beatles and the Stones, who are in turn respectively cited in 'Murder Most Foul' ('The Beatles are coming, they wanna hold your hand'), and 'I Contain Multitudes' ('them British bad boys, the Rolling Stones') (Dylan 2020). The last two lines of 'Black Rider' are: 'Some enchanted evening I'll sing you a song, / Black rider, black rider, you've been on the job too long' (Dylan 2020). The latter phrase channels the traditional American song 'Duncan and Brady', also known by its chorus line 'Been on the job too long' (see Dylan 2000); this could be the song the singer offers to sing the black rider. This might suggest that the persona is saying, covertly, that he is threatening to kill the black rider, because 'Duncan and Brady' is a murder ballad. But it could also be preparing the ground for 'Key West (Philosopher Pirate)' and 'Murder Most Foul', also murder songs (involving presidential assassinations).

In terms of poetic and stanzaic form, most of the song-lyrics are written in rhyming couplets. This template confirms the lyricist's dual allegiance here to the blues and English-language poetry. As Paul Muldoon writes in his Foreword to Van Morrison's selected lyrics: 'At the heart of the blues is the couplet, the mainstay of poetry in English from Chaucer, through Dryden, Pope, Byron, Yeats and Owen to Eminem and Kendrick Lamar' (Morrison 2020). It is true that, as Muldoon says in relation to Morrison, this grants the lyricist the 'flexibility' to range widely in terms of subject matter. That said, the couplet can become a limitation, if it is followed too closely. At times certain pairings strike a note of glibness, as when Dylan teams up Indiana Jones with the Rolling Stones in 'I Contain Multitudes', a triteness compounded by the fact that it's Anne Frank who opens that particular couplet. Sure, it may well be the persona talking, and the poor taste of that line, combining as it does Anne Frank and Indiana Jones, may well be his or hers, but it's a line that's 'out there' and no amount of Dylanology or filter signalling can dictate what listeners take away. All right, it's a bum note. A footnote. We contain multitudes. Beyond the couplet, two of the *Rough and Rowdy Ways* song lyrics in particular have more idiosyncratic rhyme schemes: the six-line stanzas of 'Key West (Pirate Philosopher)' rhyme aabccb throughout, while those of 'False Prophet' rhyme abcbdd.

Dylan extends the expressive possibilities of the blues form technically on several of the songs on *Rough and Rowdy Ways*. He truncates the final bar of the last line of each stanza of 'Goodbye Jimmy Reed', thus beginning, as it were, early, the next twelve-bar round. The band set up a complex rhythmic pattern on the riff-based 'Crossing the Rubicon', on which the drummer plays the off-beat, designed perhaps to highlight the conflicting feelings expressed by the singer as he growls his way through the lyrics, a mixture, or confusion, of vengefulness and adherence to 'the holy spirit'. The dynamic of the song is reinforced by the fact that the guitar riff builds up to a climax on the first quatrain and then falls silent on the second, opening space before the next onslaught. 'False Prophet' has the overall shape and rhythm of a slow blues but the brief *glissandi* of the rhythm guitars on the off-beat, and snaky lead guitar played down the neck at the end of the verses, give the song a jauntiness slow blues do not usually have. In fact 'False Prophet' takes its cue from Billy 'The Kid' Emerson's 'If Lovin' is Believing' (Sun Records #195B, 1954). Unadorned production pulls off a convincing rootsy rendition of drums and guitar in a room *somewhere*, with some of the un-over-wrought ease of those early Sam Phillips cuts. The twelve-bar structure of the Emerson song is modified in 'False Prophet',[2] giving Dylan some justification in not crediting Emerson, and we'd be foolish to expect otherwise. Dylan is probably right in giving body to the belief that popular music is owned by one and all, that we're all borrowers and lenders, and that ironically enough, proprietariness and the litigiousness it feeds are perhaps best opposed by cocking a snook. I ain't no false prophet. I'm a philosopher pirate. Publish and be damned.

[2] On the way in which the blues 'form' is 'truncated' here, see Moon 2020.

Popular music reviews – or Dylan reviews, at least – are a funny business, reflecting the hypertrophied celebrity culture within which most popular music artists are obliged to work. Somehow, with Dylan, the music sometimes gets left behind, and writing about Dylan's work actually means writing about Dylan, or writing about his work as though it were a reflection of his personality, something he has denied and continues to deny. Q: 'Do you think about mortality often?' A: 'I think about it in general terms, not in a personal way' (Brinkley 2020). Strange to say, the best review of a Dylan album could well be by someone who was willing and able to forget it was by Dylan, or by an artist of any particular stature, and consider it just as work in itself – though whether this piece, and the book as a whole, have succeeded in differentiating the artist from the icon remains an open question. There may indeed be Dylan agnostics out there and, after thirty-nine albums, it would be interesting to know what someone who had never heard any of them thought of this one. What would they say? Maybe the answer's in the music somewhere, the music being made now by listeners tapping into Dylan without the baggage, without the name, accidentally/blindly tuning in through a freak of Spotify *algorhythms*. Maybe that's why Dylan (and his minders) have allowed this album to proliferate freely on YouTube, all twelve tracks sinking into the sound of 2020, no questions asked.

The songs on this album form a set of blues and ballads, with no rock songs (hence there is no equivalent of 'Things Have Changed', for example); none of them can be described as up-tempo, even if the locomotive rhythm of 'Goodbye Jimmy Reed' will doubtless get some of its listeners up on their feet and out on the floor. 'I Contain Multitudes' makes the perfect prelude since, although generically similar, as has just been said, the songs are thematically and atmospherically varied. The ballads are imbued with lyricism, above all 'Key West (Philosopher Pirate)' which leaves the first disc unresolved because the chorus-line stays on the minor chord. This song, alluding to the assassination of President William McKinley (1843–1901; in office from 1897 until his death), paves the way perfectly for 'Murder Most Foul': in both songs, melodic and instrumental restraint enables the emotions in the piece to come to the fore, as befits, perhaps, such meditations on tragic moments in American history. As the album pivots from one disc to the other, from one side to the other, we get a distinct sense that the overriding feel of the whole sound is slow moving, even sleepy, but aggressive nonetheless and, of course, broken. That the stories and concerns it sings of are those from the South: from the Poe-styled gothic horror of 'My Own Version' to the starry-eyed porch-perfect love song 'I've made up my mind'. There's Texas killings and Tennessee waltzes, and there's rivers that become Rubicons, to cross or to travel north upon in search of the future.

Even when the personae are on the rampage – they are rough and rowdy, after all, though the hint of an ironic chuckle one hears from time to time coming from the singer's throat suggests his snarl is worse than his bite – the music is informed by hints of old-time European quaintness. The appearance of the accordion right from the beginning of 'Key West' brings a delightful, aquarelle tone to the album, just at the right moment. It shifts the album into a more melodic space, to the extent that the tune is carried by more than just the solo voice; since its invention in about 1829, the instrument has been linked to many different types of American music, including blues, bluegrass, zydeco, and country and western. The lyrics of 'Mother of Muses' set out a cohesive, not to say quasi-providential, view of history, according to which Sherman, Montgomery, Scott, Zhukov and Patton, 'and the battles they fought', paved the way for both 'Presley to sing' and for the achievements of Martin Luther King (they were both, like John F. Kennedy, 'kings'), achievements which were driven by, and inseparable from, the pastor's faith. This historical perspective is already suggested in the lyric of the first song, 'I Contain Multitudes': 'I go right where all things lost are made good again' (Dylan 2020).

Which is not what 'Black Rider' does. This track, slotted into the middle of disc one, between a ballad and a foot-tapper, is perhaps the least amenable to analysis on the whole album. One line that sticks out – not the one with the obscenity, though that too is unexpected – is the quote from Rodgers and Hammerstein's *South Pacific*: 'some enchanted evening' (Rodgers and Hammerstein 1949). This line is the clincher in the love scene between the American nurse Nellie and the expat French plantation owner Emile, who proclaims that love is life's greatest reason, overcoming all vices of affection, like the racial prejudice which forms the backdrop to the 1949 Broadway musical. This nudge allows us to grasp Dylan's abstract song in a more concrete way and hear it in connection with questions of colour and race. 'You been on the job too long', says the speaker to the black rider, horseman of a very Southern – but not only – apocalypse. That Dylan should allude to conflicts of ethnicity, and suggest something of Manson's race war revisited on twenty-first-century America at precisely the time when the murder of George Floyd brought such nightmares to life, is a point of some prescience that Dylan himself would no doubt have preferred not to be capable of.

With *Rough and Rowdy Ways*, Dylan seems to have become his music in some sense: though we are used to his absence (since the *Tempest* album Dylan had not brought out any original recorded material), unlike *"Love and Theft"* (2001),

Modern Times (2006) and *Tempest* (2012), the artist does not appear in the cover art at all: the front cover is a 1964 photo, touched up with the photographer's permission (Greene 2020) of a dancing scene in a London club; the back cover is the photo of President John F. Kennedy which accompanied the online release of 'Murder Most Foul' on 27 March 2020.[3] The inside photo is uncredited, and shows two men and two women (the men are smoking cigarettes, but not the women) formally dressed and wearing hats, standing outside a building with a sign on it saying 'For Rent' as well as 'Louisville' in tiny letters. The photo could have been taken in the forties or fifties. The three photos all suggest a link with the past which the sound of the album corroborates, shorn as it seems to be of strong production values (no hint of technical wizardry, echo or extensive use of overdubbing is discernible to our ears), and the sparse liner notes (to call them minimalist would be an understatement) carry no production credit. Dylan seems to be trying for a sound which, as it were, takes no prisoners: a sound you (the singer, or even the musicians themselves) cannot hide behind. It is not yet clear how all the contributors to the album's sound were coordinated but it does seem clear that no sound guru such as Daniel Lanois was at work in the studio, since no producer or arranger is credited. If we're right in this, Dylan seems to have orchestrated things live in the studio, with a makeshift musical bonhomie reminiscent of the living-room-style recordings he made with his Traveling Wilburys partners. This might be stretching a point, but the sound of *Rough and Rowdy Ways* is sparse, and there are gaps, even Beckettian silences, especially so in the recitatives. If the mix is even across the instruments, the voice is pushed straight to the front, clear and without ambient effects. Possibly the sound you might wish for if you wanted nothing to get in the way of what it is you do. Words and music. Wasn't that always the way?

One aspect of the album that gives it its singularity is the fact that it can be considered as a tribute and an expression of gratitude, and an explicit fusion or synthesis of influences some of which have only become apparent in recent years. Thus, the phrase 'I Contain Multitudes' is drawn from Poem 51 of Whitman's 'Song of Myself', while the first two lines of the song (and therefore of the album, since 'I Contain Multitudes' opens the album), 'Today, and tomorrow, and yesterday, too / The flowers are dyin' like all things do' specifically allude to the emotion of the opening of Poem 51: 'The past and present wilt – I have fill'd them, emptied them, / And proceed to fill my next fold of the future' (Moore 186). The verb

---

[3] On 8 May 2020 Dylan announced the release of a new album for 19 June, for which 'Murder Most Foul' and 'I Contain Multitudes' turned out to be teasers, also releasing 'False Prophet', on 8 May.

'dyin'' evokes Whitman's 'wilt', as Whitman's alliterative attack – 'Past ... present ... fill ... fold ... future' – echoes in 'Today ... tomorrow ... dyin' ... do' (Moore 186). 'I'm a man of contradictions' may allude to the same poem: 'Do I contradict myself? / Very well then I contradict myself' (Moore 186). This could even be an indirect response to Mick Jagger's remark at the Coachella Festival just after the announcement of that year's Nobel Prize in Literature: '"I want to thank Bob Dylan for an amazing set," he said. "We have never shared the stage with a Nobel Prize winner before. Bob is like our own Walt Whitman"' (Willman 2016). To Whitman, we may add the 'Key West (Pirate Philosopher)' line, 'Like Ginsberg, Corso and Kerouac' for the American poetic tradition, and Poe for the narrative tradition in American literature. Jimmy Reed can here stand for the blues influences on the songs, while the phrase 'Go tell it on the mountain' (in 'Goodbye Jimmy Reed') is just one reference among several to Christian spiritual and Biblical culture. The lyrics of 'False Prophet' allude to 'Something's Gotta Give', the Johnny Mercer standard associated with Sinatra (1959; other singers have recorded it): 'When your smile meets my smile, something's gotta give' (Dylan 2020). The phrase 'When your smile meets my smile' is a telescoping of several lines of Mercer's song. After a succession of albums of songs composed *by* others, *Rough and Rowdy* is an album composed *of* others, other voices, other times, true, but it is also an album of Dylan himself. The jukebox which lights up the dancers on the album cover is the lodestone behind n°39: Dylan's mind precipitated into a world.

Dylan may be rough and occasionally rowdy in these songs. But above all, the songs themselves are rough and ready – ready for the listener to the record, but above all ready for the road. And what do we find here, finally? A musician and poet still developing, allowing himself to have fun, albeit serious fun. The last line of Whitman's 'Song of Myself' (Moore 186) comprises two questions with which we might continue a dialogue with *Rough and Rowdy Ways*. 'Will you speak before I am gone?' Yes, we will. We hope not, we reply to the second question: 'will you prove already too late?'

References

American Graffiti (1973) [Film], Dir. G. Lucas, USA: Universal Pictures.
Brinkley, D. (2020), 'Bob Dylan Has a Lot on His Mind' [Interview], *New York Times*, 12 June. Available online: https://www.nytimes.com/2020/06/12/arts/music/bob-dylan-rough-and-rowdy-ways.html (accessed 23 June 2020).

Cott, J., ed. (2017), *Bob Dylan: The Essential Interviews*, New York: Simon and Schuster.

Dylan, B. (2017), 'Nobel Lecture', *The Nobel Prize* website. Available online: https://www.nobelprize.org/prizes/literature/2016/dylan/lecture/ (accessed 3 April 2020).

Dylan, B. (2000), 'Duncan and Brady' [Live], *YouTube*. Available online: https://www.youtube.com/watch?v=BGcUaxYGg60 (accessed 23 June 2020).

Dylan, B. (2020), *Rough and Rowdy Ways* [Album], USA: Columbia Records.

Grafe, A. (2020), 'Time out of joint: Is "Murder Most Foul" Dylan's *American Graffiti*?', *TLS*, 15 May. Available online: https://www.the-tls.co.uk/articles/time-out-of-joint/ (accessed 23 June 2020).

Greene, A. (2020), 'How a 56-Year-Old Photo Wound Up on the Cover of Bob Dylan's Upcoming LP', *Rolling Stone*, 11 May. Available online: https://www.rollingstone.com/music/music-news/how-a-56-year-old-photo-wound-up-on-the-cover-of-bob-dylans-upcoming-lp-997105/ (accessed 23 June 2020).

Heylin, C. ([1991] 2001), *Bob Dylan: Behind the Shades Revisited*, New York: HarperCollins.

Moon, T. (2020), 'Trickster Treat: Bob Dylan's New Song Sounds Awfully Old . . . And Familiar', *NPR*, 12 May. Available online: https://www.npr.org/2020/05/12/853992774/trickster-treat-bob-dylans-new-song-sounds-awfully-old-and-familiar (accessed 29 June 2020).

Moore, G., ed. ([1977] 1979), *The Penguin Book of American Verse*, Harmondsworth: Penguin.

Morrison, Van (2020), *Keep 'Er Lit: New Selected Lyrics*, foreword P. Muldoon, ed. E. Hughes, London: Faber and Faber (Kindle edition).

Rodgers, R. and O. Hammerstein (1949), 'Some Enchanted Evening' [Song], sung by E. Pinza, *South Pacific* [Album], USA: Columbia Records.

Sinatra, F. (1959), 'Something's Gotta Give' [Song], *Come Dance With Me!*, USA: Capitol Records.

Sisario, B. (2017), 'A Really Cool Gig': Playing Piano for Bob Dylan's Nobel Lecture', *New York Times*, 7 June. Available online: https://www.nytimes.com/2017/06/07/arts/music/bob-dylan-nobel-prize-lecture-alan-pasqua-piano.html (accessed 23 June 2020).

Willman, C. (2016), 'Desert Trip Weekend 2: Rolling Stones Mix It Up, Nobel Prize Winner Bob Dylan Stays Stoic', *Billboard*, 15 October. Available online: https://www.billboard.com/index.php/articles/news/festivals/7542023/rolling-stones-bob-dylan-nobel-prize-mick-jagger-weekend-2-desert-trip (accessed 23 June 2020).

Index

Adorno, Theodor W. 17, 43, 46, 47, 136, 139, 143, 145
advertising 74, 77–8
All Quiet on the Western Front 207
allusion 16, 22, 51, 89, 126, 144, 156, 160, 176, 190, 212
American Graffiti 219
'American Pie' (song) 219
(Approximately) Complete Works 180–2
Armitage, Simon 207
'As Time Goes By' (song) 144
audience 2, 4, 9, 15, 16, 18, 21–4, 28, 31, 43–5, 47–9, 52–3, 61, 63–5, 67–8, 71, 85–8, 91–2, 102, 108, 114–16, 132, 139–40, 170–1, 172, 174, 184, 193, 209
Aufray, Hughes 190
authenticity 9, 10, 18–19, 24–5, 50, 58–61, 68, 72–7, 79, 84–7, 89, 92–5, 104
autobiographical, autobiography 4, 28, 36, 40, 135–7, 140, 144, 146, 170, 206
awards 95, 165–78
    American Academy of Arts and Letters 168
    Commandeur des Arts et des Lettres 165, 169, 175–6
    Nobel Prize 5, 10, 27, 72, 95, 152, 165, 168, 170–2, 175, 180, 197–8, 200, 203–7, 209–10, 212–13, 218, 225
    Polar Music Prize 166, 170
    Premio Príncipe de Asturias de las Artes 167
    Presidential Medal of Freedom 95, 167–8
    Princeton University Honorary Doctorate of Music 73–4, 166, 169–70
    Pulitzer Prize 167
axis 156, 208–9

Baez, Joan 4, 32, 36, 48, 62, 76, 84, 93, 104, 109, 114; 'Diamonds & Rust' 36
Baker, LaVern 'Jim Dandy' 190
'Barcarolle' (Offenbach) 218
Barthes, Roland 15–19, 21–3, 25, 45, 53–4
Beatles, The (including Lennon & McCartney) 66, 86, 104, 174, 203, 210, 220
Beethoven 17, 143, 156
Bennett, Tony 145
Bergson, Henri 205
Bible, biblical 50, 77, 158, 160, 162, 211, 225
Blake, William 210
Blanchett, Cate 53–4, 205
Blind Lemon Jefferson 4, 28
blues 3, 6, 7, 35, 78, 83, 88, 101, 103, 106, 111, 117, 121, 130, 138–42, 145, 151, 156, 158–9, 185, 206, 213, 217, 220–3, 225
Bowie, David 75, 77, 220
Burns, Robert 130
Byron, George Gordon, Lord 6, 173, 175, 220

Cash, Johnny 8, 146
Charles, Larry 30, 43, 49–50, 52, 54
Charles, Ray 154, 156
Chobani 72, 93–4
Christianity 2, 126, 162, 170, 225
Chrysler, Cadillac 72, 77, 80, 89–93, 95
Churchill, Winston 205
cinema *see* film
cinéma vérité 57, 59–60, 64, 66
Clark, Kenneth 135
Cohan, Steven 43–6, 48
Cohen, Leonard 174, 204
Cole, Nat King 145
commercialism 27, 61, 72, 74–6, 79, 84–7, 91, 94–5, 168
controversy 45, 47, 165, 170–1, 204–5

creativity 8, 11, 24, 29, 30, 54, 99, 122–4, 128–32, 135, 143, 145, 150, 171, 199
cummings, e. e. 7

death 2, 6–7, 33–4, 39, 52, 79, 124–5, 129–30, 132, 135, 150, 156, 158, 191, 219
Declaration of Independence, American 89
Detroit 77, 92
'Diamond Joe' (song) 28
'Dixie' (song) 28
documentary, rockumentary 9, 47, 57–9, 61, 63, 67, 69, 104, 210
Donne, John 5–7, 197, 208
'Duncan and Brady' (song) 220
Dylan, Bob
  literary works:
    Chronicles, Volume One 7, 23, 27, 29–31, 33–9, 52, 75, 84, 135, 142n, 170, 173n, 179, 210
    Tarantula 191, 198
  lyrics:
    Lyrics: Since 1962, The 187
    Lyrics: 1961–2012, The 179–93
    Lyrics: 1962–1985, 186, 189
    Lyrics: 1962–2001, The 190
    Writings and Drawings 180, 182–3, 186, 188
  released albums:
    Blonde on Blonde 94, 153, 185
    Bootleg Series, The 152, 183
      Vols 1–3 (Rare & Unreleased) 24
      Vol. 8: Tell Tale Signs: Rare and Unreleased 1989–2006 137
      Vol. 12: The Cutting Edge 1965–1966 185
      Vol. 14: More Blood, More Tracks 15
    Christmas in the Heart 8, 79, 143–4
    Desire 153, 203
    Empire Burlesque 149, 203
    Fallen Angels 143–4, 212
    Freewheelin' Bob Dylan, The 45–6, 50, 76, 102, 105–6, 203
    Good As I Been To You 1, 157
    Infidels 153, 203
    "Love and Theft" 29, 139–41, 146, 149, 153, 158–9, 204, 223
    Modern Times 88, 139–40, 149, 158–9, 161–2, 224
    Oh Mercy 30, 157, 203
    Rough and Rowdy Ways 5n, 11, 149, 217–26
    Self Portrait 143
    Shadows in the Night 143–5, 212
    Slow Train 203
    Tempest 139, 155, 204, 218, 220, 223–4
    The Times They Are A-Changin' 11, 46
    Time Out of Mind 1, 9, 78, 87, 123–5, 135–6, 140–1, 145, 149, 151, 153, 156–8, 163, 203
    Together Through Life 139, 204
    Triplicate 24, 135, 143–4, 212
    Under the Red Sky 1
    World Gone Wrong 1, 137, 157
  recorded songs:
    'A Hard Rain's A-Gonna Fall' 46, 211
    'Absolutely Sweet Marie' 180
    'Ain't Talkin'' 141, 149, 156–62
    'All Along the Watchtower' 23, 208
    'All the Tired Horses' 184
    'Ballad of a Thin Man' 35, 156, 162
    'Ballad of Hollis Brown' 46
    'Beyond Here Lies Nothin'' 204
    'Beyond the Horizon' 141, 159
    'Black Rider' 218, 220, 223
    'Blind Willie McTell' 121, 153, 204
    'Blowin' in the Wind' 46, 99–120
    'Brownsville Girl' 39
    'Buckets of Rain' 21–2, 149
    'Can't Wait' 137–8, 145, 158
    'Cold Irons Bound' 28, 137, 204
    'Cross the Green Mountain' 204
    'Crossing the Rubicon' 218, 221
    'Down in the Flood' 28
    'Drifter's Escape' 28
    'Early Roman Kings' 2
    'Eternal Circle' 24
    'Every Grain of Sand' 203
    'False Prophet' 217–18, 221, 224–5
    'Forever Young' 38, 90
    'Fourth Time Around' 184–5

'Gates of Eden' 188
'Goodbye Jimmy Reed' 217, 219–22, 225
'High Water (for Charley Patton)' 141, 159, 211–12
'Highlands' 39, 130, 138, 149
'Highway 61 Revisited' 210
'Honest With Me' 142, 222
'Huck's Tune' 3, 210
'Hurricane' 39, 203
'I Contain Multitudes' 11, 219–24
'Idiot Wind' 40, 165, 203
'I've Made Up My Mind to Give Myself to You' 218
'Is Your Love in Vain?' 170, 175
'It's All Over Now, Baby Blue' 149
'It's Alright Ma (I'm Only Bleeding)' 44, 111, 180, 184
'Joey' 39
'Jokerman' 203
'Just Like Tom Thumb's Blues' 207
'Key West (Pirate Philosopher)' 219–23, 225
'Knocking on Heaven's Door' 203
'Leopard-Skin Pill-Box Hat' 185
'The Levee's Gonna Break' 159
'Let's Keep It Between Us' 188–9
'Like a Rolling Stone' 3, 61, 63, 65, 67–8, 85, 129, 155
'Lonesome Day Blues' 142, 159
'Long and Wasted Years' 2
'Love Sick' 2–3, 71, 78, 87–8, 124, 137, 211
'Maggie's Farm' 39, 76, 85
'Masters of War' 46
'Mississippi' 25, 29, 141, 204
'Moonlight' 204, 211
'Mother of Muses' 218, 223
'Mr Tambourine Man' 10
'Murder Most Foul' 10–11, 149, 218–20, 222, 224
'My Version of You' 219
'Nettie Moore' 35, 142, 159
'Not Dark Yet' 123–5, 127–8, 130, 137–8
'Only a Pawn in their Game' 46
'Pay in Blood' 2, 142, 218
'Political World' 203
'Precious Angel' 203, 210
'Queen Jane Approximately' 180
'Rainy Day Women #12 & 35' 191
'Red River Shore' 18, 125–7, 129
'Roll on John' 155, 210
'Rollin' and Tumblin'' 159
'Sad-Eyed Lady of the Lowlands' 149
'Scarlet Town' 3
'Shelter from the Storm' 203
'Simple Twist of Fate' 28, 213
'Someday Baby' 88, 159
'Spirit on the Water' 141, 211
'Stack a Lee' 174
'Standing in the Doorway' 137
'Sugar Baby' 8, 149
'Sweetheart Like You' 210
'Tangled Up in Blue' 22, 203–4
'Tell Me Momma' 187
'Tell Ol' Bill' 184, 193
'Tempest' 39, 142, 190, 204, 211
'Things Have Changed' 3, 77, 80, 91, 171, 204, 222
''Til I Fell In Love With You' 137–8, 211
'Times They Are A-Changin', The' 46, 94
'Tin Angel' 39, 211
'Tryin' to Get to Heaven' 8, 138
'Tweedle Dee &Tweedle Dum' 190–1
'Wedding Song' 149
'What Was It You Wanted?' 23–4
'When I Paint My Masterpiece' 210
'When He Returns' 149
'When The Deal Goes Down' 142, 144, 159, 210
'Where Are You Tonight? (Journey through Dark Heat)' 136, 149, 173
'Workingman's Blues # 2' 159
'You're a Big Girl Now' 203
'You're Gonna Make Me Lonesome When You Go' 5, 210
visual art and exhibitions
   Beaten Path 4
   Brazil Series, The 10, 121, 127
      'Chrysanthemums' 128
      'Ventriloquist, The' 127–8
   Revisionist Art 15–25

230 Index

editing, editor 57, 62, 65–9, 90, 179–80, 184, 188, 191–3, 208
Eliot, T. S. 3, 7, 197–9, 204, 208
Elliott, Ramblin' Jack 4–5
ending 65, 67, 149–64, 193, 211
eschatology 9, 142, 150, 156, 160–3
exhibition *see* Dylan, visual art

Faithfull, Marianne 76
fame 24, 57, 61, 63, 65, 74, 83, 87, 166, 174
fanhood *see* audience
Fate, Jack 11, 28–9, 32–6, 38–9, 43, 49–51
Fell, Cliff 6
Ficino, Marsilio 122
film
    Dont Look Back 9, 47, 57–69, 87
    I'm Not There 31, 43, 52–5, 85, 205
    Masked and Anonymous 27–9, 33–9, 43, 49–52, 54
    No Direction Home 9, 54, 57–71, 74, 83, 85, 93, 102, 103, 129, 210
    Renaldo and Clara 136n, 139
    Rolling Thunder Revue: A Bob Dylan Story 2, 66n, 69
Fitzgerald, Ella 145, 169
folk music 3–4, 6, 9, 29, 46, 48–50, 60–4, 68, 72, 75–6, 78–9, 83–6, 88, 92–3, 102–4, 108, 110, 112, 139, 142, 144–5, 158, 206–7, 210, 213

Gagosian Gallery (New York City) 16, 19
Gates Jr., Henry Louis 75, 200
gender 44, 48–9, 53
Ginsberg, Allen 11, 174, 207, 213, 225
Girl from the North Country (musical) 213n
Great American Songbook, The 143–5, 212, 218
Guthrie, Woody 4, 30, 50, 61–2, 75–6, 84, 103n, 173, 213

Hamlet, Hamlet 199
Harrison, George 66, 104
Haynes, Todd 31, 43, 52–4, 85
Hendrix, Jimi 28
'Here's That Rainy Day' (song) 144
hermeneutics 8, 22, 136
Hibbing, Minnesota 31–2, 34, 57, 61, 83, 89, 219

Hit Factory, The 213
Holiday, Billie 145
Holly, Buddy 206, 213
Homer – *Odyssey* 17, 173, 207, 192, 212, 219
honours 165–78
Houston, Cisco 7
humour 130–2, 175, 189

IBM 72, 93, 95
icon, iconic 9–11, 22, 29, 43, 50–1, 57, 71–4, 90, 92–3, 191
image, imagery 2, 9, 15–18, 20, 22, 24, 28, 39, 44–5, 47, 49–50, 54, 59, 62, 67, 72, 76, 78, 84, 88–95, 115, 137, 143, 146, 149, 165, 191
interpretation 3, 19, 36, 46, 52, 62–3, 68, 94, 100–2, 117, 143–5, 159–60, 184, 192
intertext, intertextuality 27, 35, 210–12
intrapretation 100, 102, 106, 111–12
iPod, iTunes 72, 88, 90, 93–5

Jagger, Mick 174, 176, 225
Jankélévitch, Vladimir 135
Johnson, Robert 7–8, 89, 101, 106, 142, 173–4
Joplin, Janis 28
journalism, journalists 8, 21, 46–7, 50–1, 53–4, 60, 65, 68–9, 79, 84, 87

kairos, 'kairotic' 155–6, 163
Keats, John 6, 123, 125–6, 208
Kermode, Frank 149–50, 154–6
Kierkegaard, Søren 123, 129–30
King, Carole 213

Larkin, Philip 73, 77, 203, 211
lateness, late style 1, 17, 22, 24, 135–48, 157, 163
Lead Belly 206
legacy 77, 144, 150, 153–4, 174
listeners *see* audience
literary criticism 208, 211
literature 35, 152, 172, 180, 193, 198, 200, 204–7, 211–12, 225

McKinley, William, US president 222
Madison Square Garden 104, 115
masculinity 22–3, 43–55
Marcus, Greil 52, 57, 66, 83, 143, 153, 158
   'invisible republic' 83–5, 87, 89, 92, 94–5
mask 24, 27, 38, 43, 45, 47, 49, 51–2, 54, 59, 74
'Maybellene' (Chuck Berry) 220
media 34, 44, 48, 51, 60, 64–5, 83–5, 94, 116, 146, 169–70
melancholia 121–32, 135, 140, 144–5
Mercer, Johnny 225
metanarrative 61, 63
Milton, John 5, 208, 212
Mitchell, Joni 204
Moby-Dick 205, 207
Modiano, Patrick 203, 206–7
Morrison, Toni 167, 170
Morrison, Van 220
mortality *see* death
Muldoon, Paul 220
Mulvey, Laura 43, 46–7, 49
myth, mythology, 5–6, 10, 27, 31–2, 39, 68, 85, 87, 89, 150, 218–19
   autho-mythology, auto-mythos 28, 39–40

narrative 21–2, 27–8, 38–40, 43, 52–3, 58–9, 61, 63, 66, 127–8, 149–52, 154–6, 159, 162–3, 191, 210, 225
Never Ending Tour 23, 105, 112, 146
Neuwirth, Bob 76
Newport Folk Festival 62, 68, 72, 76, 79, 85–8, 104, 108, 110–11, 114, 117, 168
New York City 4, 16, 30, 37, 62, 103–4, 125, 159, 172
Nobel Prize, Nobel Laureate *see* awards
nostalgia 32, 88–90, 91–2, 135–6, 138, 143–5, 158, 193

'O Little Town of Bethlehem'
O'Brien, James 10*n*
Obama, Barack 91, 95, 165, 170
Olson, Charles 186–7

oral performance, orality 179–80, 182, 184–8, 192
Ovid 6–7, 137

painting, paintings v, 4, 10, 17, 79, 121, 123, 125, 127–9, 131–2, 141, 174, 199, 209, 217
Pasqua, Alan 218
pastiche 35, 91
Pennebaker, D. A. 9, 47, 57–60, 62–5, 87
performance 1–5, 9, 16, 21–3, 25, 28–9, 33–4, 39, 43–5, 47–8, 50–6, 59, 61, 64–6, 75, 76, 79, 83, 85–7, 91–2, 94–5, 99–102, 112, 114–15, 146, 149–50, 152–4, 183–7, 192–3, 204
persona 2–3, 5, 8–9, 13, 25, 27, 29, 43–5, 49, 54, 58, 60, 63, 68–9, 72, 94–5, 102, 116, 132, 138, 140–1, 143–5, 150, 158, 218–21, 223
philosophy 23, 54, 121–2
Poe, Edgar Allan 213, 219
poet, poetry 2–3, 5–7, 9, 22, 25, 34, 43, 64, 73, 77, 83–4, 93, 95, 121–6, 128–32, 135, 146, 151–2, 166–8, 186, 190, 193, 197, 199, 200, 204, 206–14, 219–20, 225
Poni-Tails, The 213
Poole, Charlie 'You Ain'tTalkin' To Me' 207
Pope, Alexander 192
popular music 99, 101, 139–40, 144–5, 151, 153, 167, 200, 219, 221–2
Porée, Marc 203*n*, 205, 212
Porter, Cole 213
posterity 189
Pound, Ezra 2, 197
Presley, Elvis 28, 37, 213
psychology 121–2
publishing *see* editing

radio 37, 71, 74–5, 83–4, 104, 174, 206, 219
   Theme Time Radio Hour 9, 74, 78, 88–9, 209, 212–13
Raeben, Norman 125
re-creation 9, 99–103, 105, 107, 109, 111, 113, 115, 117, 199

Reed, Jimmy 217, 219–22, 225
Rembrandt 2, 18, 146
resources 197–9
Ricks, Christopher 9, 17, 75, 151, 167, 172, 174–5, 187, 192, 197–201, 203–13
  Dylan's Visions of Sin 151, 205, 208
Riley, Billy Lee 7
'Rime of the Ancient Mariner, The' (Coleridge) 204
Rings, Steven 101, 111, 184
rock 'n' roll, rock and roll 29, 78–9, 88, 104, 213, 217
Rodgers, Jimmie 219
'Rollin' and Tumblin'' (song) 159
Rolling Stones, The 28, 59, 220–1
Rushdie, Salman 205
Russell, Bertrand 205

Said, Edward 1, 17, 136
Schatzberg, Jerry 191
Scorsese, Martin 2, 9, 54–5, 57, 61, 63, 66, 68–69, 74, 210
screen 29, 43–9, 61, 90
Shakespeare, William 1–2, 5–6, 33, 51, 173, 180, 185, 198, 207, 212–13
shyness 175
Simon, Paul 151
  'Fifty-Ninth Street Bridge Song' 210
Sinatra, Frank 20, 144–5, 154, 218, 225–6; songs associated with:
  'It Gets Lonely Early' 144
  'Melancholy Mood' 144
  'September of My Years' 144
  'Something's Gotta Give' 225–6
  'What I'll Do?' 144
  'Where Are You Now?' 144
  'Why Try to Change Me Now?' 144

'Somewhere Along the Way' (song) 144
Sondheim, Stephen 213
Soyinka, Wole 200–1
speech, speeches 7, 34, 50–1, 75, 170–2, 175, 179, 205–7
'Stormy Weather' (song) 144
style 36, 50, 59, 76, 85, 135–6, 139, 168, 176, 206, 220, 222, 224
Sun Records, Sun Studio 140, 213, 217, 221
Super Bowl 72–3, 76–9, 90–1, 93
Szymborska, Wislawa 205

technology 68, 85–9, 93–5, 150, 153
Telegraph, The (fanzine) 188–9
television 32, 34, 84, 87–8, 103–4, 108, 111–12, 117–18, 170
Tench, Benmont 218
Tennyson, Alfred, Lord 197, 208
Timrod, Henry 17, 135
Tin Pan Alley 158, 204, 211–12
Titanic 142, 190, 197, 204
transcription 182–4, 187, 189–90
Traveling Wilburys 224

Vaughan, Sarah 145
vernacular 157–9, 206–7
Victoria's Secret 71–2, 78, 87, 95
voice, vocal style 2–5, 10, 22, 25, 32, 109, 111, 137, 142, 144–5, 184, 187–8, 197, 204, 218, 224

Western Governor's University 93–4
Whitman, Walt 84, 92, 213, 225
Williams, William Carlos 22
'When the World Was Young' (song) 144

Yeats, W.B. 5, 34, 205–6, 220

www.ingramcontent.com/pod-product-compliance
Lightning Source LLC
Chambersburg PA
CBHW072147290426
44111CB00012B/2000